Breakin' into Nashville

Breakin' into Nashville

*How to Write and Sell
Country Music*

Jennifer Ember Pierce

MADISON BOOKS
Lanham • New York • Oxford

Published by Madison Books
4720 Boston Way
Lanham, Maryland 20706

12 Hid's Copse Road
Cumnor Hill, Oxford OX2 9JJ, England

Edited by Miccinello Associates, Branford, CT, U.S.A.
Text design and layout by RPC Desktop Publishing, Milford, CT, U.S.A.

Distributed by National Book Network

Library of Congress Cataloging-in-Publication Data

Pierce, Jennifer Ember.
    Breakin' into Nashville : how to write and sell country music /
Jennifer Ember Pierce.
        p.   cm.
    Includes bibliographical references (p.   ) and index.
    ISBN 1-56833-110-X (pbk.)
        1. Country music—Tennessee—Nashville—Vocational guidance.
    2. Music trade—Tennessee—Nashville—Vocational guidance.
    I. Title. II. Title: Breaking into Nashville.
    ML3790.P54 1998
    781.642'023'73—DC21   97-44501
                                                          CIP
                                                          MN

∞ ™ The paper used in this publication meets the minimum requirements of
American National Standard for Information Sciences—Permanence of
Paper for Printed Library Materials, ANSI Z39.48–1984.
Manufactured in the United States of America.

To all those who dream and believe all their dreams will come true.

Jennifer Ember Pierce

Dedication

This book is dedicated to a number of special people.

To my late father, Michael, who read to me from Shakespeare, Tolstoy, Poe, Robert Service, and many others when I was very small.

And, to my late mother, Emma. May God hold you in the palm of His hand.

To Bev, my sister, for always putting the needs of others before her own.

To my two brothers, Ted and David, and my beautiful daughter, Kellie, who have given me their support.

To Edith O. Toombs, my first university English instructor. Edith told me I was, and always would be a writer. She helped me and believed in me. She was and is my very good friend.

To John, there are no words to thank you for all your support.

And, to all songwriters, whoever you are, wherever you are. God bless you all.

Jennifer Ember Pierce

Table of Contents

Foreword

There have been a few books written on how to write a song, but none as *comprehensive* as *Breakin' Out of Nashville*.

You say you want to be a songwriter. That is all you are dedicating your life to. You know you will make it. You have given your heart, mind, and soul to the art and craft of being a professional songwriter. You know you have what it takes, if only someone would listen.

If you have a talent for the love of words and composition, and you are willing to put hours into studying, you may have a slight chance. *Breakin' Out of Nashville* will help you achieve your dreams and aspirations.

I have worked with the greatest and the least, and sometimes have received the *best* from the *least*.

I have endeavored to cover all the bases in this book. However, I *cannot* give you the tenacity and willpower that is necessary for you to excel in this undertaking. I *cannot* give you the talent it takes from the innermost part of you that forces you to write, whether or not you are paid for doing so.

I *cannot* give you hits. I *cannot* give you the realism necessary to understand the music business. I *cannot* give you the fortitude you will need not to quit. I *cannot* comfort you when you cry out in frustration, and I will not be there to share your joy when you finally make it. But, I will be with you in spirit.

I *can* give you all the knowledge I have acquired from 15 years of learning, working, and, on a daily basis, understanding more and more about songwriting and the music industry. I *can* give you tips on what to do and what not to do. This is a quiet business.

I *can* do my best to explain what the industry considers to be a *hit*, even when they themselves do not know.

Preface

This is not a book of *fluff* and *nonsense*. There are no unnecessary fillers in *Breakin' Out of Nashville*.

After each chapter is a direct quote from some of the great and knowledgeable people who make country music happen. They are the ones the business could not do without. Their input is of vital importance to this business.

Music is a business just like any other business. If money was not made, no one could stay in business.

Managers, producers, artists, writers, composers, studios, engineers, publicists, photographers, fan clubs, secretaries, song pluggers, publishers, bus drivers, road managers, and many more involved in the music business must make money—or there would be no music business.

In order to simplify matters, the masculine gender is used throughout this book, although many women are also in positions of authority, power, and control in the music industry.

The phrase "the bottom line is money" is not used negatively but positively in this book. Record companies spend a great deal of money releasing the music they have so carefully chosen. They should expect a return on their investment. They must make a return on their investment or they would go bankrupt.

The music business is a very complicated one. I cannot possibly touch on all facets here, but, perhaps, after reading and studying this book, you will have a clearer and truer understanding of how the many different divisions of the music industry function.

Acknowledgments

I would like to extend a special thank you to Barry Beckett, Beckett Productions; Maggie Cavender, founder of Nashville Songwriters Association International (NSAI); and Gilles Godard, producer, publisher, and songwriter for not only adding their credits and insights to this book, but also for their endorsements.

My appreciation is also extended to:

Richard Leigh, EMI Music and Fred Knobloch, Almo Irving Music, professional songwriters;

Dan Wilson, creative director, Sony/Tree Publishing Company, and Sam Ramage, RCA;

Kevin O'Neal, former operations director, WSM-FM Radio, and Buddy Killen, Buddy Killen Enterprises, for allowing me to interview them for this book;

Vincent Candilora, president and chief executive officer, SESAC, and Roger Sovine, vice-president, BMI, for their contributions to this book;

ASCAP's Eve Vaupel, director of public relations, Merlin Littlefield, associate director, and Connie Bradley, Southern Regional executive director;

Doyle Brown, head of creative services, Polygram/Island Publishing Company;

Terje Brattsveen, owner and engineer, Sound Zone Studio, for helping with the charts and numbers section of this book.

Terrell Tye, president and partner, Forerunner Music Group;

Clay Myers, director of publishing, Starstruck Writers Group; and

Ron Twist, program director and disc jockey, KTAK-FM Radio, Riverton, Wyoming.

Finally, it takes a team to make any endeavor work. The following people are as important as anyone else named or credited in this book: Robbin Ahrold, vice president of corporate relations, BMI (New York); Pat Rogers, executive director, NSAI (Nashville); Ian Dove, NARAS (Burbank, California); Tammy Genovese, CMA (Nashville); Bill Boyd, ACM (Hollywood, California); Paul Adler, ASCAP (New York);

Rob Senn, general manager, NARAS (Burbank, California); Ed Benson, CMA (Nashville); Janet Boseman, CMA (Nashville); Janet Williams, CMA (Nashville); Teressa George, CMA (Nashville); and Ellen L. Wood, director of publicity, BMI (Nashville).

About the Author

Jennifer Pierce grew up in South Texas. She moved to Nashville in 1988.

In 1975, Pierce graduated magna cum laude from Texas A&I University. She majored in political science and history.

Pierce has been an avid reader since the age of 14. She also began to write seriously at that time.

Pierce has had her songs recorded by Johnny Cash with Hank Williams, Jr., Janie Frickie, The Wood Brothers, and others. She has co-written with several notable writers, including Garth Brooks.

Pierce is a member of the American Society of Composers, Authors and Publishers (ASCAP), the Country Music Association (CMA), the Academy of Country Music (ACM), is a member of the pro-writer division of Nashville Songwriters Association International (NSAI), and is a voting member of the National Academy of Recording Arts and Sciences (NARAS). She is also a member of Kappa Delta Pi, a national academic honor society. She is the recipient of two Texas Music Appreciation Awards and is in *Who's Who in Entertainment 1992-93.*

The quote by Garth Brooks on cover of book was taken from a picture Garth autographed for Jennifer when they were co-writing "Heaven Sent" in 1989.

Partial Discography
of Jennifer Pierce

"That Old Wheel" (Single), 1988–1989; Artists: Johnny Cash with Hank Williams, Jr. Label: Polygram/Mercury; Album: Water From the Wells of Home; Producers: Paul McCartney and Jack Clement; Charted for 21 weeks, Billboard Singles Charts; Nominated for four preliminary Country Music Association Awards, went top five for Vocal Event of the Year; Polygram 1988 (Album No. 422 983 778-1) (Single No. 870 688-7 DJ) (Cassette No. 834 778-4) (CD No. 834 778-2); Jennifer Pierce (ASCAP).

"That Old Wheel" (Re-released), August 13, 1991; Artists: Johnny Cash with Hank Williams, Jr.; Album: Best of Johnny Cash (One and Only Series); Label: Curb Burbank, California. (Cassette No. D4-77494) (CD No. D2-77494); Jennifer Pierce (ASCAP).

"That Old Wheel" (Re-released), June 24, 1991; Artists: Johnny Cash with Hank Williams, Jr.; Album: Best of Hank Williams, Jr. (One and Only Series); Label: Curb Burbank, California. (Cassette No. D4-77418) (CD No. D2-77418); Jennifer Pierce (ASCAP).

"How Long Did It Take You" (To Stop Lovin' Me), 1992; Artists: Tim Stacy and Ricky Wood; Label: K-Tel Records; Album: The Wood Brothers; Release date: August 1992; Writers: Jennifer Pierce (ASCAP) and Keith Palmer (ASCAP); (Cassette No. 1042 4) (CD No. 1042 2).

"Love," 1992; Artists: Tim Stacy and Ricky Wood; Label: K-Tel Records; Album: The Wood Brothers; Release date: August 1992; Writers: Jennifer Pierce (ASCAP) (lyrics), and Terry Bell (BMI) (music); (Cassette No. 1042 4) (CD No. 1042 2).

"What Do I Do" (With All This Love), 1991; Artist: Janie Frickie; Album: Janie Frickie; Label: Intersound; Producer: Gilles Godard; Executive Producers: Randy Jackson and Gilles Godard; (Cassette No. PDI 9105) (CD No. DCI 9105); Writers: Jennifer Pierce (ASCAP) and Bob Kitchener (BMI).

Partial List of Co-writers
with Jennifer Pierce

I would like to thank my co-authors and co-writers for helping me to grow as a person and as a writer.

Aaron Barker. Barker was the sole writer on "Baby Blue" and "Love Without End, Amen," two number one songs for George Strait. Barker and I co-authored "God Bless Texas, God Bless Tennessee."

Terry Bell. Bell is a great pop singer, composer, and lyricist. He was recently hired by Cornelius Company's president, Ron Cornelius, as professional manager for the company. Bell and I co-wrote "Love" on The Wood Brothers album.

Terje Brattsveen. Brattsveen composed the great composition for the song we wrote together, "You Believed."

Garth Brooks. Brooks and I have completed two songs together: "Heaven Sent" and "Some Things Never Change."

Barbara Cloyd. Cloyd sings beautifully and runs the sound and MC's some writers' nights at the famous Bluebird Cafe. Cloyd co-authored with John Robbin "I Guess You Had To Be There," the number one song for Lorrie Morgan.

Ed Ford. Ford has the determination and courage all songwriters need to have. Ford and I have penned several fine songs together. Ford wrote the music to "The Hands of Time."

Sonny George. George is the lead singer and plays acoustic guitar for the Planet Rockers.

Jackie Gulledge. Gulledge is another Texas writer/composer/singer, and professional chef.

Randy Jackson. Jackson managed Janie Frickie.

Tamie Jones. Jones is past president of the Texas Music Association, San Antonio Division.

Bob Kitchener. Kitchener and I co-authored "What Do I Do with All This Love," which was recorded by Janie Frickie.

Kellie Michele (Mann) Gilpin, my daughter, and I wrote "The Hands of Time" with Ed Ford.

Keith Palmer. Palmer co-authored "My Broken Heart" for Reba McEntire. Palmer and I co-authored "How Long Did It Take You" (To Stop Lovin' Me) on The Wood Brothers album.

Danny Parks. Parks plays lead guitar, acoustic guitar, mandolin, and fiddle on "Be a Star," and wrote the single "You Called," for and with Daniele Alexander.

Ron Twist. Twist is a former DJ for KJ97 in San Antonio, Texas, and is currently Program Director and morning DJ for KTAK Radio in Riverton, Wyoming.

I have written with many more fine songwriters, too numerous to mention here. Each has taught me a great deal.

Interview with
BUDDY KILLEN
Buddy Killen Enterprises

Author: You're a producer, a manager, a writer, an artist, and a publisher. What would your advice be to the up-and-coming artist?

Killen: My advice to anyone, even if they were not in music, would be to prepare yourself. Become the best you can at what you do before you go out and try to sell yourself.

Know what you are about as much as possible. Fine-tune yourself. Don't expect anyone to dig out all of your wonderful talents for you. Know yourself and know your strong points. Work on them.

So when you present yourself to a producer, a publisher, a manager, or whomever, make sure that you present yourself in the best light possible. Make sure you are showing the best that you are.

So many people bring tapes to me or they sing for me. Then they say, "You know, I can do better than this." I say, "Then why didn't you?"

Everyone wants to tell you that they can do better than what you are hearing. If *I'm* going to audition for somebody, then *I'm* going to "blow them away."

Don't expect someone to try to determine how good you are without you putting forth all the effort. Many times we can do that. In fact, I've done that many times throughout the years. I've discovered people because I've heard through the bad tapes and songs. Today you can't get by with as much as they used to because they have the facilities today to make your presentation terrific.

Author: Do you think age has anything to do with becoming an artist today?

Killen: There seems to be a tremendous thrust today toward young people. Audiences are not excited anymore about the older acts (people who have been around awhile, 10 or 15 years). Radio doesn't care unless the act is an absolute monster.

Record labels want to start with these kids who are young. Then they try to build a future with them, and an audience for them.

I think that to a great degree video has something to do with younger artists. Before video became so popular older acts tended to not have the problems they're having right now. Think about it. When you watch a video, you want to see handsome guys and pretty girls.

Although you certainly can be very attractive as you grow older, the audience is becoming younger. The record buyers are younger now. The Willie Nelsons, the Waylon Jennings, and those people who have become older, their audiences have grown older with them. Most of them no longer even buy records. What we have today is a wonderful opportunity to take young people and get nice long careers out of them.

Author: What motivates the labels to become excited enough about a new artist to give them a record deal?

Killen: You go into the studio and make a fabulous tape of great songs. You know that you have elicited from that artist or writer the best of his ability so that you don't have to make excuses.

I don't get turned down very many times for the simple reason that I won't go in unless I really feel that I am going to sell. I don't like to close doors. Once you've been through a door and fail, more than likely, you won't get a second shot. The response might be, "Oh man, what are you doing bringing me this. I've already heard it. What are you doing coming back again?" In most cases, the excitement goes out when you miss the first time.

I prefer to have my act together. I know that I would personally take that artist into the studio and record him if it were my label. Or I would sign a person as a writer. If they're not good enough for me, why would they be good enough for anybody else?

Author: If a middle-aged person asked you what his chances were of becoming an artist, what would you tell him?

Killen: I don't like for age to be a factor. If that were the case, then I should probably pull in my shingle and go home because I'm no longer a teenager. Age has never meant anything to me.

I still think as young as I did when I was 19. I have more sense now than I did when I was 19, but I'm not intimidated by age and yet I'm not naive enough to think that the world is not attuned to youth, especially in the music business. Branson, Missouri, is full of people who have been "up on the mountain" and continue to perform because they're performing to that audience that will come to them. The mountain comes to Mohammed. That makes a difference. There's a difference in working in Branson or Dollywood, or wherever.

As an artist, you gain a certain amount of notoriety, and people remember you and they're there to see you. There's a difference though in cutting a record that's competitive enough to get on the radio today. The longer you've been around, the less people care about hearing you on the radio for some reason. They'll keep playing those big hits you once recorded, but they don't care about playing your new records. They just don't care.

Author: Does radio want the new artists?

Killen: Yes. Radio does not seem to think the older artists do much for their ratings. And record labels do not think that there's much of an audience out there for most of the people who have been around a long time. They go with the fresh acts.

Today is the best time I've ever seen for new young artists. There was a time when all they wanted was the tried and proven. They wanted the people and the names that everybody recognized. Today, however, you can break an artist "faster than a speeding bullet." There was a time when you couldn't do that.

Radio used to think that if they played anything but the big hits they'd lose their audience. Today the audience has changed so much that it wants new things. The new audience is saying to radio, "Hey, don't just keep crammin' these old records down my throat and the same acts over and over. Give me something new and I'll buy it. And, I'll help your ratings because I'll listen to your radio station."

It's all changed. The industry is much more sophisticated than it was. Video has had a lot to do with the changes. The modern sound is what's wanted today. These new young singers are singing strong and surround themselves with shows that are comparable to the rock shows and big pop shows. You can no longer be "Ned" in the first grade reader. You've got to go out there and you've got to have this unbelievable show that knocks people out. If you don't, you're not on the "cutting edge" and you won't last. The "dye is cast." The standard has been set.

If you can't play the game, you're not going to become a major star. It's that simple.

Author: How much of a role does TNN (The Nashville Network) and CMT (Country Music Television) play in the country music industry today?

Killen: They both play very important roles.

TNN is playing a much more vital role than it did at first. In the beginning it was a bit "hokey." It was more nostalgic than it was on the cutting edge. The producers were just trying to get it on the air, and they were putting shows on that were not quite "today." Now when you watch TNN they're getting more and more in tune with "today." They're getting more aggressive. They're reaching out. I think TNN is a vital part of what we're doing.

CMT has become an unbelievable source to sell country music. Even VH1, with their country shows, is important.

Television, in general, with all the networks have really become an important part of our selling records. Television is also important in breaking acts.

Author: Does television coordinate with radio?

Killen: I think they both determine things for themselves. If a record is strong enough to be a hit, then the program directors of both radio and television will play it. It's all a matter of opinion.

Author: Are more country artists going to be like George Strait and Garth Brooks and get involved in the motion picture industry?

Killen: Absolutely. There's no doubt about it. I think there will be more country acts in the movies and on television than ever dreamed of. And, it's happening as we speak.

Country music is hot. When it's that hot, the world is lovin' it. How can you go wrong?

The main thing we have to be careful about is emulating ourselves. You can't keep copying what you did. You've got to keep coming up with fresh new ideas and fresh new approaches.

One of the things that has made country music as hot as it is, is the sound, digital. It's a really great sound instead of that old-fashioned, dead kind of sound that didn't sparkle. Today it's really sparkling. And it's wonderful.

Author: The title of this book is *The Bottom Line Is Money.** Would you not agree that what we're talking about is a product?

Killen: It is a product. That's all it is. And, if you start trying to make it anything else and get up on that ethereal plain, you're lost. A singer is a singer. He may not be carrying a plate around. He's not a waiter or she's not a waitress. He's not driving a truck or digging a ditch. He's singing. That's what he does for a living.

When you get beyond all of that and start thinking that it's so special that you can't keep your feet on the ground anymore, it will be taken away from you. I've seen it happen so many times. You've got to approach it as a business.

The new artists today are bright. They're much better businesspeople today than they were when I came up here. We were all "babes in toyland." We were writing the book and didn't even know it. It hadn't happened before. We made it happen.

Today's young artists have patterns to follow. We set the example and they're smarter than we were. They come in with business degrees and music degrees behind them. They come

*Now titled *Breakin' Out of Nashville.*

in with managers, lawyers, and a multitude of things that many of us in the early days never thought of.

We're here because we love it. That doesn't mean that they don't love it. They're just better prepared than we were.

Author: Would you say the competition is much greater now?

Killen: The competition is unbelievably big plus the fact that the business is unbelievably bigger. When I came to Nashville it was a small business money-wise. Today it's increased thousands and thousands of times.

When you've got something as big as this business, you're going to attract more intelligent people. I don't know if they're more talented but they have their act together. They have tremendous savvy of the business.

Author: What do you believe the difference is in Nashville, New York, and Los Angeles insofar as new artists and writers approaching the industry?

Killen: Nashville is still the hub for country music. The finest country songwriters eventually come to Nashville. The big money may come from the home offices in New York or Los Angeles, but the music originates and is created in Nashville.

Nashville is a very good place to be to learn all phases of the music business. This city is geared to offering a helping hand to new people coming in. There are many writers' organizations here with an open door policy. I believe Nashville is more accessible than New York or Los Angeles when it comes to breaking into the industry. Each of these three cities has a very definite place in the business. However, the "grass roots" of country music, from a creative standpoint, is still in Nashville.

Author: Are any labels still held by American interests?

Killen: Warner Brothers and Mike Curb. When I sold Tree International, I sold it to the Japanese because they offered me about twice the amount that anybody in America would give me.

Author: The bottom line is money.

Killen: You said that yourself. The bottom line is money. I worked for many years to build the company, why would I be stupid enough to give it away?

I wasn't pleased that I would sell it to someone outside this country, but why would I want to give it away? That wouldn't have been good business. I've always been bothered that more American businesspeople, especially here in Nashville, don't get involved in the music business.

Author: If there was a turning point in Buddy Killen's career that brought you to where you are now, what would that be?

Killen: I had a couple of turning points in my life. One was when I went to Wheeling, West Virginia, back in 1953. I stayed there for three months. I nearly starved to death. GMAC came and took my little Pontiac Coupe and drove it away. I hitched a ride back home to Nashville in the back of a van with my wife and my little baby and I went to work. I went to work as a musician and I went to work with a brand new company called Tree Publishing Company. I stayed with it and I worked more hours than you'd ever dream of.

I made my living as a bass player with the Grand Ole Opry and traveling on the road with every person that was a major star on the Grand Ole Opry. One day in the mid-1960s we had Roger Miller breaking wide open with "Dang Me," "Chug-a-lug," "King of the Road"—all those great songs he had. We had "Green, Green Grass of Home." We had Joe Tex exploding all at one time.

And, we were generating money, really good money for the first time. I felt that the time had come for me to determine what I wanted to do. I was still recording as a bass player, recording as a back-up singer, anything I could to generate income.

I gave it some thought and decided that I would concentrate on Tree, which gave me the opportunity to do all of those things that I wanted to do anyway. I could produce records. I could write hit songs. The only thing that I would give up was the playing on other people's sessions. I never looked back. From there Tree became the biggest publishing house in the world.

I don't know that I just sat back one day and said, "This is what I'm going to do." Decisions take time. It takes that little osmosis to get you where you are. There are always a lot of factors. I guess I've always known that I was in the right place. I had struggles. Tremendous struggles. But from the moment I came home, I never looked back. I never quit during the roughest times in my career. And, I don't care how tough it got, I still wouldn't quit.

You must believe in yourself. You must believe in your mission. You must believe in what you are reaching for.

My mission is to continue achieving. I know that I haven't done all I'm going to do. That's why every day I'm open to whatever hits me. I'm bombarded every day with all kinds of things.

You just sort of "cherry pick." You pick this one out without even realizing why you picked it. You don't know. Why do you eat a certain candy or certain food? Why do you fix your hair that way? It doesn't matter. Something down inside of you says, "This is me today. This is what I'll be doing." You make mistakes sometimes, but you can afford a mistake every once in a while.

Author: One of the great things about the music business is the immortality of the great songs. What songs do you like to listen to the most? And of the songs *you* have written, which ones are your favorites?

Killen: I love so much music. I've always said that the best of any kind of music is great. When I listen to something I don't say, "Oh, that's a country song, or that's a pop song, or that's a rhythm and blues song." Unless I'm recording an artist, then I have to determine if I'm going in the proper direction with this act.

For my own musical tastes it absolutely runs the gamut. It can be a great symphony. It can be the funkiest rhythm and blues record that you've ever heard or it can be the countriest country. I've always had that kind of diversified taste in music. So many, many songs have been written that I love.

One of my favorite songs—one that I wish I had written—is "I Believe." "I believe for every drop of rain that falls a flower grows . . ." I wish I had written that song because it's so inspirational. It says everything that I really believe inside. I tried to write a song comparable to that one called "When I've Learned Enough to Really Live" (I'll Be Old Enough To Die). I sort of patterned it after "I Believe."

I like songs with meaning, with a philosophy that will never die. I like a song that will be just as good 50 years from now as it was 50 years ago. Those are the kind of songs I like.

I can get frivolous, I like funny songs. But for myself, I like it to have a lyric that will hold up forever and ever.

I wrote a song called "We Love Each Other," I like a lot. It's been recorded 40 or 50 times by many big names.

THEY ASKED ME HOW WE DO IT
AND I TELL THEM WE LOVE EACH OTHER
THERE'S REALLY NOTHING TO IT
IT'S EASY WE LOVE EACH OTHER
SO WE ALWAYS WILL I KNOW
WE FOUND IT LONG AGO
AND NOW THAT WE'RE SURE
THAT IT'S THE KIND TO LAST FOREVER

THEY ASKED ME CAN WE MAKE IT
AND I TELL THEM WE LOVE EACH OTHER
IF THERE'S TROUBLE WE CAN TAKE IT
I TELL THEM WE LOVE EACH OTHER MORE
THEN WE EVER DID BEFORE AND THEY SHOULD KNOW
THAT WHEN THEY ASK ME HOW WE DO IT
I'LL JUST TELL THEM THAT WE LOVE EACH OTHER SO

I wrote that in 15 minutes. "Forever," has been a pop hit three times. I wrote it without even realizing I'd written it. I was just sitting here humming.

Bill Anderson and I wrote a song called "I May Never Get to Heaven." I like that song. I've been fortunate enough to have written a number of hits, and I like many of the songs I've written. My tastes are so diversified that there's no one particular kind of song, just substance.

Author: What about the gospel music industry?

Killen: I'm one of the largest independent holders of gospel music. I started those companies with Joe Huffman and Randy Cox. Donna Hilly was working with us at that time. We built Meadowgreen. Then I bought all of those great songs of Andre Crouch and Ralph Carmichael. We've had a lot of gospel music.

Author: Tell us about your book.

Killen: My book is called *By the Seat of My Pants* [published in May 1993].
  One day I realized that so many people I knew were dying. You know what I mean—you knew them but you didn't even realize they were dead until somebody wrote about them in the newspaper. Then you start thinking about all of the wonderful anecdotes, all of the wonderful stories that died with them that nobody even knew.
  Through the years when I tell these little stories about what happened to me in the music business, people say, "Why don't you write a book?" I'd say, "I don't know."
  One day I was reading a column by Bob Oermann of *The Tennessean*. He was talking about all of the people who had died that year. I glanced down through it and said, "Oh, look at all my friends. I didn't even know they were gone." I hadn't known they were dead because they had lived all over the country. Then I started thinking about writing that book and thought "maybe I should."
  About that time Tom Carter kept calling me and calling me and calling me. I finally took his call. He said, "You have the best story in town, you ought to write a book. And I'd like to help you do it." I said, "Oh, I don't know, let me think about it."
  At any rate, we got together and we wrote the book. I wrote it with Tom's wonderful help. We finished it after two and a half years. I'm very proud of it. It's warm. It's painful. It's entertaining. I tell about the abject poverty that I grew up in. I tell about my unhappy marriages. I tell about my happy marriage. I tell about disappointments in my children when they were growing up. I tell lots of things. It's an

autobiography. I talk about a lot of people . . . Paul McCartney, who I've spent a lot of time with . . . Jim Reeves, who was one of the best friends I ever had . . . Hank Williams, who I was working with when he died . . . George Morgan, . . . and many of the people I worked with on the Grand Ole Opry. A lot of it I wrote with trepidation. I tried hard not to step on toes too badly. I did not want to be cruel in the book. But sometimes just by virtue of the fact that you have to be honest, as honest as possible, you might crush a feeling, but you don't really mean to. You can't give them baby food if you're going to write a book. It's a pretty diversified kind of book.

It's called *By the Seat of My Pants* because that's how I've flown all of my life. I've had no formal training. Everything I've done and everything I've learned, I've learned by the seat of my pants. When I started out the title was going to be *The Truth of the Matter*. That never did excite me. Then one day I was just going through the book and I said, "Everything I've ever done has just sort of been by the seat of my pants." I thought, "Hey, that might be a title." I called my publisher and he said that's good. Then he ran it by everybody up there and they liked it.

Author: Did you enjoy writing it?

Killen: No. I never got any pleasure out of putting it down. It was almost painful. You have to admit things that you don't want to admit. You have to face things that you thought were out of your life forever. It took so much energy.

Author: What do you do just for fun?

Killen: My wife Carolyn and I enjoy taking cruises. I enjoy the time that I can spend at home, which is not much.

I like to perform. I like to go over to the Stockyard, my restaurant, and entertain the people when I have the time. I like to write songs. I like to produce records. That's all part of what I do but in a way I guess it's sort of an avocation. I don't even know what my vocation is anymore. I really don't because I have about 20 companies and I do all kinds of different things. I don't really know how to separate them. Whatever I am that's me.

I used to snow ski. Carolyn and I like to fish. We fish and catch these huge bass. I like to read. I'm not much of a television person. I like to create. When you're as diversified as I have to be with all of my different businesses, each one of them takes so much of my time each day, I don't have time to get bored. I'm never bored. I'm trying more and more to delegate. I keep saying, "I'd like to reduce myself down to 'mono'."

Author: What's your favorite hands-on activity?

Killen: I enjoy producing records. I enjoy writing. The Stockyard's been a source of joy for me because I took it out of bankruptcy and made it one of the top restaurants in the United States.

I like taking something that's ailing and make it well. Like my travel agency. It was sick when I got it and we turned it around. I like to take an artist who hasn't had a hit in years and have a hit with him. Or take a songwriter who never really got off the ground or nobody even recognizes and turn him into the hottest writer in town.

There's always a mountain to climb. I love climbing mountains.

Buddy Killen

Without question, Buddy Killen has always been a man of vision . . . and goals . . . but most important of all, he is a big dreamer. And ultimately, it's because Killen has had the gumption to go after his dreams that he has also been able to enjoy them . . . to make them happen . . . to see them through.

Even as a kid, back in Florence, Alabama, Killen used to skip school to play music gigs, only imagining his success at the time. But it was just 24 hours after his high school graduation that young Killen was already seeing his first real dream-come-true. That's when he was offered a job on the Grand Ole Opry playing bass for a couple of black-faced comedians called Jam Up and Honey.

He took the job immediately, moved to Nashville, and went to work as a free-lance musician. He traveled with many big-name acts, such as Jim Reeves, Ray Price, Moon Mullican, George Morgan, Cowboy Copas, and Hank Williams, Sr.

However, Buddy Killen was not happy. His music wasn't making his life a dream after all and he was, in fact, struggling to survive. Success simply seemed to elude him. Then, during the time he was pickin' as a sideman on the Wheeling Jamboree, in Wheeling, West Virginia, his life changed.

GMAC took away his car.

Killen vividly recalls:

I was just standing there with big tears in my eyes, and I immediately made up my mind to never let that happen again. I moved back to Nashville, and began working at every music job in sight. I played on the Opry. I played on the road. Sometimes I played all night for only $10. But believe me, I've never been without work for even one day since that terrifying time.

Killen never stopped hustling. He was always eager to work. Jack Stapp spotted that unique quality in him right away, and hired him. Stapp put him on the payroll for $35 a week to plug songs for a new publishing company he was starting called Tree.

In the beginning, neither Stapp nor Killen even knew what a music publishing company was all about. But by the time they had their first international hit, "Heartbreak Hotel" by Elvis, it was Katie-bar-the-door all the way.

Killen's keen taste for talent brought such names to the Tree family as Dottie West, Roger Miller, Joe Tex, Dolly Parton, and countless others. He also added his own writing skills to the Tree clan and created a number of big songs for their catalog including the gigantic hit "Forever."

In 1959, Tree was doing so well that one week they owned seven of the top 10 hits on the country charts. In 1964, the company had its first million-dollar year. And 11 successful years later, in 1975, Killen was named president. In 1980, when Stapp passed away, Killen purchased sole ownership of Tree and continued to nurture its growth as chief executive officer.

Over the years, Killen also made a name for himself as one of the industry's most highly acclaimed record producers. Among artists he has put in-the-grooves are Exile, T.G. Sheppard, Bill Anderson, Doug Kershaw, Dinah Shore, Burt Reynolds, Jack Palance, Diana Trask, Louise Mandrell, Ronny Robbins, Paul Kelly, Clarence "Frogman" Henry, Bonnie Guitar, Jimmy Holliday, Gunilla Hutton, Dolly Parton, Donna Meade, and Ronnie McDowell.

In 1989, Killen sold Tree International to CBS and was to remain at the helm for at least five years. But that plan did not pan out. Killen never seemed to hear the drum of corporate life. So, he managed to negotiate his way out of the contract, and began pursuing Buddy Killen Enterprises in 1991.

In essence, he was starting over. Starting a fresh new slate. And at the time, he was making a statement about himself, his pride, his determination, his ambition, and his never-faltering belief in his very own dream.

Today, Killen sits in control of his multi-faceted corporation, still working 14-hour days, while never blinking an eye. His focus is fine-tuned, but far reaching, encompassing everything from numerous music publishing companies, to record production, to talent management, to owning a major state-of-the-art recording studio, to owning a restaurant that's ranked in the nation's top 50, to co-owning a large travel agency, to writing books, and raising Arabian horses.

A seemingly tireless individual, he also spends an enormous amount of time serving his "adopted" hometown, working with Nashville's Chamber of Commerce, city officials, financial institutions, charities, the arts, state government, and has literally dedicated his life toward helping the Easter Seal Society.

His ambition knows no boundaries. His enthusiasm knows no end. And his example, as a high school graduate, should not go unnoticed. Buddy Killen remains among us as positive proof that the American dream lives on.

Buddy Killen

Part 1

◆ ◆ ◆

The Creative Beginning

Chapter 1

An Overview

Terms Used in This Chapter

Business: Commercial practice or policy; business is business sentiment, friendship, etc., cannot be allowed to interfere with profit making. *(Webster's Dictionary)*

Compose/Composition: To create (a musical or literary work). 1a. The act of composing, or putting together a whole by combining parts; specifically. 1b. The putting together of words; art of writing. 1c. The creation of musical works. *(Webster's Dictionary)*

Hold: Your song or your material, as it is called, is retained by a music industry professional to possibly be recorded by an artist.

Manager: 1a. One who manages a business, institution, etc. 1b. One who manages affairs or expenditures, as of an entertainer. *(Webster's Dictionary)*

Material: Important, essential, or pertinent (to the matter under discussion). *(Webster's Dictionary)* Music, lyrics, and songs on a cassette, usually including typed lyric sheets. *(Jennifer Pierce)*

Music: 1. The art and science of combining vocal or instrumental sounds or tones in varying melody, harmony, rhythm, timbre, especially so as to form structurally complete and emotionally expressive compositions. 2. The sounds or tones so arranged, or the arrangement of these. 3. Any rhythmic sequence of pleasing sounds, as of birds, water, etc. 4a. A particular form, style, etc. of musical composition or a particular class of musical works or pieces [folk music]. 4b. The body of musical works of a particular style, place. *(Webster's Dictionary)*

Song: 1. The act or art of singing [to break into song]. 2. A piece of music sung or as if for singing. 3a. Poetry; verse. 3b. A relatively short metrical composition for, or suitable for, singing, as a ballad or simple lyric. 4. A musical sound like singing [the song of the lark]. *(Webster's Dictionary)*

Universal: 1. Of the universe; present or occurring everywhere or in all things. 2. Of, for, affecting, or including all or the whole of something specified; not limited or restricted. 3. Being, or regarded as, a complete whole; entire; whole. 4. Broad in knowledge, interests, ability, etc. 5. That can be used for a great many or all kinds, forms, sizes, etc., highly adaptable. 6. Used, intended to be used, or understood by all. *(Webster's Dictionary)*

Video: 1. Of or used in television. 2. Designating or of the picture portion of a telecast, as distinguished from the audio (or sound) portion. *(Webster's Dictionary)*

The Lord is my strength and song . . .

Exodus 15:2

Song and *music* are as old as history itself. Plato and Socrates spoke of art and music. Music and song are presented all throughout the Bible. It would be indeed a sad world without song and music.

Believe in Yourself

My first suggestion to anyone embarking on a career in the music industry is never think you are better than anyone else. And, at the same time, never think you are less than anyone else. You are you. You are unique. There is no one on this earth with your feelings, insights, experiences, knowledge. You, and only you, can express all of these unique qualities like no one else can because they belong to you. No one can ever take them from you.

Music is *universal*. A C chord is a C chord throughout the entire world. Music is universal. A great song is a great song now and forevermore.

Once you have a very clear understanding of professional writing, once you know you have given your all to a composition and lyric, do not doubt yourself or let others make you doubt. Everyone has an opinion and you are sure to hear those opinions. Listen quietly and go your way, still believing in yourself and your song. Never defend or explain your material. If it needs explaining, it is either not there or you are presenting it to a person in the industry who does not have ears for your particular kind of music. Don't give up.

Think Like a Songwriter

Read all the lyric writing books you can get your hands on. Study! Type out lyric sheets from the greatest writers. Study what they have done and why they have done it.

Your forte is words, improve your vocabulary. You'll need a thesaurus, a good dictionary, and a good rhyming dictionary for your constant tools.

Always think like a songwriter, observing everything around you. Use your mind, your heart, your eyes, your ears, and your senses of smell and touch.

Go over all letters, old and new, you have written and received. There may be ideas there you never thought about before. Look through bookstores for possible ideas.

This is a difficult *business* to break into. But, if you really want to be a songwriter, you will be one.

Make Yourself Be Heard

Once you have your material completed, sing and play your songs at the various writers' clubs around the city. Let your songs be heard. It is highly unlikely that majors in the industry are going to be knocking at your door or calling you up when they don't even know you exist. So, get out there and do your thing. Try to link up with other artist/writers who are at your level or above. Put your heads together and try to find ways of getting the attention of the industry people.

Teamwork

There is a great deal to know about this industry. You will need to have an understanding of *managers*, and what their function is, producers and what they do, studios and engineers, and which best suit your needs. You will need to understand the difference between a *good* musician and a *great* musician. (A great musician plays with his heart and soul. He gives his all, even in a demo session, for *your* music. They are perfectionists.) Remember it takes a team to make a great song.

I view a *lyric* as the drawing of a child. That child could be quiet, loving, rowdy, or dreamy. I see the *composition* as the personality of that child. The picture (lyric) and the composition (personality) are cohesive. Then when the music plays and the marriage between lyric and music is there, the great musicians give that kid a slap on the bottom and give it life and motion. It takes a team—a great team all giving their all. Make sure the vocalist you use has the vocal range and qualities to give your song the feeling it needs to begin, build, grow, expand, and still have hope at the end.

If you don't feel a good rapport with your team, find another team.

Your job as the writer is to express those emotions which others cannot express. That's a big job. Also, you must write universally. That is, you must express a universal feeling. What you write must be identified with in Germany, Texas, Sweden, Canada, Japan, and around the world. Records are released internationally. A great deal of thought is given to each album and each single. Record companies would be out of business if they did not want a return on their investment. Most major publishing houses and record labels *will not* take unsolicited *material*. There are literally thousands of songs "pitched" (played for executives in the industry for possible recordings) each year by *professional writers*, right in Nashville. The competition is the toughest and the odds are slim for single cuts or album cuts.

Providing Synthesized Sounds

When you have completed your material, lay it down on an eight track, four track, or whatever. Some entities (producers, labels, artists, managers, publishers) *will not* accept synthesized sounds, others will.

We all want to keep our great pickers picking. No one hates "(canned) drum tracks" more than a great drummer, who puts his heart, soul, and special magical touch into his sounds. It is better to just do a piano or guitar vocal, rather than to use machines. After all, we need to keep our great musicians working.

Try to use a recommended studio, where you feel comfortable with the engineer. (I have worked with the same musicians for more than four years. They understand how I write and this cohesiveness makes everyone more comfortable in the studio, and always speeds up the process. I don't produce.) If you have great musicians let them know basically what you feel and/or the sound you want, then let them do their thing. And, if the engineer and you have established a good working relationship, he will know exactly how you want your material mixed. Keep the vocals clearly out front and never leave any holes in the material. Great musicians will take care of all of that for you.

You will need to know what type of system your studio uses so you will know what kind of reel and mix reel to purchase if the studio does not supply them. Then, have clean copies of your session made on cassettes, either there in the studio, or use one of the tape copying facilities in your area where there are professionals who run clean cassettes with no hiss off of your mix reel.

Get it all together and start making appointments to pitch your material.

This book deals with some very technical material, not addressed in most lyric writing books. It presents and defines the highly technical jargon used in the industry.

Pitching Your Material

Find an artist, publisher, manager, or producer who believes in your material. Send it to them on a cassette (usually no more than three songs and accompanying lyric sheets, typed). Also, be sure that your name, address, and phone number is on each label and lyric sheet. If you are affiliated with the American Society of Composers, Authors and Publishers (ASCAP), Broadcast Music Incorporated (BMI), or Society of European Stage Authors and Composers (SESAC), include your affiliation on the label and lyric sheet as well.

(While most people in the music industry are helpful, remember it is a highly competitive business. A good source of information and advice is a professional writers' organization. For a discussion on these groups, see Appendix 1.)

When your material is accepted to be listened to, prepare yourself for a lot of waiting! Do not bother the industry people who have your material. Just wait. If they are interested, they will find you.

Copyright Registration

Be careful who you write with. Have a clear understanding, with your co-writers, who will register your material with the Copyright Office in Washington, DC, and if it is to be registered at all.

It costs $20 to copyright a song. You can register a volume of works or you can register your material song by song, or, by volumes of your material. (For lyrics only, fill out form TX; for lyrics and music use form PA.) I register each song separately, enclosing a cassette and lyric sheet.

For more information on copyright registration or to request forms, contact: the Register of Copyrights, Washington, DC, 20066, (202) 479-0700.

Maintaining a Pitching Log and Files

Keep a pitching log. A pitching log is a file listing the title of your material, to whom you have pitched it, and the date and time it was pitched.

Keep individual files on co-writers and/or co-authors, with their names, addresses, social security numbers, dates of birth, and phone numbers. (The Copyright Office will need this information if you are the one registering the material.)

Signing with a Company

If you are asked to sign with a major company, be careful. Read your contract carefully. Find a qualified music attorney to help you with your signing. Be cautious you are not buried underneath 50 to 70 other writers who have first priority with the company. Your draw may be anywhere from $100 to over $500 per week. Remember this draw is against your own royalties. The higher your draw, the more likely your chances are that the company will try to get you cuts (releases) in order for them to recoup their money.

Holds

If a company puts a *hold* on your material, that means they are interested in possibly recording your work.

This process takes a lot of patience. First, you must have written or co-written a *great* song. Next, that song must get through the producer, the manager, the artist, and lastly the record label. The record label usually ultimately determines, along with the artist and producer, what the singles will be. It is out of your hands at this point. There are three types of holds (molds): soft, hard, and cut. You may feel your material is growing moldy when the interim is long before someone calls you back on your material.

1.   A *soft hold* means perhaps the company will listen again.

2.   A *hard hold* means the listener believes in your material, and will try to have the people in Artist and Repertoire (A&R), or the producers and/or managers, and perhaps, even the artist, listen to your material. It takes a long time to have your material heard and approved by all of these entities. *Be patient.* (I've had songs on hard hold for more than a year.) Once a song is on hard hold, you cannot pitch that material to anyone else, you must ethically wait until you hear back from those holding your material.

3.   A *cut hold* means everyone believes you will have a cut. Your song has gotten through all of the above entities and is to be recorded. Even though your song is recorded in the studio it still may not make the record. If it makes the record, it still may not be a single release.

Retaining Publishing

Based on my experience, I suggest that unless you are a very major writer, don't retain publishing. If a company has two songs of equal greatness and one song has publishing retained by the writers and the other does not, which song do you think will get the cut? If my material is with a major publisher, I trust that major publisher to handle the publishing splits, if any.

The producers, managers, and record labels need your publishing money in order to pay record promoters, buy advertising, press the material, make cassettes and CDs, pay for videos, etc. Usually publishing is split by publishing companies just as writing is split by two or three writers. Just look at *Billboard* magazine and see how many publishers are on one song.

The worst thing that can happen is after all is said and done, and all the contracts are signed, you don't even make the album. This happens. Then your material is "dead in the can." It is very difficult to get someone else interested in previously published material. And, of course, if your material was recorded, even though it did not make the album, you had to have signed a publishing contract prior to the session in which your song was recorded. You can still pitch it and one day it may surface again. But, it is a done deal. Hopefully whatever entity or entities hold your publishing right will continue to try to get your song recorded. Chalk it up to a learning experience and get on with your next song.

Attitudes

Never "cop" an attitude. Be humble, even if you think you are the best writer in the world or the best writer/singer in the world. There are so many great writers in Nashville, New York, and Los Angeles that no one needs someone with an attitude. There will always be those better than you and those still climbing.

There is always more to learn each day, each moment. So, never think you know it all. Keep writing, playing, and making great music.

Music has been called the speech of the angels; I will go farther and call it the speech of God Himself.

Charles Kingsley

Insights of
DOYLE BROWN
Professional Manager
Polygram/Island

The music business is real tough, but you can get there if you persevere and work at it. Look at the masters, see who's in the charts and why they're there in the charts.

Take a look at the "greats," like Dave Loggins, Max D. Barnes, Rory Burke, and Bob McDill. Study their material. They are consistent writers. Ask yourself why. Analyze their lyrics.

One secret to songwriting is consistency. McDill has written hits in four generations; the 1960s, 1970s, 1980s, and 1990s. He has had 26 number one songs. That is a hit songwriter.

You may need to get a day gig to eat, live, and sleep. Just keep writing, and try to write with people who are better writers than you are.

Get a plan as to how to approach the people in the industry.

Keep your lyrics simple and conversational. Be able to talk your lyrics. Your lyrics must have a beginning, a middle, and an end, like in the *Harbrace Handbook*. A song is a story with a melody coupled with it. Study Don Pfrimmer, who wrote "Meet Me in the Middle."

The music business is like two businesses. Publishers make their money from performance and mechanicals. Labels make their money from units sold. The other business is the radio business. Radio stations make their money by selling advertising, they charge for air time, they formulate their programs to make money. So be sure that you are also writing your songs for radio.

You must combine all the things you have learned and stay in it for the long haul. Remember, lyrics are only words on a piece of paper until they're recorded and earning money.

Doyle Brown, a native of Nashville, Tennessee, has been with Polygram/Island Music Publishing Group (formerly the Welk Music Group) for 15 years. He began his career as tape copy librarian and sole song plugger in a small office headed by the late Bill Hall, and is now the professional manager in Polygram/Island's Nashville publishing complex.

Brown attended Middle Tennessee State University, Columbia State, and the University of Tennessee at Knoxville where he was an English education major. He left his studies and worked in sales while trying to land a job in the music business. Soon he was hired by Ernie's Record Mart, an R&B mail order house, which advertised on WLAC's clear channel station. B.J. McElwee, who was working at ABC Records at the time, told Brown about a position available with Bill Hall working for Hall-Clement Publications and Jack and Bill Music Company. Hall was impressed with the young man and hired him.

Brown is responsible for many of Polygram's major country cuts including, "Ya'll Come Back Saloon," recorded by the Oak Ridge Boys, Anne Murray's "A Little Good News," T.G. Sheppard's "Slow Burn," and Keith Whitley's "Don't Close Your Eyes." When asked about his career as a song plugger, he remarked, "It definitely is not a 9-to-5 job. I like to go out on the road with acts and see exactly what they do and sound like, what makes them tick. Otherwise, you're just guessing what songs to pitch. You've got to know as much as possible about an artist and the business in general in order to pitch the tunes that best suit that artist."

Brown has served as National Vice President on the Board of Governors of the National Academy of Recording Arts and Sciences, and as First Vice President of the Nashville chapter. He is a member of the Country Music Association, the Gospel Music Association, and the Nashville Entertainment Association, and is frequently asked to lecture or serve on panels at music industry seminars and workshops.

Doyle Brown *(Photo by Beth Gwinn)*

Chapter 2

◆ ◆ ◆

The First Line

Terms Used in This Chapter

Alliteration: Repetition of an initial sound, usually of a consonant or cluster, in two or more words of a phrase or line. *(Webster's Dictionary)*

Commercial: Made, done, or operating primarily for profit; designed to have wide popular appeal.

Commercialize: To run as a business; apply commercial methods to.

Mood: The feeling in the content of words and music (i.e., sad, happy, etc.).

Rhetorical Question: A question asked only for effect, as to emphasize a point, no answer being expected. *(Webster's Dictionary)*

Rhyme: 1. Correspondence of end sounds, especially at the ends of lines. 2. A regular recurrence of corresponding sounds, especially at the end of lines. 3. Correspondence of end sounds in lines (assonance and consonance). 4. A word that corresponds with another in end sound. *(Webster's Dictionary)*

Tone: Music: 1a. A sound that is distinct and identifiable by its regularity of vibration, or constant pitch (as distinguished from a noise), and that may be put into harmonic relation with other such sounds. 1b. The simple or fundamental tone of a musical sound as distinguished from its overtones. 1c. Any one of the full intervals of a diatonic scale; whole step. 1d. Any of several recitation melodies used in singing the psalms in plainsong. *(Webster's Dictionary)*

Vernacular: The common, everyday language of ordinary people in a particular locality. *(Webster's Dictionary)*

The first line must make the hearer want to hear more. It must be fresh. In the first line, and throughout the lyric, you must draw the pictures and paint the words. Remember, *show it*, don't *tell it*.

If the first line isn't there, then don't expect anyone to listen any further.

Importance of The First Line

The song's first line is extremely important. It is the power pack for the rest of the song.

The first line sets the entire song up. It lets the professional listener know a little bit of what's to come. It sets the *tone* (energetic or slow) and the *mood* (happy or sad) of the underlying feeling of the song.

Now that you understand the importance of the first line, all of your other lines must live up to that first line or you'll lose the song.

Some Famous First Lines

"I GREW UP 'A DREAMIN' OF BEIN' A COWBOY AND LOVIN' THE COWBOYS WAYS."

> From "My Heroes Have Always Been Cowboys"
> (written by Vaughn)

This first line does it all. It lands on all the right vowels, in all the right places, and uses alliteration. It makes you want to hear more.

"I HAVE SEEN THE MORNIN' BURNIN' GOLDEN ON THE MOUNTAIN IN THE SKY."

> From "Lovin' Her Was Easier"
> (written by Kris Kristofferson)

This first line used the *R* sounds for flow and color. And, it lands on a beautiful word for the singer: "sky."

"HOW OLD DO YOU THINK I AM HE SAID, I SAID, WELL I DIDN'T KNOW."

> From "Old Dogs and Children and Watermelon Wine"
> (written by Tom T. Hall)

This first line again lands on all the right vowels for smoothness. It uses alliteration and asks a *rhetorical question,* requiring the listener to want to hear more.

"SEE HIM WASTED ON THE SIDEWALK IN HIS JACKET AND HIS JEANS."

From "The Pilgrim"
(written by Kris Kristofferson)

This first line is so great! It does it all again. It makes the listener ask for more, it alliterates, and makes great use of the vowel sounds.

"COWBOYS AIN'T EASY TO LOVE AND THEY'RE HARDER TO HOLD."

From "Mammas Don't Let Your Babies Grow Up
To Be Cowboys" (written by Ed Bruce and Patsy Bruce)

This first line uses opposites, alliterates, and lands on all the right vowels—all seemingly with great ease. It's not easy.

"UPTOWN GOT ITS HUSTLERS, THE BOWERY GOT ITS BUMS."

From "Don't Mess Around With Jim"
(written by Jim Croce)

Jim Croce was a great writer. I studied everything I could get my hands on that he wrote. He, in my opinion, was a true genius. This first line covers everything with great freshness and alliteration. Croce also makes use of each vowel and consonant with superb expertise. He also uses opposites in uptown and bowery.

"BUSTED FLAT IN BATON ROUGE, WAITIN' FOR A TRAIN, FEELIN' NEARLY FADED AS MY JEANS."

From "Me and Bobby McGee"
(written by Kris Kristofferson)

This first line by Kristofferson is pure genius too. He makes incredible use of alliteration, he draws all the pictures, and he knows exactly how to make use of vowel sounds.

"MIRACLES APPEAR IN THE **STRANGEST** OF **PLACES**."
From "Yesterday's Wine"
(written by Willie Nelson)

Here, in this first line, Nelson uses internal alliteration, and appropriately uses vowels to alliterate rather than using only consonance. And, he makes use again of those wonderful vowels.

(Chorus) **"WELL THAT'LL BE THE DAY WHEN YOU SAY GOODBYE."**
From "That'll Be the Day"
(written by Holly, Allison, and Petty)

These writers knew how to write a lyric. They alliterate and make use of vowels to create the rowdy cadence this song needed. Also, they make you want to hear more.

"RAPID ROY THAT **STOCK CAR BOY HE TOO** MUCH TO BELIEVE."
From "Rapid Roy"
(written by Jim Croce)

Again, the brilliance of Croce. This first line is like a miracle to me. Not only does Croce use all of the aforementioned craft of lyric writing, he also writes in the vernacular.

"NIBBLIN' ON SPONGE CAKE, WATCHIN' THE SUN BAKE."
From "Margaritaville"
(written by Jimmy Buffett)

Buffett's first line is unquestionably one of the finest first lines ever written. Buffett paints all the pictures. He puts you right where he wants you to be. He uses *rhymes* within rhymes as in *bake* and *cake*, and, of course, you want to hear more.

"WHEN LOVE IS **GONE** AND THE **ONE YOU** THOUGHT **WOULD STAY, DOES YOU WRONG** AND **YOU'RE** LEFT ALONE TO PAY."
From "That Old Wheel"
(written by Jennifer Pierce)

This first line also makes use of alliteration and vowels. Since I wrote it, I'll say no more. However, "That Old Wheel" was nominated for four preliminary Country Music Association

The First Line

(CMA) awards and nominated in the top five for vocal event of the year.

All of these great first lines have one thing in common. They are all fresh. They all make the listener want to hear more and they are all professionally and properly written.

Each line lands on the vowel sounds which makes even a rowdy song easy to hear. Each line alliterates, making use of consonants to establish evenness of flow and cadence.

Type out about 50 great first lines and analyze them.

Making Your First Line Count

Be sure your first line sets the mood or feeling you want to create throughout your song. Keep in mind all the tools of your craft and art.

Twelve first lines were presented above. There are hundreds more. Remember to type out and study these lines. Do not handwrite them because you won't be able to see the flow and the patterns. When you set up your first line, make sure you have a time frame (past, present, future). In one line you can set up a conflict situation or you can write to internal monologue or direct dialogue.

Your first line may ask a question or give an answer. Make sure you stick to your subject, do not vary. You only have 12 to 16 lines to write an entire mini-motion picture. Select each word like you're panning for gold. Make sure it's not fool's gold. Make every word count. You may use contrast in your first line or you may use comparison.

Whatever you write, make sure you are setting up a visual image. Keep your song ongoing. Build suspense in your lyric. Never give the end away too soon. Twist the hook to mean two different things, if possible. For example, "After all we've been through together" . . . I guess you didn't love me after all." Note the two meanings to *after all.* Then *end* it with hope always, always leave hope.

Your title should lend itself to the first line in some form. Nothing is carved in stone, but until you really understand the 100 or more things to remember about songwriting, it's better to be safe and stick to proven methods. You can be daring later. Keep your title short, if you can. It will be more easily remembered.

The Value of Teamwork

It takes a team to make it in this business. Gather a team of trusted writers around you. Co-writing is good, it keeps you fresh. Remember, the old adage "two heads are better than one."

I'm not saying you shouldn't write alone. Of course, you should. But you also need to learn how to co-write. Again, look at *Billboard* magazine and see how many writers there are on many of the hit songs, usually at least two. And, they have formed friendships and teams and usually stick with those who are on their same wavelength. They may write with others from time to time, but they usually always go back to the first ones who they got cuts with. "If it works, why fix it?"

Evolution of a Professional Songwriter

Songwriting must become a part of you, just as much as eating, drinking, and breathing. If you do all of your homework, eventually you'll go on automatic. And, believe it or not, you won't always have to be looking things up. They'll be right there, a part of you, the professional songwriter.

Professional listeners listen to between 50 and 200 songs a day on their listening days. If you send in one bad song, the chances are you won't get another chance. Make sure you have written a *great* song.

As soon as a professional listener sees your lyric sheet, he will instantly know whether or not you are a songwriter. These listeners are too busy to waste their valuable time with amateurs or artistes. (I define an artiste as a person who writes for himself and believes he is the best in the world. He doesn't want anyone to tell him what to do or how to change his material to make it better and/or more commercial.)

Some have told me, "I am going to write what I feel" and "like it or not, no one is going to tell me how to write." Well, to me this person is unable or unwilling to learn, or both, and is already copping an attitude.

A true artist is able to write uniquely, from a fresh point of view, touching everyone in the world with the beauty of his lyrics and music. Such artists are the true professionals—the commercial songwriters.

Others have told me they think the word *commercial* is a sell out. To me commercial means you are great enough that the world wants to hear what you have to say, and even better, you will be well paid for your professionalism.

Summary

Keep the first line conversational. Set a time frame. Know where you want to go. Be sure the world will want to hear what you have shown (not told). Remember you are writing a mini-motion picture. Paint your song.

Make every word count. Avoid words like *just, but, because,* if possible. Sometimes certain songs need these words; however, try not to use them unless absolutely necessary. Do not write backwards, reaching for a rhyme.

Observe everything that is going on around you. You might pick up a great first line overhearing a conversation at a restaurant. You may find a first line on a billboard while you're driving along the highway. Or, you may see one in the want ads.

Ideas are everywhere. How many times have you heard a great song, and said to yourself, "Now why didn't I think of that?"

The competition is fierce, but without great competition songs would not continue to improve. Songwriting is a great challenge. If you like challenges of the toughest kind, don't give up.

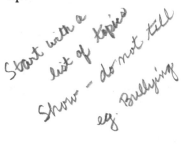

Start with a list of topics
Show - do not till
eg. Bullying

Insights of
MAGGIE CAVENDER
Maggie Cavender Enterprises

Maggie Cavender is, and has always been, interested in helping the songwriter.

Cavender's best advice is: "Know you really want to be a songwriter. Then, look for the people who write better than you do, and write with them."

Don't come to Nashville until you are ready. Don't come thinking you will walk in and see someone, because you won't. Not anymore. The population of songwriters has grown faster than anything else in the music industry. You must be taken seriously and take yourself very seriously. You must get to know the people who have already proven themselves.

Your life can be made or unmade in Nashville or in any other music town, for that matter. You must be terribly devoted to your writing. Listen carefully, but be careful not to act too hastily on that advice.

You have got to work to eat, and even with a number one song, how long do you think that will keep you alive?

You have got to be better than the best, the ones who are already there, the ones who are the best. They are your competition.

Remember, you are only as good as your last recorded song. This applies to every songwriter out there.

Since 1964, when Maggie Cavender returned to her hometown of Nashville, Tennessee, she has made an ongoing major contribution to the growth of the city as a music center.

As one of the most respected leaders of the Nashville music community, she owns and operates Maggie Cavender Enterprises, a company as diverse and effective as the woman herself. Throughout her career, she has worked in music publishing, record production, public relations, and artist management. She is best known as the executive director of the Nashville Songwriters Association International (NSAI), which she has nurtured into a worldwide organization of over 3,000 members. In the spring of 1989, Cavender handed the reins of

NSAI over and became an active member of the NSAI board of directors, and assumed the title of director emeritus. She continues her work for and with songwriters with the same care she has always shown.

In addition to NSAI, Cavender is an active member of The National Academy of Recording Arts and Sciences, The Country Music Association, The Nashville Entertainment Journalists Association, The Nashville Entertainment Association, The Black Music Association, The Gospel Music Association, The Coalition to Save America's Music, The National Academy of Popular Music, the W.O. Smith Community School, and many others.

She has played a key role in the careers of Charley Pride, Alabama, Willie Nelson, Johnny Paycheck, and Ronnie Dove, among others. In addition, there are entertainers and songwriters too numerous to list whom Cavender has helped with words of encouragement or sound advice.

Under her gentle but firm guidance, the NSAI became an international hub for similar organizations, disseminating information and education through workshops, seminars, and newsletters. With Cavender as its chief spokesperson, NSAI has been an advocate of songwriters' rights, a struggle which she has often led in the nation's capitol.

Cavender was one of the first women to assume a leadership role within the previously male-dominated Nashville music industry.

After graduating from Vanderbilt University with a law degree, she moved to California where, with her husband Pete, she involved herself totally in the aviation industry as Lockheed Aircraft's liaison officer, and to this day she still maintains her pilot's license.

But even at that time, prior to World War II, Cavender harbored a love of and interest in music. "It started in the California days," Cavender says of her interest in music. "I'd spend all my evenings with composers, writers, and musicians at the Hangover Club, right off of Hollywood and Vine. They didn't call it hanging out then, but that's what I did. I enjoyed it and learned a lot about those people who wrote and how much courage it took, even back then."

After the war, she and Pete formed their own aviation/business consulting firm. They traveled throughout the country, specializing in making businesses more efficient and profitable.

By 1964, Cavender was ready for both a career change and a return to her home of Nashville. "I had left Nashville because it had nothing to offer," she notes. "I thought music might have something to offer, not money-wise, but challenge-wise. I saw it as a way to give something of myself."

Cavender's first music job was with Pamper Music in copyright administration. At the time Pamper (for whom Willie Nelson and Hank Cochran wrote, among others) was the largest publishing company in the southeast.

After a year there, she worked in executive capacities for CMA, Jack Music, and Shelby Singleton Music, Inc., before forming her own company in 1970.

Today Cavender's reputation is that of a progressive thinker and activist, an astute entrepreneur who is known internationally for her honesty, sincerity, and knowledge of the music industry.

But beneath her credentials and accomplishments is Cavender's unadulterated love of music. "It's been a labor of love, as far as I'm concerned," she says. "I don't think it's the money you have or the money you make. I think it's the things you do that make you successful."

She had both the vision to see Nashville as a major internationally acclaimed music center and the grit to help make that dream a reality.

Today, the word Nashville is magic. So too is the name Maggie Cavender.

Maggie Cavender

Chapter 3

◆ ◆ ◆

Structure, Terms, and Usage

Terms Used in This Chapter

Assonance: A partial rhyme in which the stressed vowel sounds are alike, but the consonant sounds are unalike, as in **late** and **make**. *(Webster's Dictionary)* The similarity of vowel sounds in words which do not rhyme [we—weep, fine—white]. *(McCrimmon)*

Bridge: A connecting passage between two sections of a composition. *(Webster's Dictionary)*

Cadence: The fall of the voice in speaking, dynamics, inflection, or modulation in tone; any rhythmic flow of sound. Example: *What* am I doing; What *am I* doing; What am I *doing*. *(Webster's Dictionary)*

Chord: A combination of three or more tones sounded together in harmony. 1. To harmonize. 2. To play chords on (a piano, guitar, etc.). *(Webster's Dictionary)*

Cliche: A "trite expression", an overused or threadbare expression, or an observation which lacks originality. *(McCrimmon)*

Consonance: 1. Harmony or agreement of elements or parts; accord. 2. A pleasing combination of simultaneous musical sounds; harmony of tones. 3. Prosody— partial rhyme in which consonants in stressed syllables are repeated, but vowels are not. (Example: **mocker, maker**. *(Webster's Dictionary)*

Design: The art of making designs or patterns.

Diatonic Scale: Designating, of, or using any standard major or minor scale of eight tones without the chromatic intervals. *(Webster's Dictionary)*

Hook: The message you are writing your song around (i.e., the words which are the most powerful attention grabbers in your lyric). Words which repeat in your chorus. Many times the hook is also your title.

Irony: A mode of statement in which the writer implies almost the opposite of what he explicitly states. The writing proceeds on two levels at the same time. Ostensibly, the writer is developing the literal meaning of his message, but he counts on the reader to see the implications of each statement in the total context and so to respond at the implied level. The most famous example in English is Jonathan Swift's, *A Modest Proposal*, which under the guise of suggesting a workable plan for improving the economy of Ireland makes an incisive criticism of England's exploitation of the Irish. Irony is difficult to handle. *(McCrimmon)*

Major: Designating an imperfect interval greater than the corresponding minor.

Terms Used in This Chapter *(cont.)*

Major Scale: Music: 1a. Designating an imperfect interval greater than the corresponding minor by a semitone. 1b. Based or characterized by major intervals, scales, etc. [in a major key]. 1c. Designating a triad having a major third. 1d. Based on the scale pattern of the major mode. *See* Major scale. *(Webster's Dictionary)*

Minor: Music: 1a. Designating an imperfect interval smaller than the corresponding major interval by a semitone. 1b. Characterized by minor intervals, scales, etc. [the minor key]. 1c. Designating a triad having a minor third. 1d. Based on the scale pattern of the minor mode: *see* Minor scale. *(Webster's Dictionary)*

Minor Scale: Music: 1a. One of two standard diatonic scales, with half steps instead of whole steps. 1b. After the second and seventh tones in ascending and after the sixth and third tones in descending (melodic minor scale). 1c. After the second, fifth, and seventh tones in ascending and after the eight, sixth, and third tones in descending (harmonic minor scale). *(Webster's Dictionary)*

Mode: A manner or way of acting, doing, or being; method or form. Music: 1a. The selection and arrangement of tones and semitones in a scale, especially any of such arrangements in medieval church music. 1b. A rhythmical system of the 13th century. 1c. Either of the two forms of scale arrangement in later music (Major mode and Minor mode). *(Webster's Dictionary)*

Order: A state or condition in which everything is in its right place and functioning properly.

Pattern: An arrangement of form; disposition of parts or elements, design.

Phrasing: 1. The act or manner of formulating phrases; phraseology. 2. The manner in which one phrases musical passages. *(Webster's Dictionary)*

Scale: Music: A series of tones arranged in a sequence of rising or falling pitches in accordance with any of various systems of intervals; especially, all of such series contained in one octave. *See also* chromatic, diatonic, major scale, minor scale. *(Webster's Dictionary)*

Structure: The arrangement or interrelation of all the parts of a whole; manner of organization or construction.

Tag: To end, tag line. *(Webster's Dictionary)*

Theory: A systematic statement of principles [the theory of equations in mathematics]. *(Webster's Dictionary)*

The first half of this chapter presents basic guitar theory and basic guitar *chord* fingering positions. These diagrams are designed to provide a clearer explanation of guitar theory and the number system.

Basic Guitar Theory

This book is not meant to teach you how to play guitar. The information provided here is for those who have no knowledge of guitar playing or guitar theory in the hopes that the music section will be more clearly understood.

In guitar theory, one method of application in using the number system is to attach a number to each note in the *scale* (i.e., A=1, B=2, C=3, D=4, E=5, F=6, and G=7, if you are playing in the key of A).

Regardless of what *major* key you are playing in, the numbers hold true. View the music *scale* as a circle. If you are playing in the key of G, your scale is as follows: G=1, A=2, B=3, C=4, D=5, E=6, and F=7. If you are playing in the key of C, C=1, D=2, E=3, F=4, G=5, A=6, and B=7. If you are playing in the key of D, D=1, E=2, F=3, G=4, A=5, B=5, and C=7. If you are playing in the key of E, E=1, F=2, G=3, A=4, B=5, C=6, and D=7, etc.

If you are playing in the key of A major, for example, the "A" is represented by the number 1. The next major chord in sequence (in the key of A major) is the D chord. It is represented by the number 4. The third major chord in the key of A major is E seventh. It would be represented by the number 5^7.

When your chords become progressively more complex, the number system will follow a logical sequence corresponding with your chord progressions. Many musicians use their own shorthand systems in numbering and charting lyrics and compositions.

By using the number system it no longer becomes necessary to transpose keys. Numbers hold true in all keys and in all chords. The vocalist simply tells the session players what key he is singing in, then the musicians, using their charted numbers, can transpose to any key. Each player has his individual charts (i.e. the drummer, the bass player, the acoustic player, and the keyboard player each have their own charts). The number system saves a great amount of studio time.

The numbers 1, 4, and 5^7 may apply to all major chords in the major keys (i.e., A, B, C, D, E, F, and G). The 1, 4, and 5^7 count may also apply to all relative *minor* chords in their respective keys. To find the relative minors in any major key, count up six, counting the major key as number 1. If A was your major key (the key in which you intend to sing and/or play), you would count A as 1, B as 2, C as 3, D as 4, and E^7 as 5^7. The three major chords in the key of A major using the number system are: A=1, D=4, and E=5^7. A major counting up the scale six notes brings you to the key of F#m, which will be your first relative minor chord in the key of A major using this system. When you find the first relative minor key, count up four to find the next relative minor chord which will be Bm=4 and C#m^7=5#m^7.

The use of sevenths and/or minors are variations in guitar theory. They may or may not be used. Variations of any chords in their respective keys are entirely up to the composer. The examples given in this book are only intended as simple explanations of very basic guitar theory and the number system.

By using numbers instead of key letters, musicians are able to transpose into any key without changing their charts. The only questions needed to be asked by seasoned session musicians is, "What key are you going to sing it in?" Professional session players usually only need to gather around the studio "deck" and listen to a work tape once or twice in order to have all their charts ready. They all use numbers.

A guitar neck is divided into frets. Figure 1 shows the first four frets on a guitar. The first fret is the one closest to the end of the guitar (the tuning end). The fourth fret is the fret continuing on toward the main body of the guitar.

The index finger is referred to as the first finger. The little finger is referred to as the fourth finger (see Figure 2).

If you were to play the A chord, you would put your first finger on the fourth string (G string) in the second fret, your second finger on the third string (D string) in the second fret, and your third finger on the fifth string (B string) in the second fret. This is the position for playing the chord of A on the guitar.

In guitar a sharp is up the neck and a flat is down the neck. A double sharp is two frets up, etc.

Figures 3 through 7 show five major keys, their major chords, and their respective relative minor chords in basic guitar theory. •An open circle means the string is open when strummed. In other words, you strum the open string. An X means the string is closed in that chord. You do not strum that string. For example, in playing the D chord, the sixth string (low E) and the fifth string (A string) are not played.

The figures represent basic fingering positions in the commonly played chords of A, C, D, E, and G along with the fingering positions of the relative minor chords. The filled-in dots indicate where your fingers belong on the strings. The numbers near each closed circle indicate the finger used on that particular sting.

Structure

In all things there is a *design*. The entire universe has a design. Each item in the universe is part of a *structure*, a hierarchical system. The stars and all the galaxies have designs or *patterns*. Without patterns there would be no *order*, no cohesiveness. The smallest flower has a pattern. All living creatures have a pattern, a design for their lives.

Maps are patterns, highways have patterns. Without patterns and designs no one would know how to get anywhere or do anything.

All songs have patterns too. All music has patterns, designs, structure, and order.

Remember, if you don't know where you are going, or how to get there, chances are you will never arrive!

Music Theory. Music theory has a great deal to do with math. Music has order, structure, design, pattern, and form. That's why there are arrangers. Just as in any work of art, there is form, design, pattern, and structure unique to that particular artist. Your music and lyrics have a form, design, and structure unique for you.

Table 1 presents the major keys and their relative minor chords. For instance, if you are playing in the key of A major, then the other major chords in the key of A are D and E^7. If you

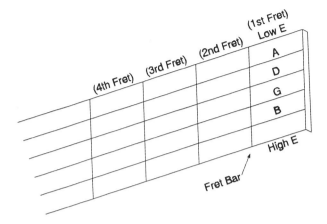

Figure 1. The first four frets on a guitar. Each string has a name. The strings range from (low) E, A, D, G, B to (high) E. The (high) E is referred to as the first string; the (low) E, as the sixth string.

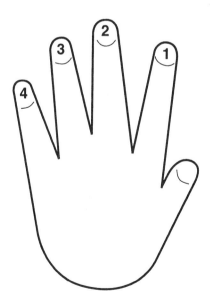

Figure 2. Finger numbering.

Key of A Major

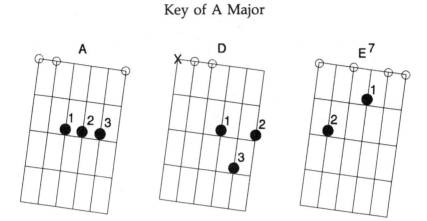

Relative Minors in A

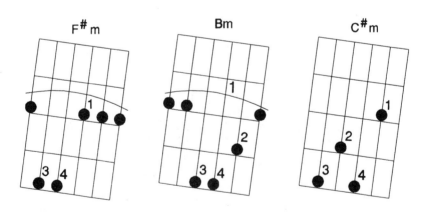

Figure 3. Key of A major. (The curved line inside the fret indicates a bar chord.)

Key of C Major

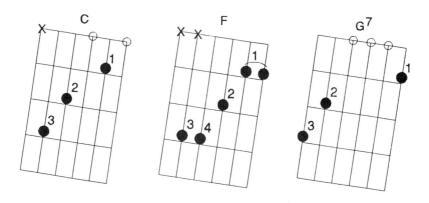

Relative Minors in C

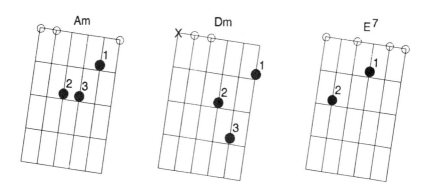

Figure 4. Key of C.

Key of D Major

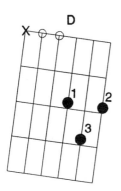 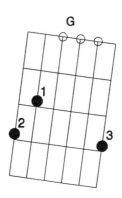 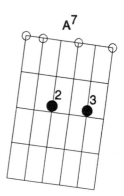

Relative Minors in D

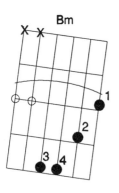 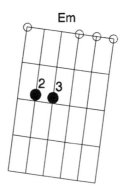 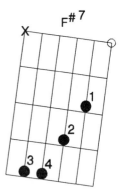

Figure 5. Key of D.

Key of E Major

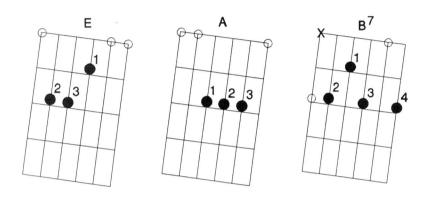

Relative Minors in E

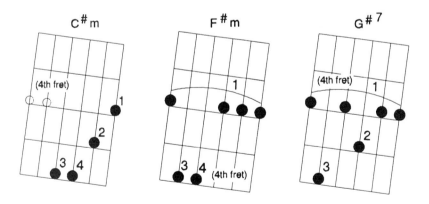

Figure 6. Key of E.

Key of G Major

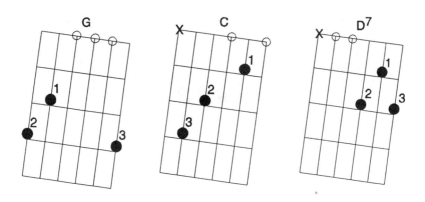

Relative Minors in G

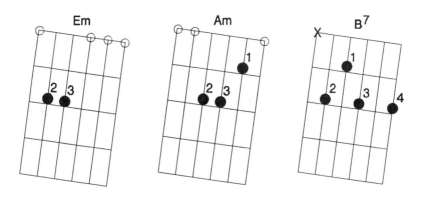

Figure 7. Key of G.

are in the key of D major, the other chords are G and A^7. If you are in the key of G major, the chords which follow are C and D^7. If you are in the key of E major, the other chords are A and B^7. These chords are built on the first, fourth, and fifth step of the major scale. Therefore, in the key of E major, E=1, A=4, and $B^7=5^7$.

Table 1. *Major Keys and Relative Minor Chords*

Major Keys			Relative Minors		
Sharp (#)	Flat (f)	Minor (m)		Seventh (7)	
(1)	(4)	(5) Count up 6	(1)	(4)	(5)
A	D	E^7	$F^{\#m}$	B^m	$C^{\#7}$
B	E	$F^{\#7}$	$G^{\#m}$	$C^{\#m}$	$D^{\#7}$
C	F	G^7	A^m	D^m	E^7
D	G	A^7	B^m	E^m	$F^{\#7}$
E	A	B^7	$C^{\#m}$	$F^{\#m}$	G^7
F	$B^{(f)}$	C^7	D^m	G^m	A^7
G	C	D^7	E^m	A^m	B^7
$A^{(f)}$	$D^{(f)}$	$E^{(f)7}$	F^m	$B^{(f)m}$	C^7
$D^{(f)}$	$G^{(f)}$	$A^{(f)7}$	$B^{(f)m}$	$E^{(f)m}$	F^7
$E^{(f)}$	$A^{(f)}$	$B^{(f)7}$	C^m	F^m	G^7
$B^{(f)}$	$E^{(f)}$	F^7	G^m	C^m	D^7

The numbered chords one, four, and five are used above because they are the most commonly used chords in commercial music, particularly country music.

There are, however, seven chords in each key. Using the key of C as an example, the chords are: first chord, C major; second chord, D minor; third chord, E minor; fourth chord, F major;

fifth chord, G major; sixth chord, A minor; and the seventh chord, B diminished.

Of course, variations may be added, which also have patterns. You need to learn the proper use of augmented chords, diminished passing chords, etc., in order to form a proper and professional musical *composition*.

Lyrics have patterns, designs, and structure. In the *aabb* pattern, for instance, the last words in the first two lines of the lyric rhyme similarly (e.g., *mine* and *time* would be the *aa* pattern part), and the second two lines of the verse end in words which rhyme differently (e.g., *you* and *true*). Each verse must follow this same pattern, once begun.

The chorus, however, may have lines that end in a quad A pattern, or rhymes of the same kind. For example, the last words of a quad A chorus might be *you, true, blue, knew*.

"I Saw the Light" is presented below as an example of a song with an *aabb* verse pattern and a quad A chorus pattern. (Choruses are indented in the song examples.)

"I Saw The Light"
Written by Hank Williams, Sr.

I WANDERED AIMLESS, LIFE FILLED WITH **SIN** *(a)*
I WOULDN'T LET MY DEAR SAVIOR **IN** *(a)*
THEN JESUS CAME LIKE AN ANGEL IN THE **NIGHT** *(b)*
PRAISE THE LORD, **I SAW THE LIGHT** *(b) (hook)*

   I SAW THE LIGHT, I SAW THE LIGHT *(a) (hook)*
   NO MORE IN DARKNESS, NO MORE IN **NIGHT** *(a)*
   NOW I'M SO HAPPY, NO SORROW IN **SIGHT** *(a)*
   PRAISE THE LORD, **I SAW THE LIGHT** *(a) (hook)*

JUST LIKE THE BLIND MAN, I WANDERED **ALONE** *(a)*
TROUBLES AND FEARS I'D CLAIM FOR **MY OWN** *(a)*
THEN LIKE THE BLIND MAN THAT GOD GAVE BACK HIS **SIGHT** *(b)*
PRAISE THE LORD, **I SAW THE LIGHT** *(b) (hook)*

The *aabb* pattern may be used throughout the entire song as was done in "Amarillo By Mornin'."

"Amarillo By Mornin'"
Written by Terry Stafford and Paul Fraser

AMARILLO BY MORNIN', UP FROM SAN ANTONE *(a) (hook)*
EVERYTHING THAT I GOT IS JUST WHAT I GOT ON *(a)*
WHEN THAT SUN IS HIGH, IN THAT TEXAS SKY, I'LL BE BUCKIN'
   AT THE COUNTY FAIR *(R/L) (b)*
AMARILLO BY MORNIN', AMARILLO, I'LL BE THERE *(b) (hook)*

[Notice the use of the rhyme within the line (R/L), which also follows in the third line, second verse, adhering to the pattern of the entire song. This song is unusual, in that no *true* chorus actually exists; but it still works because the pattern and design are so beautifully adhered to.]

THEY TOOK MY SADDLE IN HOUSTON, BROKE MY LEG IN SANTA
   FE *(a)*
LOST MY WIFE AND A GIRLFRIEND SOMEWHERE ALONG THE
   WAY *(a)*
I'LL BE LOOKIN' FOR EIGHT WHEN THEY PULL THAT GATE AND I
   HOPE THAT JUDGE AIN'T BLIND *(R/L) (b)*
AMARILLO BY MORNIN', AMARILLO, YOU'RE ON MY MIND
   (b) (hook)

   AMARILLO BY MORNIN', UP FROM SAN ANTONE *(a) (hook)*
   EVERYTHING THAT I GOT IS JUST WHAT I GOT ON *(a)*
   I AIN'T GOT A DIME, BUT WHAT I GOT IS MINE, I AIN'T
      RICH, BUT LORD I'M FREE *(R/L) (b)*
   AMARILLO BY MORNIN', AMARILLO, IS WHERE I'LL BE
      (b) (hook)

The following songs represent more complicated writing patterns. We'll start with Jim Croce's "Operator."

Croce's expertise with totally natural conversation makes all of his songs work and made all of his songs and music great. However, with the exception of a few of his songs ("Leroy Brown," "Time in a Bottle," "Operator," and a few others), not too many other people recorded Croce's songs because he wrote so differently, both lyrically and musically.

Note that a *c* denotes conversational line. Boldface words indicate his own individual pattern or use of vernacular speech patterns.

"Operator"
Written by Jim Croce

OPERATOR, COULD HELP ME PLACE THIS CALL *(hook)*
YOU SEE THE NUMBER ON THE MATCHBOOK IS OLD AND
   FADED *(b)*

[Croce alliterates the hard *c* sound and a hook in line 1. In line 2, he draws the pictures.]

SHE'S LIVING IN **L.A.**, WITH MY BEST OLD EX-FRIEND **RAY** *(R/L)*

[Notice Croce's use of irony. Obviously Ray wasn't really his best friend at all *(my best old ex-friend Ray)*. And, notice Croce's sense of truth. He is dealing with a real-life situation.]

A **GUY** SHE SAID SHE KNEW WELL AND SOMETIMES **HATED** *(b)*

[Again, Croce is using irony *(a guy she said she knew well and sometimes hated)* and truth (playing real-life games). Also, Croce uses the word *guy*, to stay in the proper framework and social class of his song. And, he rhymes *faded* (line 2, verse 1) with *hated* (line 4, verse 1).]

ISN'T THAT THE **WAY** THEY **SAY** IT GOES, LET'S FORGET ALL
   THAT *(R/L)*
AND GIVE ME THE NUMBER, IF YOU CAN **FIND** IT *(c)*
SO I CAN CALL JUST TO TELL 'EM I'M **FINE,** AND TO **SHOW** *(c)*

[Irony is used again. The caller obviously has not overcome the blow. Also, Croce uses vernacular speech, saying *'em* instead of *them*.]

I'VE OVERCOME THE **BLOW,** I'VE LEARNED TO TAKE IT **WELL** *(R/L)*

[Croce uses R/L phrasing in line 1 *(goes)*, line 3 *(show)*, and line 4 *(blow)*.]

I **ONLY WISH** MY WORDS WOULD **JUST CONVINCE** MYSELF *(R/L) (c)*

[*I only wish* and *just convince* are near rhymes used to express frustration and sadness.]

THAT IT JUST WASN'T **REAL**, BUT **THAT'S** NOT THE **WAY** IT
    FEELS *(R/L)*
OPERATOR, COULD YOU HELP ME PLACE THIS CALL *(hook)*
I CAN'T READ THE NUMBER THAT YOU JUST **GAVE ME** *(c)*

[This last line is one of the most brilliant ever written to say someone has tears in their eyes.]

THERE'S SOMETHING **IN MY EYES**, YOU KNOW IT HAPPENS **EVERY
TIME** *(R/L)*

[Again, *in my eyes* and *every time* are near rhymes. (Croce uses near rhyme phrases to clarify, without saying, that he is crying. Crying over whom? The next line follows seamlessly. Remember in professional songwriting the listener should never know where a line begins or ends. Lyric writing is conversational!]

I THINK ABOUT A LOVE THAT I THOUGHT COULD **SAVE ME** *(R/L)*

[Again, the use of near rhyme phrasing in line 2, verse 2 *(gave me)*, with line 4, verse 2 *(save me)*.]

(Repeat chorus)

[However, after finishing the second chorus, Croce uses a bit of the blues by saying, *No, No, No, No, That's not the way it feels.* Croce gives added emphasis to the fact that he's not feeling too good about this whole situation. He is expressing a *universal* feeling that *everyone* can identify with.]

OPERATOR, LET'S FORGET ABOUT THIS CALL *(hook)*

[Here, Croce involves the operator on a personal level in dealing with his loneliness, and begins to bring us to the *wrap*.]

THERE'S NO ONE THERE I REALLY WANTED TO TALK TO *(c)*

[Although this is a conversational line, notice all the alliteration Croce uses. Content-wise, Croce is deciding not to risk talking to his old love.]

THANK YOU FOR YOUR **TIME**, YOU'VE BEEN SO **MUCH** MORE
THAN **KIND** *(R/L)*

[Here he shows his humility by thanking the operator and
also by complimenting her. Again, he makes use of *assonance,
consonance,* and alliteration.]

YOU CAN KEEP THE **DIME** *(R/L)*

(Repeat chorus)

[Again, Croce uses R/L phrasing in line 3 *(time* and *kind)* and
line 4 *(dime).* He even tells the operator to keep the dime. How
humble. How sad. And it's all in keeping with the *mode,* the
mood, and the entire content of Croce's brilliant song.]

Now this was, and still is, the work of a genius. He uses
almost every lyrical device. He not only *knew* all the lyrical
devices, he knew how to use them effectively.

Croce was able to deal with irony to a great extent. Irony is
very difficult to deal with and few lyricists understand the
mechanics of just how to use it. Croce knew.

Let's take this song line for line on corresponding verses. In
the first line of all three verses, Croce *hooks* each verse with his
title—a one-word title. He then follows the first line of each
verse to its totally conversational and seamless next line.

In the second line of each verse, Croce draws all the pictures
for the listener to see. You can clearly see that faded matchbook
cover (line 2, verse 1). You can see the tears in the caller's eyes
(line 2, verse 2). And, you can feel the loneliness, sadness,
frustration, and hopelessness the caller feels in line 2, verse 3.

Croce writes from the first person, direct dialogue to the
operator, which is the strongest way to write a song. He makes
use of all the senses: sight (matchbook), touch (feel the tears in
his eyes), hearing (as he speaks on a personal level with the
operator), sense of smell (the odor of [what seems to be] a
phone booth the caller was standing in; and taste (taste as well
as feel the tears). In the third lines of each verse, Croce uses the
technique of rhymes within lines: line 3, verse 1, *L.A.* and *Ray;*
line 3, verse 2, [near rhyme] *eyes* and *time;* and line 3, verse 3,

time and *kind*. Then Croce concludes with a beautiful and sad wrap: "You can keep the dime," again rhyming with *time* and *kind*.

Croce word paints an entire story. One that is unforgettable. This is a sad and gentle song. A song of truth. A song of pain. A song that all can relate to.

Croce uses a lot of words, but they are all necessary to complete this hit song.

[I have been told by some in the music industry not to use too many words. That is a matter of opinion and preference. If your song calls for every word you use, then you must use all of those words to complete your entire content, thought, and feeling. Stick to your guns. Once you know you have written the best song you can write and there is no more that can be done to improve it, leave it alone.

I've found that rewrites asked of me by those in the industry only tend to water down my lyrics. I've learned to stick to what I know I've done correctly. I pitched "That Old Wheel" 22 times and was turned down. Then it was recorded by Johnny Cash with Hank Williams, Jr., and remained on the singles charts in *Billboard* for a run of 21 weeks. It was nominated for four preliminary Country Music Association (CMA) awards and it was nominated in the top five for vocal event of the year.

A song on the album was co-produced by Paul McCartney. (One man's junk is another man's jewels). No one can get into my head or heart anymore than they can get into your head and heart. Everyone has an opinion! But, you are the writer. It's your opinion of your own creation that counts the most. This does not mean you should not listen to what those in the industry have to say. You should. You'll always learn something.]

Now back to "Operator." In line 4, verse 1, Croce wrote: *"A guy she said she knew well and sometimes hated."* *Hated* is a near rhyme with *faded* (line 2, verse 1). In lines 2 and 4 of verse 2, Croce rhymes *gave me* with *save me*. This is acceptable because it flows so easily and naturally (usually it is best not to end a verse line with the same word). In lines 2 and 4 of verse 3, rather than rhyming with line 2, Croce wraps the song with the rhyme word *dime*.

Croce also makes use of vowels (assonance) all through the song. Notice all of the *I*s and *O*s he uses. These sounds are great for the singer to sing and pleasant for the listener to hear.

In the chorus, Croce makes a universal statement: "Isn't that the way they say it goes." We can all relate to universal truths. Be careful not to get too clever or use too many *cliches*. They can get boring. Use common sense and if you use a cliche, make sure it flows naturally with your lyric.

Croce also utilizes a rhyme within the line in the last line of each chorus *real* and *feels*. Then he struggles to come to grips with a virtually hopeless situation. When he finally realizes it is senseless and probably would be humiliating to be rejected by his old love, who already did him wrong, he decides to bear his pain. However, the listener still has hope through the courage of the singer for at least trying, and, most of all, for being so entirely honest with his feelings.

The next song analyzed is Jimmy Buffett's "Margaritaville."

"Margaritaville"
Written by Jimmy Buffett

NIBBLIN' ON SPONGE **CAKE**, WATCHIN' THE SUN **BAKE** *(R/L)*

[*Cake* and *bake*—a rhyme within the line in line 1, verse 1. Buffett is drawing all the pictures. He is *nibblin'* not eating or chewing on a specific type of cake. You can taste it (sense of taste). You can feel the sun baking those tourists (sense of touch). He also makes use of assonance which is a vital part of the structure throughout his song.]

ALL OF THOSE TOURISTS COVERED WITH **OIL** *(b)*

[He's painting the pictures. You can see and feel the oil on all of those tourists.]

STRUMMIN' MY **SIX STRING**, ON MY FRONT PORCH **SWING** *(R/L)*

[*String* and *swing*, a rhyme within a line in line 3, verse 1. He is *strummin'* not playing his *six string* (a nice way of saying guitar without saying it. Buffett makes use of alliteration with the *S*s.]

SMELL THOSE SHRIMP THEY'RE **BEGINNIN'** TO **BOIL** *(b)*

[Line 2, verse 1: *oil* rhymes with *boil*, line 4, verse 1. He makes use of assonance. Also, you can smell those shrimp, again, making use of alliteration with *S*s and shows the sense of taste.]

I'M **WASTIN'** AWAY AGAIN IN **MARGARITAVILLE** *(hook)*

[Buffett is telling you, the way great lyricists would tell you, he is gettin' drunk. Again, he makes great use of assonance and consonance. He uses all the proper *idiomatic* phrasing necessary for the mood and tone of this particular song, which he writes as a mini-motion picture.]

SEARCHIN' FOR MY LOST SHAKER OF SALT *(a)*

[Here Buffett makes use of alliteration and assonance. He again lets us know he is gettin' wasted because he can't find the salt.]

SOME PEOPLE **CLAIM** THERE'S A WOMAN TO **BLAME** *(R/L)*

[*Claim* and *blame*, a rhyme within the line in line 3 of the chorus. Buffett is telling us that obviously he is hurtin' over a woman but, since this song calls for the attitude of being cool, his next line states:]

BUT I **KNOW** IT'S NOBODY'S FAULT *(a)*

["Margaritaville" is unusual in that Buffett *tags* the chorus with three different attitudes. And it works. Buffett again uses alliteration with *K* and *N* in this chorus line. He rhymes *salt* in line 2 of chorus with *fault* in line 4 of chorus.]

DON'T KNOW THE **REASON**, I STAYED HERE ALL **SEASON** *(R/L)*

[*Reason* and *season*, a rhyme within the line in line 1, verse 2. Buffett is letting us know content-wise that he is a laid-back beach bum. He again uses assonance *reason* and *season*, leaning on vowels, which make the song easy to listen to and easy to sing.]

ALL I CAN SHOW IS THIS BRAND NEW TATOO *(b)*

[Here he alliterates with Ss and Ts, and uses internal assonance with the *an* in *can* and the *and* in *brand*. And, again staying glued to his content, as all great songs are, he paints a picture of a tattoo which blends seamlessly into the next line.]

BUT IT'S A REAL BEAUTY A LITTLE MEXICAN CUTIE *(R/L)*

[Here he uses alliteration with Bs, and consonance with Ts. And he let's us know he still has that laid-back attitude.]

BUT HOW IT GOT HERE I HAVEN'T **A CLUE** *(b)*

[Line 2, verse 2, *tattoo*, rhymes with *a clue*, line 4, verse 2. Again, he uses alliteration with the Hs, and consonance with the ending Ts. Buffett tells us he was wasted in that he has no idea where that tattoo came from.]

BLEW OUT MY **FLIP-FLOP** STEPPED ON A **POP-TOP** *(R/L)*

[This is another great picture, and another rhyme within the line, line 1, verse 3. Notice also the F alliteration.]

CUT MY HEEL HAD TO CRUISE ON BACK **HOME** *(b)*

[Here he alliterates with Hs and Cs (*cut* and *cruise*). Cruise, what a great word to fit the mood of this man in "Margaritaville."]

BUT THERE'S BOOZE IN THE **BLENDER** AND SOON IT WILL **RENDER** *(R/L)*

[He alliterates with Bs and internally rhymes *blender* and *render*, line 3, verse 3.]

THAT FROZEN CONCOCTION THAT HELPS ME **HANG ON** *(b)*

[Alliteration with Ts and *hang on* is a near rhyme with *back home*, line 2, verse 3. He is most definitely back in "Margaritaville." *Frozen concoction* is the professional way to write about a frozen margarita without saying it.

Then Buffett repeats the chorus after each consecutive verse using three different attitudes for each chorus tag.]

IT'S NOBODY'S FAULT *(first chorus tag)*
IT COULD BE MY FAULT *(second chorus tag)*
IT'S MY OWN DAMN FAULT *(third chorus tag)*

So ends "Margaritaville," a brilliant hit song. Buffett, like Croce, knew how to make use of all of his knowledge and use all the devices available to him.

We have analyzed four songs: "I Saw the Light," for its simplicity of pattern and structure; "Amarillo by Mornin'," for its difference in not having a true chorus; "Operator," for all of the complexities within this great song; and "Margaritaville" not only for all of its complexities, but also for the unusual way Buffett dealt with the chorus tag lines.

There are specific ways to write strictly commercial songs. When a writer knows enough about songwriting so that he has truly mastered the craft, then some license may be taken. In order to do something different, as Buffett did, you must know what you are doing and exactly why you are doing it, or it will not work. Stick to the basics unless and until you are one of the few great masters of songwriting.

The following song is one of my favorites.

"No Easy Horses"
Written by Fred Knobloch, Thom Schuyler, and Don Schlitz

I REMEMBER AS A **CHILD** DADDY TAUGHT ME HOW TO **RIDE** *(R/L)*

[Near rhyme *child* and *ride* in line 1, verse 1.]

TWO CHROME WHEELS, SOME HANDLEBARS, YOU COULD NOT BREAK THE **CHAIN** *(b)*

[Great picture of a bicycle without saying bicycle.]

IT WAS A SUMMER DAY AS **I RECALL**, WASN'T LONG 'FORE I **TOOK A FALL** *(R/L)*

[In line 3, verse 1 the writers rhyme *I recall* with *took a fall*, notice the exact syllable count on rhyming words.]

DADDY SMILED HE DUSTED ME OFF, I GOT BACK ON **AGAIN** *(b)*

[*Again*, line 4, verse 1 is a near rhyme with *chain*, line 2, verse 1.]

THERE AIN'T **NO EASY HORSES** BUT YOU GOTTA LEARN
  TO **RIDE** *(a) (hook)*
YOU MAY FALL YOU WILL STUMBLE BEFORE YOU HIT
  YOUR **STRIDE** *(a)*
MOTHER EARTH WILL CATCH YOU DON'T BE AFRAID TO
  TRY *(a)*
THERE AIN'T **NO EASY HORSES** BUT YOU GOTTA LEARN
  TO **RIDE** *(a) (hook)*

[This song is written with a quad A chorus.]

THE FIRST TIME THAT I LEFT **HOME** TO TRY TO MAKE IT IN THIS
  WORLD **ALONE** *(R/L)*

[Again, as in line 1, verse 1, the writers use a rhyme within the line with *home* and *alone* in line 1, verse 2.]

FIGURED I WOULD BE A STAR ONCE THEY HEARD ME **SING** *(b)*

[What is so appealing here is pure honesty of content.]

THOUGHT I WAS ONE OF THE **BEST** FOUND OUT I WAS ONE OF
  THE **REST** *(R/L)*

[Here, staying with their pattern of lines 1 and 3, verse 1, the writers use rhymes within the lines in lines 1 and 3, verse 2.]

NOW I SPEND ALL MY SUNDAY NIGHTS WAITIN' FOR THE PHONE
  TO **RING** *(b)*

[*Sing*, line 2, verse 2, rhymes with *ring*, line 4, verse 2, following the *bb* pattern of verse 1, with the rhymes or near rhymes of *chain* and *again*, lines 2 and 4, verse 1. Also, this song has great appeal due to the humble nature of this man.]

[Since this last verse ends on such a sad note, and, hope should always be encouraged, the writers make use of a *bridge*, which brings the lyric back to the chorus.]

Bridge:

DREAM ON 'TIL YOU GET IT **RIGHT** *(a)*
WHEN YOU FINALLY GRAB HOLD YOU BETTER HOLD ON **TIGHT** *(a)*

[Note the double *a* bridge, makes a very strong drive back to the chorus.]

(Repeat chorus and tag)

A *tag line* simply means to repeat a line (usually the last line, or the last two lines of the chorus) when the song has ended.

"No Easy Horses" is a professionally written song. The writers manage, with seemingly no effort, to incorporate philosophy and realism all at the same time. A truly masterful song!

The next song analyzed was musically and lyrically written in three-quarter time, a waltz. (Timing is further discussed in Chapter 4.) Lyrics often lend themselves to the timing of a song like *cadence* lends itself to *phrasing* (i.e., the rise and fall of the voice on certain words).
Do a syllable count on the previously analyzed songs and on the following one. See how tight each line matches its corresponding line (e.g., line 1, verse 1 should be very close in syllable count to line 1 in each verse). The same should hold true for each consecutive line for each verse. The chorus will also have a very tight syllable count.

"Amazing Grace"
(Public Domain)

[This song has an *abab* pattern and begins with the chorus.]

AMAZING GRACE HOW SWEET THE **SOUND** *(a)* *(hook)*
THAT SAVED A WRETCH LIKE **ME** *(b)*
I ONCE WAS LOST BUT NOW I'M **FOUND** *(a)*
WAS BLIND BUT NOW I **SEE** *(b)*

'TWAS GRACE THAT TAUGHT MY HEART **TO FEAR** *(a)*
AND GRACE MY FEARS **RELIEVED** *(b)*
HOW PRECIOUS DID THAT GRACE **APPEAR** *(a)*
THE HOUR I FIRST **BELIEVED** *(b)*

(Repeat chorus)

THROUGH MANY DANGERS TOILS AND **SNARES** *(a)*
I HAVE ALREADY **COME** *(b)*
'TIS GRACE HATH BROUGHT ME SAFE THUS **FAR** *(a)*
AND GRACE WILL LEAD ME **HOME** *(b)*

[Verse 2 of lines 1 and 3, respectively, do not rhyme. Bear in mind that this song was written a long time ago. However, stretching it, we could call *snares* and *far* near rhymes. In lines 2 and 4, however, *come* and *home* are a bit closer.]

(Repeat chorus)

WHEN WE'VE BEEN THERE TEN THOUSAND **YEARS** *(a)*
BRIGHT SHINING AS **THE SUN** *(b)*
WE'VE NO LESS DAYS TO SING GOD'S **PRAISE** *(a)* *(R/L)*
THEN WHEN WE FIRST **BEGUN** *(b)*

[Again *years* does not rhyme with *praise*, however, the *sun* does rhyme with *begun*. In fact, the entire rhyme scheme was done away with when the writer used a rhyme within a line of line 3 of the last verse. It's still a great old hymn. Today, however, you need to be much closer in your rhyming scheme than the old songs were.]

(Repeat chorus and tag)

"Amazing Grace" is a wonderful song, with a beautifully written melody. It's what I call a sing-song song. It flows so naturally. Everyone enjoys singing this song. Also, the content is very comforting. The song has great appeal in making the listener and/or the singer have a feeling of great strength.

The next song analyzed, "Mammas Don't Let Your Babies Grow Up To Be Cowboys," is another favorite "standard." (A "standard" song is one that has been recorded by many different artists. A "classic" song is usually attributed to one artist (e.g., "There's a Stranger in My House" by Ronnie Milsap.) The following song is a song of truth, a song of philosophy, and a song we can all feel in our hearts.

This song is also a waltz. In this particular song the rhyming pattern is rather complex; however, it works beautifully.

"Mammas Don't Let Your Babies Grow Up To Be Cowboys"
Written by Ed Bruce and Patsy Bruce

COWBOYS AIN'T EASY TO LOVE AND THEY'RE HARDER TO
   HOLD *(a)*
THEY'D RATHER GIVE YOU A SONG THAN DIAMONDS OR GOLD *(a)*
LONE STAR BELT BUCKLES AND OLD FADED LEVI'S AND
   EACH NIGHT BEGINS A NEW DAY *(b)*
IF YOU DON'T UNDERSTAND HIM AND HE DON'T DIE YOUNG
   HE'LL PROBABLY JUST RIDE AWAY *(b)*

[Verse 1 is an *aabb* pattern. The writers use opposites in line 1 (*easy* and *harder*). They also make use of alliteration with *belt buckles*.]

MAMMAS DON'T LET YOUR BABIES GROW UP TO BE
   COWBOYS *(hook)*
DON'T LET 'EM PICK GUITARS AND DRIVE THEM OLD
   TRUCKS *(a)*
LET 'EM BE DOCTORS AND LAWYERS AND SUCH *(a)*
MAMMAS DON'T LET YOUR BABIES GROW UP TO BE
   COWBOYS *(hook)*
THEY'LL NEVER STAY HOME AND THEY'RE ALWAYS
   ALONE EVEN WITH SOMEONE THEY LOVE *(a) (R/L)*

[In the chorus, *trucks, such,* and *love* are near rhymes.]

COWBOYS LIKE SMOKY OLD POOL ROOMS AND CLEAR MOUNTAIN
   MORNINS' *(c)*
LITTLE WARM PUPPIES AND CHILDREN AND GIRLS OF THE
   NIGHT *(a)*
THEM THAT DON'T KNOW HIM, WON'T LIKE HIM AND THEM
   THAT DO SOMETIMES WON'T KNOW HOW TO TAKE HIM *(c)*
HE AIN'T WRONG HE'S JUST DIFFERENT BUT HIS PRIDE WON'T
   LET HIM DO THINGS TO MAKE YOU THINK HE'S RIGHT *(a)*

[The writers break into more of a philosophical mood in verse 2; and very expertly changes the pattern, using (C) conversational lines, but the song still works out beautifully. Throughout the song, they use opposites, rhymes within lines, and comparisons of what cowboys like, comparing puppies, children, and girls of the night. The writers really set the mood. There's probably not one cowboy that would disagree with the truth in the great song.]

The preceding songs were chosen to understand how to analyze a great song and how to write a great song. Willie Nelson said, "If songwriting were easy everybody would be doin' it." It's not easy!

The seven songs analyzed in this section are very different in character, pattern, design, structure, and content. If you study them, you will learn a great deal about songwriting.

Insights of
CLAY MYERS
Director of Publishing
Starstruck Writers Group

Nashville's music community has a very strong sense of friendly competition. Persistence, talent, and some luck are the key elements to success in this industry.

The best advice I can give to anyone pursuing a career in the country music industry is to become a "sponge" and soak up everything you can, learn every facet of the music business, and never give up on your dream. My observation of those who have been successful is they all have one strong characteristic—a true passion for what they do, regardless of whether they are an artist or work behind the scenes.

Clay Myers, a Jacksonville, Florida, native, received a degree in commercial music from the University of North Alabama. In 1986, following his graduation, Myers went to work in Nashville as an administrative assistant for Maypop Music Group, a publishing company owned by the group Alabama.

In spring 1988, Myers left Maypop to work for Don King Music and Production Company as professional manager.

His next position was in creative services for Malaco Records, a black rhythm and blues label out of Jackson, Mississippi.

Myers worked for Malaco a short time when in fall 1989, he was offered the position of director of publishing for Reba McEntire's newly formed publishing company, Starstruck Writers Group.

Starstruck Writers Group had been operating successfully for a little over a year and in that time had had cuts by Lee Greenwood, Eddy Raven, Cee Cee Chapman, Reba McEntire, Linda Davis, Les Taylor, Trader-Price, The Outlaws, Cleve Francis, and several others. Starstruck Writers Group has a small but very talented staff of writers.

The publishing company is the newest branch of the Starstruck Entertainment organization which handles the management for Reba McEntire, RCA recording artist Aaron

Tippin, and Capitol's new artist Linda Davis. Starstruck Entertainment also includes a concert promotion company, a booking agency, a public relations department, and Reba's fan club and merchandising department.

Clay Myers *(Photo by Cindy Owen)*

Songs Chorded

Below are portions of some of the songs already analyzed with their basic chord progressions. This section explains how to transpose from one major key to another. (See Table 1 on major keys, chords, and relative minors.)

Following the chorded songs are charts with the numbers instead of the keys. This is necessary in major recording sessions so that no one needs to take time to transpose keys. Each number represents the same chord for all the musicians.

The following is a portion of "Amarillo By Mornin'," in the key of G. Remember, G counts as 1, C as 4, and D⁷ as 5⁷.

This same pattern applies to all other keys.

"Amarillo By Mornin'"

[4/4 time. Four beats to the measure.]

ᴳAMARILLO BY ᴮᵐMORNIN', ᶜUP FROM SAN ANᴳTONE
EVERYTHING THAT ᴮᵐI GOT IS ᶜJUST WHAT I GOT ᴰ⁷ON
WHEN THAT SUN ᶜᴹᵃʲ⁷IS HIGH IN THAT ᴰ⁷TEXAS SKY, I'LL BE
ᶜBUCKIN' AT THE ᴮᵐCOUNTY ᶜFAIR
ᴳAMARILLO BY ᴰMORNIN', ᶜAMARILLO ᴰ⁷I'LL BE ᴳTHERE

[You do not need to use all of the major or minor chords in your composition. Use only what your composition calls for. Transposed to the key of D, G, and A⁷. (Relative minors: Bᵐ, Eᵐ, and F♯ᵐ.) The fifth minor (i.e., F♯ᵐ) may also be F♯⁷, if that is what your composition calls for.]

ᴰAMARILLO BY ᶠ♯ᵐMORNIN', ᶜUP FROM SAN ANᴰTONE
EVERYTHING THAT ᶠ♯ᵐI GOT IS ᶜJUST WHAT I GOT ᴬ⁷ON
WHEN THAT SUN ᴳᴹᵃʲ⁷IS HIGH IN THAT ᴬ⁷TEXAS SKY, I'LL BE
ᴰBUCKIN' AT THE ᶠ♯ᵐCOUNTY ᶜFAIR
ᴰAMARILLO BY ᴬMORNIN', ᶜAMARILLO ᴬ⁷I'LL BE ᴰTHERE

The following is a portion of "Mammas Don't Let Your Babies Grow Up To Be Cowboys" in the key of A.

"Mammas Don't Let Your Babies Grow Up To Be Cowboys"

[3/4 time waltz. Three beats to the measure.]

^{A}COWBOYS AIN'T EASY TO LOVE AND THEY'RE HARDER TO ^{D}HOLD
^{E7}THEY'D RATHER GIVE YOU A SONG THAN DIAMONDS OR ^{A}GOLD
LONE STAR BELT BUCKLES AND OLD FADED LEVI'S AND ^{D}EACH
    NIGHT BEGINS A NEW DAY
IF YOU ^{E7}DON'T UNDERSTAND HIM AND HE DON'T DIE YOUNG HE'LL
    PROBABLY JUST RIDE ^{A}AWAY

[Transposed to the key of G. The changes are G, C, and D.]

^{G}COWBOYS AIN'T EASY TO LOVE AND THEY'RE HARDER TO ^{C}HOLD
^{D7}THEY'D RATHER GIVE YOU A SONG THAN DIAMONDS OR ^{G}GOLD
LONE STAR BELT BUCKLES AND OLD FADED LEVI'S AND ^{C}EACH
    NIGHT BEGINS A NEW DAY
IF YOU ^{D7}DON'T UNDERSTAND HIM AND HE DON'T DIE YOUNG
    HE'LL PROBABLY JUST RIDE ^{G}AWAY

The following is a portion of "I Saw The Light" in the key of C.

"I Saw The Light"

[4/4 time. Four beats to the measure.]

^{C}I WANDERED AIMLESS, LIFE FILLED WITH SIN
^{F}I WOULDN'T LET MY DEAR SAVIOR ^{C}IN
THEN JESUS CAME LIKE AND ANGEL IN THE NIGHT
PRAISE THE LORD, ^{G7}I SAW THE ^{C}LIGHT

[Transposed to the key of E.]

^{E}I WANDERED AIMLESS, LIFE FILLED WITH SIN
^{A}I WOULDN'T LET MY DEAR SAVIOR ^{E}IN
THEN JESUS CAME LIKE AND ANGEL IN THE NIGHT
PRAISE THE LORD, ^{B7}I SAW THE ^{E}LIGHT

The following is a portion of "That Old Wheel" in the key of A.

"That Old Wheel"

[2/4 time. Two beats to the measure.]

(Chorus)

ᴬTHAT OLD WHEEL IS GONNA ᴰROLL AROUND ONCE ᴬMORE
AND WHEN IT DOES IT WILL EVEN UP THE ᴱ⁷SCORE
DON'T BE ᴬWEAK AS THEY ᴰSOW THEY WILL ᴬREAP
ᴰTURN THE OTHER ᴬCHEEK AND DON'T GIVE ᴱ⁷IN
THAT OLD WHEEL WILL ROLL AROUND ᴬAGAIN

ᴬWHEN LOVE IS GONE AND THE ᴰONE YOU THOUGHT WOULD
   ᴬSTAY
DOES YOU WRONG AND YOU'RE LEFT ALONE TO ᴱ⁷PAY
THE PRICE IS ᴬHIGH BUT ᴰSOMEHOW YOU'LL ᴬSURVIVE DON'T
   GIVE ᴱ⁷IN
ᴱ⁷THAT OLD WHEEL WILL ROLL AROUND ᴬAGAIN

[Transposed to the key of B.]

(Chorus)

ᴮTHAT OLD WHEEL IS GONNA ᴱROLL AROUND ONCE ᴮMORE
AND WHEN IT DOES IT WILL EVEN UP THE ᶠ#⁷SCORE
DON'T BE ᴮWEAK AS THEY ᴱSOW THEY WILL ᴮREAP
ᴱTURN THE OTHER ᴮCHEEK AND DON'T GIVE ᶠ#⁷IN
THAT OLD WHEEL WILL ROLL AROUND ᴮAGAIN

ᴮWHEN LOVE IS GONE AND THE ᴱONE YOU THOUGHT WOULD
   ᴮSTAY
DOES YOU WRONG AND YOU'RE LEFT ALONE TO ᶠ#⁷PAY
THE PRICE IS ᴮHIGH BUT ᴱSOMEHOW YOU'LL ᴮSURVIVE DON'T
   GIVE ᶠ#⁷IN
ᶠ#⁷THAT OLD WHEEL WILL ROLL AROUND ᴮAGAIN

The following examples of chord transposition will give you a better understanding of how to transpose chords.

(The following sections on theory, *diatonic* chords, and chord progressions and the number charts were composed in their entirety by Terje Brattsveen, musicologist, composer, studio engineer, and owner of Sound Zone Studio.)

Table 2. Diatonic Chords in Each of the Twelve Key Centers

Major (M) Minor (m) Diminished (dim) Sharp (#) Flat (f) Double [#]-(x)						
(1)	(2)	(3)	(4)	(5)	(6)	(7)
C Maj	D min	E min	F Maj	G Maj	A min	B dim
D Maj	E min	F# min	G Maj	A Maj	B min	C# dim
E Maj	F# min	G# min	A Maj	B Maj	C# min	D# dim
F Maj	G min	A min	B(f) Maj	C Maj	D min	E dim
G Maj	A min	B min	C Maj	D Maj	E min	F# dim
A Maj	B min	C# min	D Maj	E Maj	F# min	G# dim
B Maj	C# min	D# min	E Maj	F# Maj	G# min	A# dim

Table 3. Enharmonic Key Centers—Five Chords
(The same pitch, chord, or key has two names)

C#M	D#m	E#m	F#M	G#m	A#m	B#dim
DfM	Efm	F m	GfM	Afm	Bfm	C dim
D#M	E#m	F×m	G#M	A#m	B#m	C×dim
EfM	F m	G m	AfM	Bfm	C m	D dim
F#M	G#m	A#m	B M	C#m	D#m	E#dim
GfM	Afm	Bfm	CfM	Dfm	Efm	F dim
G#M	A#m	B#m	C#M	D#m	E#m	F×dim
AfM	Bfm	C m	DfM	Efm	F m	G dim
A#M	B#m	C×m	D#M	E#m	F×m	G×dim
BfM	C m	D m	EfM	F m	G m	A dim

It is equally common in many songs that the two, three, and six minor chords have been exchanged for major or dominant seventh chords. These are called secondary dominants.

Remember, theory is just the writing down of common practice. In the end there are *no rules* other than the composer's own "two ears." This section is designed to give you a basic understanding of chord progressions and how they come about. It is in no way meant to be an in-depth or extensive study of harmony and theory.

Chord Progressions

Chord progressions are to songs, as canvases are to paintings. It's the harmonic backdrop on which you "paint" the melody and the lyric.

Most commercial chord progressions are very similar. A chord usually contains three notes (triad) and is named by its lowest note (root). Chords come from "stacking" (harmonizing) the major scale in thirds (skipping every other note). For example, to create the C chord, begin with the note C (root) because it is the lowest note. The next note in the scale would be D, which you will *skip*. The following note is E. You should now have the combination C/E. To complete the triad, you will need one more note. The next note *up* from E is F, which you will *skip*. The following note, G you will *add to* your existing C/E, for a C (triad) reading C/E/G.

On the number chart, a diamond (<>) is the same as a fermata. An (x) is a double sharp. Now, try writing out your own chord progressions on your own lyric sheets, and see how well you do. Also, transpose each chord to its proper corresponding number charts in Tables 4, 5, and 6. Note in the tables that (-) indicates minor; (__) a split bar; and (<1>) a fermata.

Table 4. "Amarillo By Mornin'" 4/4 time

Intro			
1	3-	4	5
1	3-	4	5 <5>

Chorus 1			
1	3-	4	1
1	3-	4	5 5
4^{Maj7}	5	1 3-	4
1	5	4 5	

Turnaround 1			
1	3-	4	5

Verse 1			
1	3-	4	1
1	3-	4	5 5
4^{Maj7}	5	1 3-	4
1	5	4 5	

Turnaround 2			
1	3-	4	3-5 modulate up 1/1 step

Chorus 2			
1	3-	4	1
1	3-	4	5 5
4^{Maj7}	5	1 3-	4
1	5	4 5	1 4 5

Tag			
1	5	4 5	

Fade			
1	3-	4	5
1	3-	4	5
1	3-	4	5
1	3-	4	5

Table 5. "That Old Wheel" 2/4 time

Intro			
1	1	1	1
Chorus 1			
1	1	4	1
1	1	1	5
1	1	4	1
4	1	5	5
5	5	1	1
Verse 1			
1	1	4	1
1	1	1	5
1	1	4	1
5	5	5	5
1	1		
Modulate up 4th Chorus 2			
1	1	4	1
1	1	1	5
1	1	4	1
4	1	5	5
5	5	1	1
Instrumental			
1	1	4	1
1	1	1	5
1	1	4	1
4	1	5	5
5	5	1	1
2	<2>	(same as "new" 5)	(same as "new" 5)
Modulate up 5th Verse 2			
1	1	4	1
1	1	1	5
1	1	4	1
5	5	5	5
1	1		

Table 5. "That Old Wheel" 2/4 time (cont.)

Modulate up 4th Chorus 3			
1 1 1 4 5	1 1 1 1 5	4 1 4 5 1	1 5 1 5 1
Chorus 4			
1 1 1 4 5	1 1 1 1 5	4 1 4 5 4	1 5 1 5 4
	Tag		
5 1	5 <1>	1	1

Table 6. "Mammas Don't Let Your Babies Grow Up To Be Cowboys" 3/4 time

Verse 1			
1 4 5 1 1 4 5 5	1 4 5 1 1 4 5 5	1 4 5 1 1 4 5 1 1	1 4 5 1 1 4 5 1 1
Chorus 1			
1 4 5 5 1 4 5 5	1 4 5 5 1 4 5 5	1 4 5 5 1 4 5 1	1 4 5 1 1 1 4 5 1 1

Insights of
TERJE BRATTSVEEN
Musicologist and
Owner of Sound Zone Studio

The Big Rip-Off

The Sting

During my first few days in Nashville, I had to, of course, check out the world-famous Music Row. Music Row is the few square blocks near downtown Nashville which is the heart and soul of the music industry. I had come from halfway across the world [from Oslo, Norway] to be a part of the country music industry.

I remember sitting in a restaurant watching in awe as the tour buses of the "Big Stars," cruised by. As my eyes took in the action on the street outside, my ear was drawn to a conversation between two men in the booth behind me. One of the men was obviously a "famous Nashville producer" and the other a green newcomer, with "stars in his eyes."

The famous producer asked the up-and-coming singer/songwriter how much money he had to spend on the recording project they were about to embark on. The newcomer answered in an innocent and naive voice, "Well, my grandfather passed away, and left me $10,000 and that money has made it possible for me to quit my job back home, and come to Nashville to pursue my dreams as a singer/songwriter. I used to have my own weekend band back in Indiana."

At this point, the famous producer interrupted. "It's funny you should mention the figure $10,000, 'cause that's exactly what it will cost you to get your songs 'demoed' and 'pitched'," he said. "And, of course, I will 'pitch' you as an artist also, to all the major labels in town. I know all the A&R (artist and repertoire) people, both here, and on the coasts, New York and Los Angeles. With your looks and talent, you will, no doubt, be a household name, like Merle Haggard and George Jones. You just stick with me. I'm the one who can do it for you."

The two men soon left the restaurant. I don't know what happened to the guy from Indiana, but, I know two things for sure: he is not a household name, and he is minus $10,000. During my seven years in Nashville, I have heard this conversation many times. Only the faces and the dollar amounts change.

Since I opened my recording studio, I have met people who put out as much as $180,000 on recording sessions that should have cost anywhere from a few hundred to a couple of thousand dollars. These "famous producers" are known in the industry as sharks! They pretend to be part of the "in crowd," but never have any connections in the legitimate music business whatsoever. Their sole purpose is to separate you from your money!

The music business is one of the most competitive businesses in the world. If something sounds too good to be true, it probably is . . . especially in the music business.

The Big Difference: Session Musicians v. Stage Players

There is a big difference between live music and recorded music. Although most musicians start out playing in bars, few move on to successful careers as session musicians.

I have had numerous situations where a songwriter will bring in the guitar player from "Bubba's Bar," to play on his session. Bubba's guitar player is amazing to watch live. He can copy licks off of any record, and sound like any of the "hip" players out there. When it comes time for him to put that special touch on your song, however, Bubba's man draws a blank. After hours of trying this and that approach, he finally settles for an intro lifted directly off a Merle Haggard record. "But he only charged me $10 a song." Is this the justification you will give yourself after the "disaster" is over? For the extra hours he cost you in the studio,you could have hired a professional session player. If your song is recorded by a major artist, the arrangement on the demo you pitched is often used on the master session.

This is not to say that every musician that plays impressively on stage is a bad session player. There are several who are at a crossover point, where they have session experience and still play the clubs.

Recording is a lot like taking a picture. It comes off the tape basically how it goes on the tape. If a great musician records your song, using professional equipment, playing great music in tune, it would be very hard for the engineer to make it sound bad. However, if a not-so-good player records your song, using noisy and inadequate equipment, playing sloppy and out of tune, it will be impossible for anyone to make it sound good.

So ask around. Ask the professional writers you meet who they use on their sessions. Ask musicians who impress you for a demo tape of the sessions they have played on. Ask the legitimate studios who they prefer to work with. Remember, as engineers, we sit through session after session and after a while we get a very good idea of what works and what does not work, who works well with whom, and so on. I feel one of my main functions is to make sure that every session runs smoothly, and no time is wasted. Then, every customer will get the most for their money.

It is out of my control if someone insists on bringing in non-session players (whose egos are showing far more than their talent) who can't get the job done.

The Big Lesson: The Right Combination

It's been said that a lot of music today is written in dollar clef. It's true that in the music business money is the bottom line. But if you think there is no art or emotions involved in the process anymore, you are dead wrong. As a recording engineer in a demo studio, I'm fortunate to be a small part of the process, and one of the first people to hear the song in its completed form. Music is a language, and when used properly, it will by-pass the listener's analytical mind and go straight to the heart. The writer will generally bring in a cassette of the song with just acoustic guitar and vocals for the musicians to write their charts from. The majority of what the song needs is felt by the best session musicians in Nashville rather than communicated verbally to them by the writers. As each instrument is added, a whole new entity comes to life.

Professional musicians take the song from its most basic form, and add just the right amount of their own magic, using the language of music. It's almost like hearing the song getting married to the music. Only when the combination is right does the song stand a chance of passing through everyone's heart all the way to the top of the charts.

Terje Brattsveen is owner of and engineer for Sound Zone Studio. The studio is located in Madison, Tennessee, a few miles from Nashville. Brattsveen studied music at some of the world's most prestigious music schools: The Conservatory of Music, Oslo, Norway, and The Musician's Institute, Hollywood, California. He composed one of the greatest compositions I have ever heard and I was honored when he asked me to write the lyrics for our song, entitled "You Believed."

Terje Brattsveen

Chapter 4

◆ ◆ ◆

Great Songs

Terms Used In This Chapter

Assonance: Vowel sounds in words which do not rhyme [we—weep, fine—white], but are similar.

Consonance: (Prosody)—consonants in stressed syllables are repeated, but vowels are not: **mocker, maker**, etc.

Alliteration: Repetition of an initial sound, usually a consonant, and/or the first letter of a word.

Analysis: 1. A separating or breaking up of any whole into its parts, especially with an examination of these parts to find out their nature, proportion, function, interrelationship, etc. 2. A statement of the results of this process. 3. Linguis: The use of word order and uninflected function words rather than inflection to express syntactic relationships.

Cadence: Vocal Phrasing, the rise and fall of the voice, inflection. Inflection and cadence are similar devices whether you are talking or singing. *Cadence* is the rise and fall of the voice; *inflection* is where emphasis is placed on certain words when phrasing. This is extremely important for the vocalist to understand in order to properly put the emotional feeling in a song where it needs to be. If a vocalist does not understand how to phrase, the song will not come across and may not be heard as it should be heard. Therefore, you may lose a cut all because you or the vocalist do not know how to phrase.

Critique: (critical) 1. A critical analysis or evaluation of a subject, situation, literary work, etc. 2. The act or art of criticizing; criticism—to analyze and evaluate (a subject, literary work, etc.) criticize. *(Webster's Dictionary)*

Inflection: 1. A turning, bending, or curving. 2. A turn, bend, or curve. 3. Any change in tone or pitch of the voice; modulation [to signal a question by a rising inflection]. 4a. Grammar: the change of form by which some words indicate certain grammatical relationships, as number, case, gender, tense, etc. 4b. An inflected form. 4c. An inflectional element, as those bound forms used in English to form the plural and possessive case of nouns (ship, ship's) and the past tense and third person singular, present indicative, of verbs [he shipped, he ships]. *(Webster's Dictionary)*

Syntax: 1. Orderly or systematic arrangement. 2a. Grammar: The arrangement of words as elements in a sentence to show their relationship to one another. 2b. The organization and relationship of word groups, phrases, clauses, and sentences; sentence structure. 2c. The branch of grammar dealing with this. *(Webster's Dictionary)*

This chapter presents songs previously discussed for you to analyze.

In the first few lines of the first song, the syllable count is broken down for you by using a slash sign (/) between syllables. Be sure to count the syllables. At the end of each line indicate the pattern with an a, b, c, R/L, etc. The parentheses at the end of each line are for your pattern letter and your syllable count.

While song lyrics are analyzed in this chapter as well as in Chapter 3, this chapter provides a more extensive and comprehensive analysis. In this chapter, opening and ending alliteration and assonance of single words and phrases (all the way through entire verses) are given. This chapter also presents consonance throughout entire verses; hence, there are more letters, words and phrases in boldface type in this chapter than in Chapter 3.

Notice the opening and closing alliterative internal letters, as in *thought*. Notice consonance, as in *maker* and *baker*. Focus your attention on all of these devices.

Remember to count the syllables after each line. Also, pay attention to the seamlessness of each line, and notice how conversational each line is. You can talk the lyrics. And, at the same time, anyone universally, can identify with the feelings and emotions in these great songs. See the pictures that are painted so clearly for all to see and identify with. These great lyricists are totally aware of everything that is going on beneath those words that seem to be so easily written.

You would be completely unaware of all the many, many devices that the great lyricists use in writing their songs, if they were not literally shown to you. That's part of what makes them great writers. Also, they are sensitive, imaginative artists—painting pictures. They are literary geniuses, telling entire stories in less than three to four minutes.

Check the glossary, and do your best to explain where metaphors, similes, analogies, etc., are used. Explain how the lines are seamless. Talk the lyrics, so you'll see that the song is conversational, and note the importance of the content and the content's universality.

See Chapter 5 for a review of syntax and tenses. You would not want to begin your lyric in the first person singular, and in versus 2 or 3 or in the chorus become confused and begin writing in the second or third person.

Also try to understand the meter in each line.

Use the glossary, if you are not sure of the meanings of the above lyrical devices. See Chapter 3 for content analysis of the following songs.

"Amarillo By Mornin'"

AM/A/RIL/LO BY MORN/IN', UP FROM **SAN AN/TONE** ( ) ( )
EV/ERY/THING THAT I **GOT** IS JUST WHAT **I GOT ON** ( ) ( )
WHEN THAT SUN IS **HIGH,** IN THAT TEX/AS **SKY,** I'LL BE BUCK/IN'
   AT THE COUN/TY **FAIR** ( ) ( )
AM/A/RIL/LO BY MORN/IN', AM/A/RIL/LO I'LL **BE THERE** ( ) ( )

[*High* and *sky,* are close representations to assonance. The *T*s, *B*s, *W*s, and *S*s represent alliteration. *Buckin'* and *county* are close to consonance.]

THEY TOOK MY SAD/DLE IN HOUS/TON, BROKE, MY LEG IN
   SAN/TA FE ( ) ( )
LOST MY WIFE AND A GIRL/FRIEND SOME/WHERE A/LONG THE
   WAY ( )( )
I'LL BE LOOK/IN' FOR **EIGHT** WHEN THEY PULL THAT **GATE** AND I
   HOPE THAT JUDGE AIN'T **BLIND** ( ) ( )
AM/A/RIL/LO BY MORN/IN', AM/A/RIL/LO YOU'RE ON MY **MIND**
   ( ) ( )

[*T*s represent alliteration, as do *W*s, *B*s, and *S*s. *Oke* and *Ope* represent assonance. *Took* and *broke* are examples of consonance. *Hope* and *long* are very close representations of assonance.]

AM/A/RIL/O BY MORN/IN', UP FROM **SAN AN/TONE** ( ) ( )
EV/ERY/THING THAT I **GOT** IS JUST WHAT **I GOT ON** ( ) ( )
WHEN THAT SUN IS **HIGH,** IN THAT TEX/AS **SKY,** I'LL BE BUCK/IN'
   AT THE COUN/TY **FAIR** ( ) ( )
AM/A/RIL/LO BY MORN/IN, AM/A/RIL/LO I'LL **BE THERE** ( ) ( )

(Same as the first chorus)

AM/A/RIL/LO BY MORN/IN', UP FROM **SAN AN/TONE** ( ) ( )
EV/ERY/THING THAT I **GOT** IS JUST WHAT **I GOT ON** ( ) ( )
I AIN'T **GOT A DIME,** BUT WHAT I **GOT** IS **MINE** ( ) ( )
I AIN'T RICH BUT LORD I'M **FREE** ( ) ( )
AM/A/RIL/LO BY MORN/IN', AM/A/RIL/LO IS WHERE I'LL **BE**
   ( ) ( )

(Same as second verse)

"I Saw The Light"

I WAN/DERED AIM/LESS, LIFE FILLED WITH SIN ( ) ( )
I WOULD/N'T LET MY DEAR SAV/IOUR IN ( ) ( )
THEN JE/SUS CAME LIKE AN AN/GEL IN THE NIGHT ( ) ( )
PRAISE THE LORD, I SAW THE LIGHT ( ) ( )

  I SAW THE LIGHT, I SAW THE LIGHT ( ) ( )
  NO MORE IN DARK/NESS NO MORE IN NIGHT ( ) ( )
  NOW I'M SO HAP/PY, NO SOR/ROW IN SIGHT ( ) ( )
  PRAISE THE LORD, I SAW THE LIGHT ( ) ( )

JUST LIKE THE BLIND MAN, I WAN/DERED A/LONE ( ) ( )
TROUB/LES AND FEARS I'D CLAIM FOR MY OWN ( ) ( )
THEN LIKE THE BLIND MAN THAT GOD GAVE BACK HIS SIGHT
( ) ( )
PRAISE THE LORD, I SAW THE LIGHT ( ) ( )

"Operator"

OP/ER/A/TOR, COULD YOU HELP ME PLACE THIS CALL ( ) ( )
YOU SEE THE NUM/BER ON THE MATCHBOOK IS OLD AND FADED
( ) ( )
SHE'S LIV/ING IN L./A., WITH MY BEST OLD EX/FRIEND RAY ( ) ( )
A GUY SHE SAID SHE KNEW WELL AND SOME/TIMES HATED
( ) ( )

IS/N'T THAT THE WAY THEY SAY IT GOES, LET'S FOR/GET ALL
  THAT ( ) ( )
AND, GIVE ME THE NUM/BER, IF YOU CAN FIND IT ( ) ( )
SO I CAN CALL JUST TO TELL 'EM I'M FINE, AND TO SHOW ( ) ( )
I'VE OVER/COME THE BLOW, I'VE LEARNED TO TAKE IT WELL
( ) ( )
I ON/LY WISH MY WORDS WOULD JUST CON/VINCE MY/SELF
( ) ( )
THAT IT JUST WAS/N'T REAL, BUT THAT'S NOT THE WAY IT FEELS
( ) ( )

OP/ER/A/TOR, COULD YOU HELP ME PLACE THIS CALL ( ) ( )
I CAN'T READ THE NUM/BER THAT YOU JUST GAVE ME ( ) ( )
THERE'S SOME/THING IN MY EYES, YOU KNOW IT HAP/PENS
  EVE/RY TIME ( ) ( )
I THINK A/BOUT A LOVE THAT I THOUGHT COULD SAVE ME
( ) ( )

(Repeat chorus)

OP/ER/A/TOR, LET'S FOR/GET A/BOUT THIS CALL ( ) ( )
THERE'S NO / ONE THERE I REAL/LY WAN/TED TO TALK TO
   ( ) ( )
THANK YOU FOR YOUR TIME, YOU'VE BEEN SO MUCH MORE
   THAN KIND ( ) ( )
YOU CAN KEEP THE DIME ( ) ( )

"Margaritaville"

NIB/BLIN' ON SPONGE/CAKE, WATCH/IN' THE SUN BAKE ( ) ( )
ALL OF THOSE TOUR/ISTS COV/ERED WITH OIL ( ) ( )
STRUM/MIN' MY SIX STRING, ON MY FRONT PORCH SWING ( ) ( )
SMELL THOSE SHRIMP, THEY'RE BE/GIN/NIN' TO BOIL ( ) ( )

   I'M WAS/TIN' A/WAY A/GAIN IN MAR/GAR/IT/A/VILLE ( ) ( )
   SEAR/CHIN' FOR MY LOST SHAK/ER OF SALT ( ) ( )
   SOME PEO/PLE CLAIM THAT THERE'S A WOM/AN TO BLAME
   ( ) ( )
   BUT I KNOW IT'S NO/BOD/IES FAULT ( ) ( )

DON'T KNOW THE REA/SON, I STAYED HERE ALL SEA/SON ( ) ( )
ALL I CAN SHOW IS THIS BRAND NEW TAT/TOO ( ) ( )
BUT IT'S A REAL BEAU/TY, A LIT/TLE MEX/I/CAN CUT/IE ( ) ( )
BUT HOW IT GOT HERE I HAV/EN'T A CLUE ( ) ( )

(Repeat chorus)

BLEW OUT MY FLIP-FLOP, STEPPED ON A POP-TOP ( ) ( )
CUT MY HEEL, HAD TO CRUISE ON BACK HOME ( ) ( )
BUT THERE'S BOOZE IN THE BLEN/DER AND SOON IT WILL
   REN/DER ( ) ( )
THAT FRO/ZEN CON/COC/TION THAT HELPS ME HANG ON ( ) ( )

In the foregoing lyric, pay attention to alliteration,
assonance, and consonance in all of the words throughout the
song.

"Delta Dawn"

DEL/TA DAWN WHAT'S THAT FLOW/ER YOU HAVE ON ( ) ( )
COULD IT BE A FAD/ED ROSE FROM DAYS GONE BY ( ) ( )
AND DID I HEAR YOU SAY HE WAS MEET/IN' YOU HERE
   TODAY ( ) ( )
TO TAKE YOU TO HIS MAN/SION IN THE SKY ( ) ( )

SHE'S FOR/TY-/ONE AND **HER** DAD/DY STILL CALLS **HER BA/BY**
  ( ) ( )
ALL THE FOLKS 'ROUND BROWNS/VILLE SAY SHE'S CRA/ZY ( ) ( )
SHE WALKS **DOWN**/TOWN WITH A SUIT/CASE IN **HER HAND**
  ( ) ( )
LOOK/IN' FOR A MY/STER/I/OUS DARK HAIRED **MAN** ( ) ( )

(Repeat chorus)

IN **HER** YOUNG/ER DAYS THEY CALLED **HER DEL**/TA DAWN ( ) ( )
PRET/TI/EST WOM/AN YOU EV/ER LAID EYES **ON** ( ) ( )
BUT A MAN OF LOW DE/GREE STOOD **BY HER SIDE** ( ) ( )
PROM/ISED **HER** HE'D TAKE **HER** FOR **HIS BRIDE** ( ) ( )

(Repeat chorus twice)

Throughout the above song, study all the lyrical devices. Specifically, look at the wonderful flow of the assonance in the second line, first verse: "'round Browns/ville." The writers were well aware that the singer would make great use of the vowel sounds.

Type out lyric sheets of your favorite hit songs, and analyze them. Learn the difference between analyzing and critiquing in order to understand how to use these terms, and how to apply them whenever you are analyzing or critiquing your songs or songs others have written.

"Mammas Don't Let Your Babies Grow Up To Be Cowboys"

COW/BOYS AIN'T EA/SY TO LOVE AND THEY'RE HAR/DER TO
  HOLD ( ) ( )
THEY'D RATH/ER **GIVE** YOU A SONG THAN DIA/MONDS OR
  GOLD ( ) ( )
LONE STAR BELT BUCK/LES **AND OLD** FA/DED **LE/VI'S**
  AND EACH **NIGHT** BE/GINS A NEW **DAY** ( ) ( )
IF YOU **DON'T** UNDER/STAND HIM AND HE **DON'T** DIE **YOUNG**
  HE'LL PROBABLY (**PROB/BLY**) JUST RIDE A/WAY ( ) ( )

MAM/MAS DON'T LET YOUR BAB/IES GROW UP TO BE
   COW/BOYS ( ) ( )
DON'T LET 'EM PICK GUIT/ARS AND DRIVE THEM OLD
   TRUCKS ( ) ( )
LET 'EM BE DOC/TORS AND LAW/YERS AND SUCH ( ) ( )
MAM/MAS DON'T LET YOUR BAB/IES GROW UP TO BE
   COW/BOYS ( ) ( )
THEY'LL NEV/ER STAY HOME AND THEY/RE AL/WAYS
   A/LONE ( ) ( )
EVEN WITH SOME/ONE THEY LOVE ( ) ( )

COW/BOYS LIKE SMOK/Y OLD POOL/ROOMS AND CLEAR
   MOUN/TAIN MOR/NIN'S ( ) ( )
LIT/TLE WARM PUP/PIES AND CHILD/REN AND GIRLS OF THE
   NIGHT ( ) ( )
THEM THAT DON'T KNOW HIM WON'T LIKE HIM AND THEM
THAT DO SOME/TIMES WON'T KNOW HOW TO TAKE HIM
   ( ) ( )
HE AIN'T WRONG HE'S JUST DIFFERENT (DIFF/RENT) BUT HIS
   PRIDE WON'T LET HIM DO THINGS TO MAKE YOU THINK HE'S
   RIGHT ( ) ( )

Notice the analysis of "Mammas," is different here than in Chapter 3. The reason for this difference is that in Chapter 3 the pattern is more conducive to understanding. Here, the syllable count proves to be closer.

Nothing is written in stone. You are the creator of your lyrics and compositions. However, the clearer the pattern and the tighter the song, the greater your chances will be for getting it cut. Unless, of course, you are Willie Nelson.

Insights of
TERRELL TYE
President and Partner
Forerunner Music Group

Music is a language which has evolved just as the spoken language has. Both forms communicate. Music, however, communicates not so much to the intellect as to the heart or to that intuitive part of our spirit that cannot quite be defined by the spoken language. Beethoven, Bach, Tchaikovsky, and other great composers have evoked intense emotions in those who listen without the necessity of putting word to music. However, in today's popular music, the written word is as important as the melody.

To write a truly great song, a songwriter must learn to speak to our innermost emotions, our memories, and our dreams through a uniqueness of melody and lyric. The writer must be able to touch the listener's heartstrings, but must accomplish this in a way that has not been done before.

As a music publisher, I have heard thousands of songs that are merely "good." The melody may be catchy and the lyric may be adequate and it might sound as good as what I just heard on the radio. But my criteria for a truly great song is that it must evoke some strong reaction. I want to feel the song, feel the hurt or the joy as if it were my own. A "good" song simply isn't enough.

There is no formula for writing a truly great song. No one can explain to you how to come up with that unique idea. No one can tell you how to keep it simple but at the same time to say something. Some writers are born with a natural ability for this, others may learn the craft after many years of writing, of rejection, of studying the styles of the truly great songwriters. Try to go inside and pull from your own experiences, no matter how painful or personal, then take the thread of that emotion and write your song in a way that the listener can identify that heartache or that joy in his or her own personal way.

Never write a song so personal that it will only mean something to you; that's boring. Paint a picture, build strong visual images. Good story songs that have managed to capture that elusive thread of emotion are wonderful ways to communicate. Don't be scared to be different.

Terrell Tye (*Photo by Alan L. Mayor*)

Chapter 5

Content and Universality

Terms Used in This Chapter

Adage: An old saying that has been popularly accepted as a truth ("Where there's smoke, there's fire"). *(Webster's Dictionary)*

Antithesis: A contrast or opposition of thoughts, usually in two phrases, clauses, or sentences (You are going; I am staying). *(Webster's Dictionary)*

Aphorism: A terse saying embodying a general, more or less profound truth or principle ("He is a fool that cannot conceal his wisdom").

Content: 1a. All that is contained in something; everything inside (the contents of). 1b. All that is contained or dealt with in a writing or speech. 2a. All that is dealt with in a course or area of study, work of art, discussion, etc. 2b. essential meaning; substance (the content of a poem as distinguished from its form). *(Webster's Dictionary)*

Degree: 1a. A line or space on the staff. 1b. An interval between two such lines or spaces.

Dialectic: Based on the principle that an idea or event (thesis) generates its opposite (antithesis) leading to a reconciliation of opposites (synthesis). *(Webster's Dictionary)*

Epigram: A terse, witty, pointed statement that gains its effect by ingenious antithesis ("The only way to get rid of a temptation is to yield to it"). *(Webster's Dictionary)*

Interval: The difference in pitch between two tones. *(Webster's Dictionary)*

Juxtapose: To move one phrase, clause, or paragraph to another place which makes that phrase, clause, or paragraph more cohesive, or causes the entire content to have a flow more easily conducive to understanding.

Maxim: A general principle drawn from practical experience and serving as a rule of conduct ("Keep thy shop and thy shop will keep thee").

Motto: A maxim accepted as a guiding principle or as an ideal of behavior ("Honesty is the best policy").

Octave: 1a. The eighth full tone above a given tone, having twice as many vibrations per second, or below a given tone, having half as many vibrations per second. 1b. The interval of eight diatonic degrees between a tone and either of its octaves. 1c. The series of tones contained within this interval, or the keys of an instrument producing such a series. 1d. A tone and either of its octaves sounded together. 1e. An organ stop producing tones an octave above those ordinarily produced by the keys struck. 2. Consisting of eight, or an octave. 3. Music producing tones an octave higher [an octave key]. *(Webster's Dictionary)*

Terms Used in This Chapter *(cont.)*
Proverb: A piece of practical wisdom expressed in familiar, concrete terms ("A penny saved is a penny earned").
Saying: The simple, direct term for any expression of wisdom or truth. *(Webster's Dictionary)*
Step: 1a. A degree of the staff or scale. 1b. The interval between two consecutive degrees.
Transposed: To transform, convert—to play music in a key different from the one in which it is written. *(Webster's Dictionary)*
Universal: 1. Of the universe; present or occurring everywhere or in all things; 2. Of, for, affecting, or including all or the whole of something specified; not limited or restricted. *(Webster's Dictionary)*
Vicarious: 1. Shared in or experienced by imagined participation in another's experience [a vicarious thrill]. *(Webster's Dictionary)*

The meaning of song goes deep. Who in logical words can explain the effect music has on us? A kind of inarticulate, unfathomable speech, which leads us to the edge of the infinite, and lets us for a moment gaze into that!

Thomas Carlyle

When you write a lyric, make sure it is universal in its content. Remember music is played throughout the world.

Be sure your song has a beginning, a middle, and an end. Always leave some kind of hope at the end. A great song should never really end at all because there is always hope.

Writing About Universal Feelings

When I hear music I fear no danger, I am invulnerable, I see no foe. I am related to the earliest times, and to the latest.

Henry David Thoreau

Writers must express those emotions everyone feels, but cannot put into words, or show the pictures. Writers have the tremendous responsibility and the great task of "hitting" emotions at a universal level. This is a big job.

If you are dealing with a feeling like "love," be sure that everyone can identify with the kind of love you are addressing in your lyric, whether it is the love between a man and a woman, a mother and her child, or a boy and his dog ("Old Shep"). Be sure it is identifiable.

Examples of various kinds of universal love in hit songs include: "Young Love" (recorded by The Judds), "I'll Love You "Til I Die" (recorded by George Jones), "All of Me" (recorded by Willie Nelson and others), "May I Have This Dance" (recorded by Anne Murray), and "Here in the Real World" (recorded by Alan Jackson). All of these hit songs address the subject content of love, whether that love is young, old, romantic, or realistic. The feelings are all universally identifiable. All listeners can relate to the feelings in these songs; that's a big part of what made them hits. The writers also knew how to write a commercial song. They followed all the rules of pattern and structure.

You might write a song about "freedom." Some great hit freedom songs are: "On the Road Again" (recorded by Willie

Nelson), "The Pilgrim" (recorded and written by Kris Kristofferson), "Amarillo By Mornin'" (recorded by George Strait), "Margaritaville" (written and recorded by Jimmy Buffett), and "Rapid Roy" (written and recorded by Jim Croce). All of these songs address different types of freedom: freedom with the boys, freedom to be a man doing his own thing, and freedom to be a rodeo cowboy (even though the cowboy loses his wife and his girlfriend, he is still free.) Buffett's man was free to do as he pleased in "Margaritaville." In Croce's "Rapid Roy," Roy was free to race around the country. All different kinds of freedom, but all universally identifiable. All listeners can relate or live vicariously through these great songs.

There should be room for the listener to place himself in the situation or in the position of the song's content and be able to apply the song's emotions to his own life. That is why people say, "This is our song," "This is the way I feel about you," or "Let's always play this song on our special day." One of the greatest compliments a professional songwriter can receive is to have his song made a part of someone else's life.

A great lyricist is a great communicator. A professional lyricist may get most of his ideas from within his own life's experience. As a professional he is able to make his experiences, feelings, emotions, joy, sorrow, happiness, etc., fall into the hearts and minds of everyone else. Remember the pros write universally. Perhaps the feeling or emotions began at a very personal level, but, the pro turns that emotion into a universal emotion. Professional lyricists and composers, for the most part, are highly sensitive and creative people who want their songs heard around the world. They want to give what they pulled out of their hearts and souls to others. It is also nice to be paid for doing what they have worked, studied, sweated over, cried over, waited for for many, many years to achieve: the ability to write a great commercial song.

"Super Glued" Content

The content of your song must be cohesive (super glued). Don't ramble, and don't jump from subject to subject. If your song is about love, keep it there. Keep it in the same emotional "room" throughout your lyric. If it is about freedom, keep it there. If it is a philosophical song, keep it there. As they say in the music business "keep it in the room."

Don't start one verse romantically and, then, begin your next verse with extreme realism. Do not make your chorus funny, if the rest of your song is serious. You can, if you really know what you are doing, twist the content, then build the tension to a relief wrap (i.e., as in Croce's "Operator" when Croce decided he really did not want to talk after all). All through "Operator" the listener is waiting to hear and see what will happen next. Croce brilliantly resolves the situation giving himself and the listener the satisfaction of knowing he has finally made a decision. But, that decision is still open-ended, giving the listener the option to decide the outcome if the song were to continue. Croce left hope. Whether that hope was for himself making a decision or the hope was for him at some later date to place that call again.

A Strong Start

Have a strong start in the content of your song. As discussed in Chapter 2, The First Line, you might start with direct dialogue: "Excuse me but I think you've got my chair." You may start out with a greeting: "Hello, walls." You might start with a specific setting: "On a train bound for nowhere." Or, you might use a visual image as in "White Christmas." You might start out with someone's occupation, "Rapid Roy that stock car boy." Whatever you do, get off to a strong start. Your opening line, if it is strong enough, will begin to write your song for you.

Don't Mix Verb Tenses or Personal Pronouns

Do not mix past, present, or future tenses. Do not mix personal pronouns. If you are writing in the first person, keep the proper pronoun throughout the lyric. For instance, if you are writing in the first person, singular, the personal pronouns will be I, my, me, and mine. Personal pronouns are inflected for gender, number, case, and person. Table 7 presents the complete inflection of the personal pronouns.

Table 7. Inflection of Personal Pronouns

Number	Case	1st Person	2nd Person	3rd Person
Singular	Subjective	I	you	he, she, it
	Possessive	my (mine)	your(s)	his, her(s), its
	Objective	me	you	him, her, it
	Reflective	myself	yourself	himself, herself, itself
Plural	Subjective	we	you	they (all genders)
	Possessive	our(s)	your(s)	their(s) (all genders)
	Objective	us	you	them (all genders)
	Reflective	ourselves	yourselves	themselves (all genders)

Know Your Audience

Know who you are writing for in your lyric. Are you writing for the blue-collar worker, the farmer, the factory worker, your lover, your spouse, your child, your mother, your father, or yourself? Who are you directing your lyric to? This does not mean you should always have someone in mind when you pick up that pen or pencil. You should, however, have something specific in mind or you will not know where you are headed and will more than likely get stuck or you will get to "ramblin'."

You should always sit down and write the best song you can possibly write, whatever your subject/content may be. But, if you do have a theme in mind, and know who you are directing your lyric to, then stick to the subject of that person or those people.

Once you decide who you are directing your lyric to, keep it there all the way through your song. Do not change emotions midstream. You will confuse the listener. If you did change midstream, your song will not be cut anyway.

A philosophical song, a great song like "The Gospel According to Luke" (Skip Ewing), addressed a person and a philosophy all at the same time and never varied from content or person.

Developing the Content

The content of your lyric should also build tension. This can be done through contrast of thoughts, as in "Ocean Front Property," "Here in the Real World," or "Lucille." Tension can bring your song to a full circle, but still with no real ending (as in "The Gambler" or "Desperado"). Remember, a great song never really ends. It leaves the listener with the opportunity to formulate some of his own conclusions.

You can find content for your songs from your own interpersonal relationships, newspapers, books, films, any and all sources your eye can see, your ear can hear, your hand can touch, you can smell, or you feel in your heart. The professional songwriter is always writing, writing in his head virtually all the time.

Remember to keep the content of your song in a time frame: past, present, and future. Furthermore, you can make it even tighter by keeping your lyric to one day, even one hour of time in a lifetime, morning, noon, night, daydreaming, or night dreaming. Train yourself to think and feel like a songwriter. Always be aware of what is going on within you and around you.

Part of your song's content is the title itself. Try to keep it short, strong, and memorable. Your title is often your hook. Therefore, in the chorus, repeat the hook at least twice or more, if possible. There are many kinds of hooks: "Sleepin' single in a double bed." A hook should never be too clever or clumsy or awkward. It should be original, fresh, memorable, and understandable. A hook does not have to be a play on words, as so many hooks were years ago. If it is, it must be dealt with very delicately. The title should encourage the listener to hear more of your song, as in "The Chair" or "Here in the Real World."

In today's music it is better to twist the content of your song, very subtly, again as was done in "Ocean Front Property" or "The Chair," rather than twist the hook.

Write every line as powerfully as you can. Do not repeat words in your lyric; that is, do not use the same words twice in your verses. For example, if in verse 1, you use the word *feeling*, do not use the word *feeling* in another verse. Use the strongest, freshest words you can think of. If you need to use a thesaurus to find a word meaning the same thing, use it.

Do not be redundant in your lyric. In other words, do not say the same thing twice in a different way. That is boring, unprofessional, and lazy. You must make new, fresh statements in every line. You must write what you have not yet written and still keep it to the flow of your content. Your entire lyric must follow a pattern to a logical and hopeful conclusion, still leaving the listeners enough room to make up their own minds as to the next part in your mini movie if there were to be a next part. Your songs must become personal to the listener. That's part of what hits are made of.

Do not be lazy when you write. Do not use the same rhyme words at the end of verse lines. And, never reach for a rhyme. Content is much more important. The rhyme will come in its own *natural way and time.*

Do not write backwards reaching for a rhyme. For instance, if your line is:

"Today I searched through my pockets for the key to our front door"

but, your next line or the line before calls for a rhyme with a key, do not write

"I searched through my pockets today for our front door key"

That is not conversational, that is not the way you would speak that line. Lyrics are conversational. Also, when writing the above line backwards, you immediately lose the time frame of today for your first line. Change the line after or the line before if need be, but don't ever write backwards.

Write what needs to be written—no more, no less. Stay to the emotional tone of your content. Do not begin the first verse happy-go-lucky and then begin the second verse down and blue. Let a happy song be happy and let a sad song be sad. Keep the emotion tightly glued throughout.

I don't begin to write until I believe I have something important to say to everyone. Then, I start jotting down emotions addressing that particular subject.

I visually and emotionally put myself right where the singer will be (in that place, time, setting, and frame of mind) and I become an actress, or actor, as the case my be. I put myself right there. I see, in my mind, a torn curtain, perhaps, a stain on the carpet, a broken gate in the garden, a swing where children used to play, or are still playing. In other words I try to paint the pictures. I try to see the details.

I usually do 10 pages, sometimes 20, of rewrites on my lyrics. Once, I didn't finish a song until I had rewritten it 60 times. I don't stop until I feel there is absolutely no more that can be done to improve it.

Words like, *but, just, so, because, that, it, these, them,* etc., are clutter and filler, taking up valuable, needed space for far more meaningful words. Therefore, unless there is absolutely no way to bend that line to leave those words out, try not to use them.

Also, do not use the vernacular way of speaking in your writing. Do not use idiomatic expressions or double negatives (i.e., "ain't," "'em" for them, "you know you done me wrong"), unless your song calls for that type of speech and "red-neck" country expressions. You only have 12 to 16 lines to write your under three-minute mini-motion picture. Every word must count. Paint as many pictures with each word as you possibly can. Show as much as you can possibly show.

When the basic writing is finished, you will also need to "polish" your lyric. Look carefully over your lyric to see if, perhaps, the last lines of your second verse might not flow better in your first verse or your third verse. Perhaps you might even move entire verses around. You need to make your lyric as forceful as possible. When you read your lyric without any music, it should move you and others emotionally. Then when you finally finish your hit lyric, you, or someone you write with who is a good composer, must write that hit composition, which must fit with your lyric like the perfect marriage.

Your music, like your lyric, should move you emotionally, without any words. Your lyric must stand alone and your music must stand alone. Then when they come together, you just might have a "hit" song.

No matter what anyone else may do, whether they are major award-winning artists or major award-winning writers, you write it right for the sake of your own integrity. Politics, power, and favoritism, unfortunately, enter into the music business just like any other business. That is why bad songs get recorded sometimes.

Usually you will want to keep your verses specific (drawing the pictures), and keep your chorus general, hooking the hook. A chorus can be somewhat of a summation of the verses, restating the verses all inclusively. In other words, covering all that needs to be covered in the chorus, while, at the same time, making the chorus cohesive to the verses.

The song "That Old Wheel" is presented below as an example:

Chorus

THAT OLD WHEEL IS GONNA ROLL AROUND ONCE MORE
AND WHEN IT DOES, IT WILL EVEN UP THE SCORE
DON'T BE WEAK, AS THEY SOW, THEY WILL REAP
TURN THE OTHER CHEEK AND DON'T GIVE IN
'CAUSE THAT OLD WHEEL WILL ROLL AROUND AGAIN

Verse

WHEN LOVE IS GONE AND THE ONE YOU THOUGHT WOULD STAY
DOES YOU WRONG AND YOU'RE LEFT ALONE TO PAY
THE PRICE IS HIGH, BUT SOMEHOW YOU'LL SURVIVE, DON'T GIVE IN
THAT OLD WHEEL WILL ROLL AROUND AGAIN

(Repeat chorus)

Verse

THERE'LL BE TIMES HARD TO CONTROL
AND YOU'LL FIND YOU'LL HURT DOWN IN YOUR SOUL
THERE'LL BE THOSE WHO'LL BE GLAD TO SEE YOU DOWN DON'T
  GIVE IN
THAT OLD WHEEL WILL ROLL AROUND AGAIN

As you can see in "That Old Wheel," the verses are specific and the chorus is general. The entire song is cohesive and gives a universal message that all can identify with. The hook is repeated at the end of each verse and twice in the chorus. The *aa* pattern is used in the first two lines of each verse. On the last line of each verse, by using the word *in*, which rhymes with *again*, all the verses were hooked.

An *aa* pattern *(more* and *score)* begins the chorus. The chorus then goes to a rhyme within the line (line 3 of the chorus) *(weak* and *reap)*. The song was hooked by rhyming *in* with *again*.

This song is both philosophical and personal. It sticks like glue to the subject/content matter. Every word counts in this song, and the content has a universal appeal.

The hook in "That Old Wheel" was developed by rephrasing the old saying, "What goes around, comes back around."

The writer must always be thinking of new ways to write old sayings, as one of many writing methods. For instance, the old saying "a stitch in time, saves nine" would not make a good hook. However, it could be rephrased to something like "take love easy" or "go slow." Do not drop any stitches. Train yourself to think and feel like a songwriter.

Pick up a book on old adages and try turning them around into great hooks.

Chord Progressions

Music has content and must flow with your lyric. Your composition, melody line, chord progressions, etc., must be as tight as your lyric. Your composition must have a pattern, structure, and design. There must be a marriage between your lyric and your composition. Your lyric should be able to stand "on its own" and your composition should be able to stand "on its own."

"That Old Wheel" is used again to demonstrate the tight chord progression that must be in every professionally written song. You cannot ramble with the chord progressions any more than you can ramble with the words of the lyric, all must be cohesive—super glued.

Also, you must be very patient in the music industry. I wrote "That Old Wheel" in 1984, but it did not get cut until 1988–89. I used only three chords and the guitar/vocal demo was much slower than the final product. Often your lyric or composition may be changed during production.

^{A}WHEN LOVE IS GONE AND THE ^{D}ONE YOU THOUGHT WOULD ^{A}STAY
DOES YOU WRONG AND YOU'RE LEFT ALONE TO $^{E^7}$PAY
THE PRICE IS ^{A}HIGH, BUT ^{D}SOMEHOW YOU'LL ^{A}SURVIVE DON'T GIVE
   $^{E^7}$IN
$^{E^7}$THAT OLD WHEEL WILL ROLL AROUND ^{A}AGAIN

   ^{A}THAT OLD WHEEL IS GONNA ^{D}ROLL AROUND ONCE ^{A}MORE
   AND WHEN IT DOES IT WILL EVEN UP THE $^{E^7}$SCORE
   DON'T BE ^{A}WEAK AS THEY ^{D}SOW THEY WILL ^{A}REAP
   ^{D}TURN THE OTHER ^{A}CHEEK AND DON'T GIVE $^{E^7}$IN
   THAT OLD WHEEL WILL ROLL AROUND ^{A}AGAIN

^{A}THERE'LL BE TIMES ^{D}HARD TO ^{A}CONTROL
AND YOU'LL FIND YOU'LL HURT DOWN IN YOUR $^{E^7}$SOUL
THERE'LL BE ^{A}THOSE WHO'LL BE ^{D}GLAD TO SEE YOU ^{A}DOWN DON'T
   GIVE $^{E^7}$IN
$^{E^7}$THAT OLD WHEEL WILL ROLL AROUND ^{A}AGAIN

Line for line, the chord progressions are exact, just as your lyric must be exact. Stay within the content of your entire song. "Keep it in the room."

The music for "That Old Wheel" was written in the key of A primarily because that was the easiest key for me to sing it in. However, keys can be transposed.

Lyrically or musically you may want the content of your music to go up a full step or a half step.

Bridges

Generally, do not use a bridge unless it is absolutely necessary. Usually bridges are used to bridge back to a chorus; however, they can be used to bridge back to verses. While a bridge does make a nice melodic change, use it only if you have no other way to drive back to your chorus. Do not bridge your lyric unless the song calls for a bridge (a transition).

One of the biggest mistakes many unprofessional writers make is to put a bridge in their song, and not really know what a bridge is for. They do it just to do it. Or they do it for the melodic change, when the lyric does not call for it.

In "No Easy Horses," a bridge was called for and the writers knew it. It was the bridge that gave the song that hope it needed; and, therefore, the writers used it for content purposes and to drive back to the chorus.

Bridge: Dream on 'til you get it right *(line 1 of bridge)*
When you finally grab hold you better hold on tight *(line 2 of bridge)*

Always drive back to the chorus. Make very sure that the listener (those in the music industry) knows exactly where your chorus is. Let the drive be distinct, understandable, and memorable. It is the chorus that the public remembers and wants to sing along with. The chorus must be very strong. It should begin and end with your hook. However, so long as the chorus is hooked, properly and consistently, there are no concrete rules. You can also use the hook to end the verses.

Usually the public remembers the chorus so don't make the chorus too complicated. They'll want to make the chorus a part of themselves. Keep the chorus simple, fresh, and understandable. And be sure no one forgets your hook.

Keep *All* Artists in Mind

Keep the artist or singer in mind when writing. Do not sit down and write for a particular artist, unless, of course, that artist has asked you to do so. Just write the very best song you can write. But, keep all artists in mind. Be sure they would want to sing your song and feel your lyric content because they are delivering your song just as though they wrote it. Your song has to feel right to that artist or it will not be cut by that artist.

Give your song the character it will need for the singer to want to sing it with feeling and emotion. You'll want that artist to identify with your song, especially if you are writing from the first person position.

Try to keep your song in both genders, so either a male or a female artist can sing it. Otherwise you will be cutting 50 percent of your pitches.

Summary

Make the content strong, original, universal, and clear. Show it, don't tell it. Have a killer first line and, if possible, a strong, short title which is memorable. Keep your entire lyric cohesive. Let it show an entire story and stick with the emotion that you started with. Never reach for a rhyme and don't write backwards.

Study the content of the great songs. Let your own emotions get involved with their lyrics. Keep studying every day. You'll never learn all there is to know.

Right now your audience is probably confined to family and friends. They are *subjective*, not *professional listeners.* Your family and your friends are not the ones who get your songs cut by major artists. Professional listeners are objective because they want to make money for you and for their companies. When the professional publishers, managers, and producers in Nashville, New York, Los Angeles, and other music hubs hear your song, they will know whether or not you know what you are doing. They know as soon as they hear that first line whether or not you are a writer.

If you are fortunate enough to have your songs listened to, don't mess up. You probably won't get a second chance. Do it right the first time. Some professional listeners follow your lyric sheet as they listen; some do not. As soon as they look at your lyric sheet, they will know if you know how to write a song. They listen to the best writers' songs in the country every day. The top writers are your competition.

So, your syllable count better be tight; your chorus better be strong; your first line better be powerful and make them want to hear more; your structure and pattern better be "super glued;" your content better be universal; and your material needs to say something fresh and different. You need to show it, don't tell it.

Remember you are writing a video. Your title better be there. It is a hard job to write, for instance, about love, and say something that has never been said before. Except for your chorus, never end a verse line with the same word. Don't be redundant in your song (don't say the same thing twice). Follow a story line (a beginning, a middle, and an end) all in less than three minutes. Don't over produce. Let the producers, produce. Don't over sing your demo (keep it vanilla), unless you have one of the greatest voices in the country, for they too are in Nashville.

Music is the harmonious voice of creation; an echo of the invisible world; one not of the divine concord which the entire universe is destined one day to sound.

                                                    Giuseppe Mazzini

Insights of
SAM RAMAGE
RCA

Alliteration, assonance, rhyme, contrast, similes, and paradoxes. These are all of the colors and shades in a painting that becomes a song. Songwriters are word painters. Sometimes the picture is clear before the writer picks up a pencil. Sometimes the pencil takes its own course. But, there is always a purpose in the songwriter's mind to evoke, to call up a memory, an emotion, or a story.

I'm not a songwriter, not because I haven't tried, but because I haven't tried hard enough to meet my criteria of a great song. I think the best songs sound like they were easy to write. That's because great songwriters are both philosophers and the average man. They are the listener and the storyteller, the poet and the musician.

It is *what* you say and *how* you say it that counts. If you write songs about things that are important to you, others will believe them. If you write them with the passion of poetry, others will respect them. Inspiration is only part of the battle. The hard part is saying it, and saying it well, using all of the colors of the language like a great artist uses all combinations of colors, like a rainbow, and uses shadows to create a masterpiece.

Great works of art are often born from inspiration; but, not completed without hard labor.

Sam Ramage has worked in music publishing since 1981. As former creative director for EMI Music, he was responsible for the exploitation of the catalog and the acquisition of new material.

Ramage has also worked for United Artists, CBS Songs, and SBK Songs.

Ramage has worked with some of Nashville's most respected songwriters including: Guy Clark ("Heartbroke," "Desperado," and "Waiting for a Train"), Richard Leigh ("Don't It Make My Brown Eyes Blue" and "Somewhere in My Broken Heart"), and Wayland Holyfield ("Some Broken Hearts Never Mend" and "Only Here for a Little While").

Sam Ramage *(Photo by Alan L. Mayor)*

Chapter 6

Lyrics v. Poetry

Terms Used in This Chapter

Abstruse: Hard to understand; deep; recondite. *(Webster's Dictionary)*

Couplet: Two successive lines of poetry, especially two of the same length that rhyme.

Esoteric: 1a. Intended for or understood by only a chosen few, as an inner group of disciples or initiates: said of ideas, doctrines, literature, etc. 1b. Beyond the understanding or knowledge of most people; recondite; abstruse. 2. Confidential; private; withheld [an esoteric plan]. *(Webster's Dictionary)*

Pentameter: 1. A line of verse containing five metrical feet or measures; especially, English iambic pentameter. Example: "He jests/ at scars/ who nev/ er felt/ a wound." 2. Verse consisting of pentameters; heroic verse having five metrical feet or measures. *(Webster's Dictionary)*

Petrarchan Sonnet: A sonnet composed of a group of eight lines (octave) with two rhymes *(abba, abba)*, and a group of six lines (sextet) with two or three rhymes variously arranged (typically: *cdc dcd* or *cde cde*). The thought or theme is stated and developed in the octave, and expanded, contradicted, etc., in the sextet. Italian sonnet. *(Webster's Dictionary)*

Quatrain: A stanza or poem of four lines, usually rhyming *abab, abba,* or *abcb*. *(Webster's Dictionary)*

Recondite: 1. Beyond the grasp of the ordinary mind or understanding; profound; abstruse. 2. Dealing with abstruse or difficult subjects. 3. Obscure or concealed. *(Webster's Dictionary)*

Shakespearean Sonnet: A sonnet composed of three quatrains, typically with the rhyme scheme *abab cdcd efef,* and a final couplet with the rhyme *gg*. *(Webster's Dictionary)*

Sonnet: A poem normally of 14 lines in any of several fixed verse and rhyme schemes, typically in rhymed iambic pentameter. Sonnets characteristically express a single theme or idea. *See* Petrarchan Sonnet; Shakespearean Sonnet. *(Webster's Dictionary)*

Stanza: A group of lines of verse forming one of the divisions of a poem or song. A stanza is usually made up of four or more lines and typically has a regular pattern in the number of lines and the arrangement of meter and rhyme. *(Webster's Dictionary)*

Anyone interested in being a songwriter has probably, at one time or another, been told that song lyrics are not poems. This chapter demonstrates why lyrics and poems differ by presenting a poem and changing it into a lyric.

Even though both lyrics and poems use many of the same devices (meter, rhyme, foot, etc.), you would not talk to someone the way a poem is written. Your speech would be very affected if you spoke like poems are written.

Also poems are usually *esoteric*. Take a close look at the following poem by Abraham Lincoln.

Memory
by Abraham Lincoln

My childhood's home I see again,
And sadden with the view;
And still, as memory crowds my brain,
There's pleasure in it, too.

O memory! thou midway world
'Twixt earth and paradise,
Where things decayed and loved ones lost
In dreamy shadows rise.

And, freed from all that's earthly, vile,
Seem hallowed, pure and bright,
Like scenes in some enchanted isle
All bathed in liquid light.

As dusky mountains please the eye
When twilight chases day;
As bugle notes that, passing by,
In distance die away.

No one would talk to someone in the manner this poem is presented. Furthermore, words such as *twixt, sadden, vile, hallowed,* etc., would never be used in a lyric.

Some people have brought me what they call their "lyrics," which are neither lyrics nor poems. They are words on a page, usually without any order, pattern, design, or structure. In order to write a proper poem, there is a great deal to study and learn, just as there is in lyric writing.

As stated in Chapter 1, there is a formula in all things. You must learn and understand the formulas if you are to write a proper poem or a proper lyric. Writing is a complicated area of study, as complex as engineering a bridge (you may take that literally and figuratively). Everything will fall apart unless you understand what you are doing. The *bridge,* the *poem,* and the *lyric* will all fall down.

If this 10-stanza "poem" by Lincoln were to be a "lyric," I would change the pattern from *abab* to *aabb* and write it something like this:

"Mem'ries All Our Own"
by Jennifer Ember Pierce

Today I looked at some old memories of when I was a child
Pictures yellowed now with age made me cry and made me smile
I know everything in life needs sunshine and some rain
One thing I've learned for certain nothin' stays the same

[The above four lines take the place of Lincoln's first eight lines.]

As I'm walkin' back through shadows to some places in my mind
I still feel the freedom in those childhood dreams of mine
Then I wake up to reality and can see those days are gone
My life right now is lovin' you we'll make *mem'ries all our own*

(Chorus)

We'll make *mem'ries all our own* 'n in time someone may see
Some faded old photographs of a younger you and me
Makin' *mem'ries all our own* we'll never be alone
We'll always have each other makin' *mem'ries all our own*

The chorus takes the place of the last stanzas of Lincoln's poem.

Try this exercise yourself. Pick out a poem and turn it into a lyric. If you do this exercise properly, you will learn how to be conversational without losing the content, theme, or the emotions in the poem.

Poems are not country song lyrics! Poems are not conversational. You would *never* speak to anyone using the words in a poem, unless, of course, you were just reciting that poem to that person or persons.

Many poems do not even have rhyme schemes. And, as you have already read, a poem's pattern (e.g., *abab, cdcd, efef*, and *gg*) are, for the most part and to a great extent, totally different from the pattern of a lyric. Also, the content of a poem is totally different from the content of a lyric.

Poems are also difficult to understand because they are very esoteric. Lyrics are plain speech. I'm not writing about nursery rhymes or comedic poetry (i.e., "She stood on the bridge at midnight as the clock struck on the town, she stood on the bridge at midnight because she couldn't sit down").

A lyricist, however, can gain some great lyrical ideas from studying poetry.

Many poems are "flowery" and/or "mushy." Lyrics must be true to life, even when philosophically written; a lyric must be earthy. A lyric must "ring" true to the realities of everyday life as we know it, see it, hear it, smell it, feel it, taste it, and touch it. Poems do not do this. And, for the most part, the poet is writing from his own personal point of view. He is not writing *universally*. Also, many poems are written in backwards speech, lyrics are not.

Summary

Poems are not conversational. They are often written in backwards speech. Poems often do not have any rhyme scheme, and, if they do, their rhyme scheme differs greatly from a lyric's rhyme scheme. Many times poems are written from the author's personal point of view (e.g., directly to someone they love without making that emotion universal). Poems utilize words which would never be used in "over-the-kitchen-table" conversation.

Poems are esoteric, recondite, and abstruse. Many times they are very difficult to understand; lyrics must be easily understood. Poems are somewhere out there in the world of clouds, the whispering branches of trees, without ever coming down to earth.

Poems don't necessarily give any hope; a lyric must give hope. Poems sometimes end; a great lyric should never end. Poems have no choruses. They have no bridges, no music, no hooks.

Insights of
VINCENT CANDILORA
President, Chief Executive Officer
SESAC, Inc., Nashville

The Bottom Line Is Money is a frightening truth to an aspiring artist. It's my observation and belief that a truly gifted artist, be he a songwriter, musician, or performer, works primarily out of pure love of his art, rather than out of love of its reward.

The business of music is recognizing what the potential consumers love to hear and providing product for consumption and profit. The music business is like any other business. People invest money to make more money. I'm sure sophisticated intellects can debate for hours on the difference between art and commercial art, but perhaps it's as simple as asking the question: "Who does your art communicate with?" The only answer from the business perspective must be that it has strong mass appeal in pre-defined distributable markets. Sounds cold? Cut and dry? Well, the sad conclusion is *the bottom line is money,* and in business that's how success is measured.

Vincent Candilora joined SESAC in February 1969. He has served as adjunct professor at New York University's Music Business Department, lecturing on performing rights.

In 1985, Candilora relocated to Nashville with the opening of SESAC's new offices. In March 1988, he was elected president of the organization.

He serves on the Country Music Association Board of Directors, the Music and Entertainment Industry Educators Association Board, and on the Jukebox Licensing Committee. He was a participant in the first class of Leadership Music and has chaired several committees for Leadership Music's 1991 class.

Vincent Candilora

Definition of Music Rights

Cable TV System: The cable TV system is a facility which receives and transmits the signals of one or more television stations or programming service to paying subscribers. Cable operators who pick up distant TV broadcast signals must pay a compulsory license fee.

Compulsory License: A compulsory license is a method of providing "automatic clearance" for specified uses of copyrighted works. The copyright law provides for four compulsory licenses: (1) for the mechanical reproduction of musical compositions on phonorecords and tapes (this was the one compulsory license that had been part of the prior copyright law); (2) for jukeboxes (no longer compulsory as of 1990); (3) for retransmission of distant broadcast signals by cable operators; (4) for public non-commercial broadcasting; and (5) for transmission of network broadcast and super station signals to home satellite dishes. Rates for each compulsory license are set under the copyright law or by voluntary negotiations and are reviewed and adjusted periodically by the Copyright Royalty Tribunal.

Copyright Owner: A copyright owner is the owner of any of the five exclusive rights granted under the law. These are the right to reproduce the work in copies or phonorecords, to prepare derivative works, to distribute the work publicly, to display the work publicly, and to perform the work publicly. The reproduction right includes the manufacturing and duplication of the composition in sheet music, musical portfolios, song books, phonorecords, tapes, and other permanent copies of the work.

The right to prepare derivative works includes adaptations such as a film version of a musical work or an arrangement of the music for radio or TV advertising commercials. The distribution right involves the distribution of copies of the composition by sale or other transfer of ownership or by renting, leasing, or lending the composition. The right of public display means the showing of a copy of the work on a slide, film, or television image. The right of public performance covers live, recorded, and transmitted uses of music.

Copyright Royalty Tribunal (CRT): The CRT was established under the Copyright Act of 1976 as an independent branch of the federal government. It consists of three commissioners appointed by the president. It is the purpose and responsibility of the tribunal to review royalty rates under compulsory licenses: mechanical, jukebox, cable, satellite, and public broadcasting. As of 1991, mechanical, jukebox, and public broadcasting rates are generally negotiated between copyright owners and users and the CRT steps in only when negotiations fail. The CRT also distributes royalties received from cable system owners to the various claimants. Among the claimants to cable fees collected under the compulsory licenses are the commercial TV stations, public broadcasters, music licensing organizations, sports programmers, and movie and film producers.

Definition of Music Rights *(cont.)*

Fair Use: Fair use is the use of a copyrighted work which does not generally require prior authorization or payment to the copyright owner and which does not constitute copyright infringement. Fair use applies to certain limited situations such as criticism, comment, news reporting, teaching, scholarship, or research.

Infringement: Infringement is a violation of any exclusive right of a copyright owner and includes the unauthorized performance of a musical composition by a user (broadcast or non-broadcast) of music. Each infringement can result in damages under the law ranging from $500 to $20,000 together with court costs and attorney's fees. When the infringement is willful, the amount of damages may be increased to $100,000 for each infringement.

Jukebox: A jukebox is a coin-operated phonorecord player.

Mechanical Right: A mechanical right is the right to reproduce a musical work on phonorecords (i.e., tapes, CDs, vinyl records). It is subject to a compulsory license rate.

Once the copyright owner of the musical work authorizes the distribution of a record, then anyone else may record the same composition by applying for a license and paying the fee set by law. For example, in order for Elvis Presley to record the song "I'll Walk Dem Golden Stairs" published by Ben Speer Music and written by Cully Holt, RCA Records had to obtain a mechanical license from the publisher or its agent.

Mechanical Rights Organizations: The Harry Fox Agency, Copyright Management Inc., and Integrated Copyright Management Inc., grant licenses for mechanical reproduction and synchronization of musical works and collect and distribute these royalties to music publishers.

Performance Right: A performance right is the exclusive right of the publisher and songwriter to perform or authorize the public performance of a copyrighted work. All music users, unless expressly exempted by law, are required to obtain authorization and pay for the performance of musical compositions. Users include radio and television stations, theaters, auditoriums, concert halls, discotheques, night clubs, country clubs, hotels, background music services, skating rinks, restaurants, dance schools, etc. Non-profit users, such as public broadcasters, colleges, and universities are also required to pay for performance rights.

Definition of Music Rights *(cont.)*

Performing Rights Society: A performing rights society is defined in the copyright law as an ". . . association or corporation that licenses the public performance of nondramatic musical works on behalf of the copyright owners, such as the American Society of Composers, Authors and Publishers, Broadcast Music, Inc., and SESAC, Inc."

Print Right: A print right is the right to manufacture, publish, print, and distribute sheet music or other music in printed form.

Public Broadcasting Entity: A public broadcasting entity is a non-commercial educational broadcast station licensed by the Federal Communications Commission as such.

Registration: Musical works are registered with the U.S. Copyright Office through completion of the appropriate form, payment of a fee, and deposit of copies of the work. While registration is not mandatory, it does grant the copyright owner additional privileges.

Synchronization Right: A synchronization right is the right to use music in synchronization or timed relation with visual images such as television programs, films, or other audiovisual materials. For example, in order to use the song "From the Cradle to the Grave" published by J.M. Henson Music Company in the motion picture *Willie & Phil*, the film producer obtained a synchronization or "synch" license to use the music.

(Used by permission from SESAC.)

Chapter 7

♦ ♦ ♦

Quiz and Exercises

Try to complete the following quiz and exercises without referring to other chapters in this book.

All of the words presented in the quiz are defined in the Glossary and in various chapters throughout this book.

Scoring: Give yourself 10 points for each correct answer. Don't worry if you didn't get all of them correct. Keep studying until these words become a regular part of your music vocabulary.

Quiz

Define each of the following writing devices.

1. Accidental _____

_____

2. Adage _____

_____

3. Alliteration _____

_____

4. Analogy _____

_____

5. Antonym _____

_____

6. Assonance _____

_____

7. Bar _____

_____

8. Beat _____

_____

9. Cadence _____

_____

10. Chromatic _____

_____

11. Coda _____

_____

12. Commercialize _____

_____

13. Consonance _____

_____

14. Content _____

_____

15. Diatonic Scale _____

_____

16. Foot _____

_____

17. Harmony _____

_____

18. Measure _____

_____

19. Melody _____

_____

20. Metaphor _____

_____

21. Meter _____

_____

22. Mode _____

_____

23. Modulation _____

_____

24. Octave _____

_____

25. Pattern _____

_____

26. Personification _____

_____

27. Pitch _____

_____

28. Prosody _____

_____

29. Rhetorical Question _____

_____

30. Rhyme _____

_____

31. Rhythm_____

_____

32. Saying _____

_____

33. Scale _____

_____

34. Simile _____

_____

35. Synonym _____

_____

36. Tone _____

_____

37. Universal _____

_____

38. Vernacular _____

_____

39. Vicarious _____

_____

40. Wrap _____

_____

Exercises

Three songs are presented below followed by the same pattern, meter, syllable count, etc., to the original song.

The songs are recorded songs you may be familiar with. The first song is completed for you. You must rework the songs with entirely new words, keeping within the same syllable count and pattern as the original.

Line 1, verse 1, should be within four syllables of line 1, verse 2, and line 1, verse 3. Correspondingly, line 2 of each verse needs to meter in the same manner and have no more than a four-syllable difference as line 3 in all other verses. The same holds true for line 4 in all your verses.

The number of syllables is given after each line so that you can see that they are no more than three to four syllables off. This is professional writer standards for commercial song-writing.

The patterns of the songs are also presented by placing a corresponding *a, b, c,* etc., after each line, so you will see the rhyme structure.

Do a syllable count after each line, and write down your pattern letters (the same will hold true for the chorus), i.e., *aabb, abba,* etc.

Remember, *c* will either stand for conversational line (you will see that it is a conversational line if the words do not rhyme) or it will be obvious, by corresponding *c*s throughout the song that *c* is part of the song's pattern, and the words will rhyme. An *s* after the number stands for syllables. Choruses are indented. R/L means a rhyme within a line.

Exercise 1

"Texas When I Die"
Written by Bruce, Bruce, and Borchers

Chorus

> WHEN I DIE I MAY NOT GO TO HEAVEN *(10s) (a)*
> I DON'T KNOW IF THEY LET COWBOYS IN *(9s) (a)*
> IF THEY DON'T JUST LET ME GO TO TEXAS *(10s) (c)*
> TEXAS IS AS CLOSE AS I'VE BEEN *(8s) (a)*
>
> NEW YORK COULDN'T HOLD MY ATTENTION *(9s) (c)*
> DETROIT CITY COULDN'T SING MY SONGS *(9s) (b)*
> IF TOMORROW FINDS ME FLAT IN DALLAS *(12s) (c)*
> I WON'T CARE 'CAUSE AT LEAST I'LL KNOW I'M HOME *(10s) (b)*

Repeat chorus twice and tag it.

Note the tightness of the syllable count which, in this lyric, is only a differentiation of no more than two syllables off per corresponding line. In addition, the pattern remains the same throughout the entire song. Each line seems seamless and easily written.

A professionally written song will somewhat dictate the underlying composition due to the meter and the cadence, and the beat (e.g., 2/4 time, two beats to the measure; or 4/4 time, four beats to the measure).

A rewritten version of "Texas When I Die" is presented below with the same syllable count and pattern *(c, b, c, b)*.

"Some Day I'm Gonna Fly"
Written by Jennifer Pierce

Chorus

> WHEN I FLY I'LL SEE SO MANY PLACES *(10s) (c)*
> HOPE SOMEDAY I'LL FIND SOMEWHERE TO LAND *(9s) (b)*
> THE NORTH WIND BLOWS BOY I'M GETTIN' COLDER *(10s) (c)*
> DOWN SOUTH I'LL FINE'LY MAKE MY STAND *(8s) (b)*

[Remember to always write to your hook.]

OVER TREES AND PASSED COOL GREEN MEADOWS *(9s) (c)*
I KNOW I'LL FIND ALL I NEED TO KNOW *(9s) (b)*
IF I GET SHOT DOWN AND MY OLD WINGS GET BROKEN *(12s) (c)*
I'LL TAKE THE BREAK 'N KEEP ON FLYIN' LOW *(10s) (b)*

(Repeat chorus)

I'LL REACH OUT AND BE TOUCHIN' HALF OF HEAVEN *(11s) (c)*
'N AS I'M SOARIN' THRU GOD'S BIG OLD BLUE WHITE SKY *(12s) (b)*
ALONE UP IN THE CLOUDS I SURE FEEL LONELY *(11s) (c)*
BUT I'LL BE IN PARADISE IF I SHOULD DIE *(11s) (b)*

Note the tightness of the syllable count, no more than two syllables off per corresponding line. The syllable count is not carved in stone. If you are a seasoned songwriter, you may take liberties.

You should be able to pick up your guitar and sing these words to the music of "Texas When I Die" because the meter, cadence, and pattern are real close.

You will need to learn how to write tight songs, with professional structure so that everyone and anyone can sing your songs. If you are a player and get into a "pocket" or a "groove" musically, you may be overlooking a great deal lyrically. Everything has to be exact so that major artists can easily sing, and, hopefully, record your songs. Don't expect the pros to deal with your melodic riff, extensions, turnarounds, instrumental breaks, or anything else you may be doing that another player or artist would have difficulty with. Keep it commercial, keep it tight, structure it right. It is easy to write just any old way at all. It is very difficult to write a professional lyric.

Also, keep your chord progressions in the exact form, line for line. If you do not, two things will happen: everyone will know you are not a professional composer, and no one will be able to record your songs.

Below is another old song with its syllable count and pattern. Write your own words to fit the pattern and syllable count exactly.

Exercise 2

"Delta Dawn"
Written by Harvey and Collins

Chorus

DELTA *DAWN* WHAT'S THAT FLOWER YOU HAVE *ON* *(10s) (R/L)*
COULD IT BE A FADED ROSE FROM DAYS GONE BY *(11s) (b)*
AND DID I HEAR YOU *SAY* HE WAS MEETIN' YOU HERE *TODAY*
(14s) (R/L)
TO TAKE YOU TO HIS MANSION IN THE SKY *(10s) (b)*

SHE'S FORTY-ONE AND HER DADDY STILL CALLS HER BABY *(13s) (a)*
ALL THE FOLKS 'ROUND BROWNSVILLE SAY SHE'S CRAZY *(10s) (a)*
SHE WALKS DOWNTOWN WITH A SUITCASE IN HER HAND *(11s) (b)*
LOOKIN' FOR A MYSTERIOUS DARK HAIRED MAN *(11s) (b)*

(Repeat chorus)

IN HER YOUNGER DAYS THEY CALLED HER DELTA *DAWN (11s) (a)*
PRETTIEST WOMAN YOU EVER LAID EYES *ON (11s) (a)*
BUT A MAN OF LOW DEGREE STOOD BY HER *SIDE (11s) (b)*
PROMISED HER HE'D TAKE HER FOR HIS *BRIDE (9s) (b)*

Now rewrite this song using the exact pattern, making sure all your syllables are the same. If there is a rhyme within a line, be sure your song has a rhyme within the same line.

Exercise 3

"I Saw the Light"
Written by Hank Williams

I WANDERED AIMLESS LIFE FILLED WITH *SIN (9s) (a)*
I WOULDN'T LET MY DEAR SAVIOR *IN (9s) (a)*
THEN JESUS CAME LIKE AN ANGEL IN THE *NIGHT (11s) (b)*
PRAISE THE LORD I SAW THE *LIGHT (7s) (b) (hook)*

I SAW THE LIGHT, I SAW THE LIGHT (8s) (a) (hook)
NO MORE IN DARKNESS NO MORE IN *NIGHT (9s) (a)*
NOW I'M SO HAPPY NO TROUBLE IN *SIGHT (10s) (a)*
PRAISE THE LORD, *I SAW THE LIGHT (7s) (a) (hook)*

JUST LIKE THE BLIND MAN, I WANDERED *ALONE (10s) (a)*
TROUBLES AND FEARS I'D CLAIM FOR *MY OWN (9s) (a)*
THEN LIKE THE BLIND MAN THAT GOD GAVE BACK HIS *SIGHT*
    (11s) (b)
PRAISE THE LORD, *I SAW THE LIGHT (7s) (b) (hook)*

Once again, using your own words, rewrite this song with the same syllable count and pattern as the original.

Insights and
Partial Discography of
FRED KNOBLOCH
Professional Songwriter

When It Hits You . . .

You might be alone;
you might be sitting somewhere imitating some lower form
of motor skill;
you might have just broken up with someone you thought
gave a damn about you emotionally or even sexually;
you could have overhead a conversation about bleach at the
laundromat while you're trying to wash your clothes;
you could even be having a good time with some people you
have never met;
perhaps you could be daydreaming in church listening to
some guy talk about censorship, when you know he doesn't
have a clue as to what it might feel like to rip a guitar in half
and have 40-odd ATOs from some SEC school go stark-raving
bonkers and try to break the world record for the largest human
pyramid;
you may be walking around some airport at the exact instant
that all airports begin to look alike and realize that you have 14
days left before you sleep in your own bed again;
and then you just might wake up every morning and pick up
a guitar and begin to strum it while you look over a page full
of ideas that it's taken you months to compile just so you have
something to do and begin the process of letting it flow until it
becomes obvious that things just don't happen by themselves
anymore and the only reasons you give yourself for doing this
are that your friends like it when you play at their parties and
you like it when they say things like "You wrote that?";
but one day, in the blue gray light of reality, you'll admit to
yourself that you are compelled by some force of inner nature

that never puts your mind completely at rest. That's when you thank God for the gift and try your damndest to never let it go.

Partial Discography of
J. Fred Knobloch

1. "Why Not Me" Co-written with Carson Whitsett. Artist Fred Knobloch.

2. "I Had It All" Co-written with Steve Allen and Terry Moretti. Artist Ray Charles.

3. "A Little More Love" Co-written with Thom Schuyler. Artist Kenny Rogers. On the "We Are the World" album.

4. "Used To Blue" Co-written with Bill Labounty. Artist Sawyer Brown.

5. "Baby's Got a New Baby" Co-written with Dan Tyler. Artist SKO.

6. "Turn of the Century" Co-written with Dan Tyler. Artist Nitty Gritty Dirt Band. On "Circle II" album.

7. "The Whole World's in Love When You're Lonely" Co-written with Dan Tyler. Artist B.J. Thomas.

8. "A Lover Is Forever" Co-written with Steve Goodman. Recorded by Etta James on Rosanne Cash Live video.

And, more of Knobloch's songs are on the Schuyler, Knobloch, and Bickhardt album "No Easy Horses."

J. Fred Knobloch

Insights of
RICHARD LEIGH
Professional Songwriter

Songwriting to me is an illusion, the illusion of combining words and music to appear as one. It is the simultaneous speaking of two distinct languages—the printed word and the printed note, to create a third separate language.

People who create songs are called writers but maybe they are really magicians. They are the slight of hand and heart masters. If they do their job well, you will be unaware of their craftsmanship. You hear a song and suddenly everything that a moment ago seemed so important has all but faded away.

We're the ones lovers turn to when they are falling in or out of love. How many times have you heard, "They're playing our song?" We make people sing, dance, laugh, cry, rethink their relationships, help them celebrate good times, and get over bad ones. And, if we are lucky, the songs live on after we do and provide incomes for loved ones long after we are gone. Not many dentists or doctors bring in a paycheck after they're dead!

A hit song can easily be played 10,000 times a day and be purchased by millions—tens of millions of people.

The songwriter has the wonderful knowledge that he was the very first person ever to have heard the song. How many times in our lives do we get to be first at anything, and be responsible for the good it has done.

If the printed word is the spoken word in chains—the song is the spoken word in flight—magically suspended above it all.

Songwriting: It's a wonderful job. It's a rewarding job. To me it's nothing short of magic.

Partial Discography of
Richard Leigh

1. "That's The Thing About Love" Co-written with Gary Nicholson. Artist Don Williams. Number one song in the country.

2. "I'll Get Over You" Written by Richard Leigh. Artist Crystal Gayle. Number one song in the country; nominated by the Country Music Association for song of the year.

3. "Don't It Make My Brown Eyes Blue" Written by Richard Leigh. Artist Crystal Gayle. Number one song in the country; nominated by ASCAP as one of the top 20 number one songs of the decade. It was the only song ever nominated for both "pop" and "country" song of the year in the same year. It won song of the year, Country Division; and won a Grammy for song of the year.

4. "Put Your Dreams Away" Co-written with Wayland Holyfield. Artist Mickey Gilley. Number one song in the country.

5. "Life's Highway" Co-written with Roger Murrah. Artist Steve Wariner. Number one song in the country.

6. "Wish I Had A Heart of Stone" Co-written with Wayland Holyfield. Artist Bailie and the Boys.

7. "Come from the Heart" Co-written with Susanna Clark. Artist Kathy Mattea. Number one song in the country. It received an ASCAP nomination for top five country songs of the year.

8. "Only Here for a Little While" Co-written with Wayland Holyfield. Artist Billy Dean. Number one song in the country.

9. "Somewhere in My Broken Heart" Co-written with Billy Dean. Artist Billy Dean. Number one song in the country.

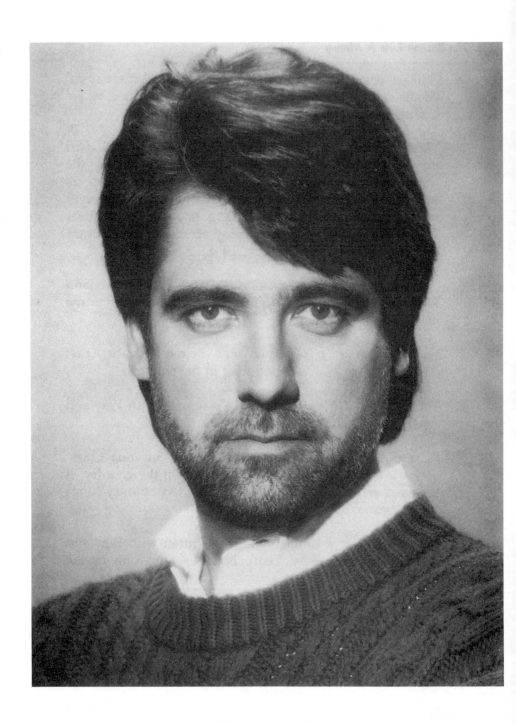

Richard Leigh

Chapter 8

◆ ◆ ◆

Keeping the World in Mind

Terms Used in This Chapter

Aesthetic: 1. Of or in relation to aesthetics. 2. Of beauty. 3. Sensitive to art and beauty; showing good taste; artistic. *(Webster's Dictionary)*

Emotion: 1a. Strong feeling; excitement. 1b. The state or capability of having the feelings aroused to the point of awareness. 2. Any specific feeling; any of various complex reactions with both mental and physical manifestations, as love, hate, fear, anger, etc. *(Webster's Dictionary)*

Empathy: 1. Feeling. 2. The projection of one's own personality into the personality of another in order to understand him better; ability to share in another's emotions or feelings. 3. The projection of one's own personality into an object, with the attribution to the object of one's own emotions, responses, etc. *(Webster's Dictionary)*

Feeling: 1. Full of or expressing emotion or sensitivity; sympathetic. 2. That one of the senses by which sensations of contact, pressure, temperature, and pain are transmitted through the skin; sense of touch. 3. The power or faculty of experiencing physical sensation. 4. An awareness; consciousness; sensation [a feeling of pain]. 5. An emotion. 6. Sensitivities, sensibilities [to hurt one's feelings]. 7. A kindly, generous attitude; sympathy; pity. 8. A natural ability or sensitive appreciation [a feeling for music]. 9. The emotional quality in a work of art. *(Webster's Dictionary)*

Impalpable: 1. That cannot be felt by touching. 2. Too slight or subtle to be grasped easily by the mind. *(Webster's Dictionary)*

Incorporeal: 1. Not consisting of matter; without material body or substance. 2. Of spirits or angels. *(Webster's Dictionary)*

Intangible: 1. That cannot be touched, incorporeal; impalpable. 2. That represents value but has either no intrinsic value or no material being [stocks and bonds are intangible property, good will is an intangible asset]. 3. That cannot be easily defined, formulated, or grasped; vague. *(Webster's Dictionary)*

Intrinsic: 1. Belonging to the real nature of a thing; not dependent on external circumstances; essential; inherent. *(Webster's Dictionary)*

Sensitive: 1. Of the senses or sensation; especially connected with the reception or transmission of sense impressions; sensory. 2. Receiving and responding to stimuli from outside objects or agencies; having sensation. 3. Responding or feeling readily and acutely; very keenly susceptible to stimuli [a sensitive ear]. 4. Easily hurt; tender; raw. 5. Having or showing keen sensibilities; highly perceptive or responsive intellectually, aesthetically, etc. 6. Easily offended, disturbed, shocked, irritated, etc., as by the actions of others; touchy. *(Webster's Dictionary)*

Terms Used in This Chapter *(cont.)*
Transmit: 1. To send or cause to go from one person or place to another; especially across intervening space of distance; transfer; dispatch, convey. 2. To pass along; impart. *(Webster's Dictionary)*
Vibration: One's emotional reaction to a person or thing as being in or out of harmony with one. *(Webster's Dictionary)*

Feelings and Emotions

People can identify with a song in many different ways. Some can identify with the lyric, finding a part of their lives in the words. Others might identify with the music which will make them feel a certain way, the way they once felt when they were with someone they loved, for instance. Music and lyrics cause people to feel a certain way. A professional writer never presumes to tell anyone how they should feel or how they are feeling.

A writer can write about how they feel about life, death, love, sadness, etc., but they should never write about how the listener should feel or be feeling about any of those subjects. In writing a song, do no anticipate how someone else might feel. In real life, you cannot tell someone how to feel so you certainly cannot tell them in your songs.

There is no right or wrong to feelings. We are all allowed the right to our own personal feelings about anything and everything.

Do not write: I know you love me too

Write: I hope you love me too

It is up to the listener to decide whether or not they love you, hate you, want you, don't want you, etc. And, unless you are writing a "duet," where the other person can respond directly, and state how they feel, you cannot and should not state their feelings for them.

Do not write: I can tell by the look in your eyes you want to leave me

Write: Does the look in your eyes mean you want to leave me?

Asking questions is a very useful songwriting device.

No one will be able to identify with what you write if you are already telling them how they feel or should feel. There have been several hit songs where a person or persons are being told how they felt or should feel. Songs have been written that way, and unfortunately, will continue to be written that way.

In my opinion, that way is wrong from both an emotional and psychological viewpoint. The writer is taking away the free choice of individuals or groups who should be entitled to decide their own feelings for themselves and to identify with what they choose to identify with. Some people are easily influenced by others. Songs, should make us all stronger. We cannot become stronger if someone is dictating how we should feel. That takes away our decision-making processes. Real life, which songs should address, should strive to leave good feelings behind them. Songs should help everyone to think more highly of themselves and be more positive.

If, however, you are writing strictly from the first person, then you have every right to declare as strongly as you like how you feel about anything or anyone.

Do not write: You'll be mine forever

Write: You'll be my forever

The former would be presuming, to state for a fact, speaking for another person, that that person will be theirs forever. The latter states the feelings, from the first person, which can be stated because that person can, of course, express how he feels. "You'll be mine forever" should not be said because the person has no way of knowing that—unless, you have that person under lock and key.

If you want your songs to help others and if you also want to make money, be very careful not to offend anyone.

An industry person once told me that I didn't need to be so careful with words. I was told that I should keep my songs simple and that I was not writing for a bunch of brain surgeons. I strongly disagree. Life is not simple, people are not simple. Therefore, I try to write for everyone.

I try to keep the world in mind whenever I write, both for the formally educated, as well as those who have no education to speak of. I have known many people with very little formal education. In many cases, they are far wiser and more intelligent than some very well-educated people. Many people who have learned from life, without the aid of a formal education, have great depth of feeling.

Songs are all about *feelings* and *emotions*. Feelings and emotions are what make each one of us unique. They are *intangible.*

Feelings cannot be held in your hand, seen with your eyes, or heard by your ears. (I'm not writing about "tears falling" and "sobs heard." I am referring to feelings in the heart, emotions in the soul, in the deepest part of all of us.)

Of course, we may believe we know someone is sad if they are crying, but then again, those tears may be tears of joy. And, many times when people act as though they are angry, they are only expressing hurt feelings.

In your songs write, "I'm sorry if I made you cry," or "last night I heard you crying in your sleep," or "is that look in your eyes love?" You are not telling that person how they feel, you are only addressing your own observations. We all observe things. We all come to our own conclusions. But, those conclusions should never be about someone else's feelings and/or emotions. Our conclusions should only involve our own observations.

Situations

You can write about sad situations. You can even write about death, if you handle the subject very delicately. You can write about any experience you or anyone else has ever had.

Do not write: Last month my father died

Write: It was a month ago today, that God
                           took him away

You must handle heavy situations very, very softly.

Do not write: I want to kill you for breaking my
                           heart

Write: Don't ever cross my heart again "Baby Don't You Cross My Heart Again," written by Jennifer Pierce, Jackie Gulledge (c1989)

Do not write: I don't want to make love to you no more

Write: Now that I know you done me wrong, I won't be layin' in your arms (vernacular speech)

The reason most songs are hits is because they hit a universal feeling, a universal emotion. The writer's job is to make the feeling real, true, deep, colorful, and at the same time depersonalized enough for the whole world to be able to identify with their songs.

If you are not writing from the first person, another device you can use to state someone else's feelings is, to write "he said" or "she said," or "I heard your message on your code-a-phone (or answering machine)." If the person you are writing about has some way to say how they feel or think for themselves in your songs, then that is legitimate, professional songwriting.

Do not write: I know you don't love me anymore

Write: Actions speak louder than words

Write from the point of view of how you feel (how you think) in any given situation. Write as deeply as you want and/or need in order to present your material the way you believe it needs to be presented. At the same time, however, stay within all the patterns, structures, designs, syllable counts, etc., addressed in previous chapters.

Another device to make your songs universally identifiable is to keep your lyric close to the subject/content. If you don't, you may lose the feeling and emotions you are trying to express. The same holds true for your composition.

I have found that people who are *sensitive* to the feelings of animals could become great songwriters. Professional songwriting is all about sensitivities and communicating those sensitivities. If a person can, for instance, get on the back of a nervous or frightened horse and *transmit* his calm feelings to such an extent as to calm the animal down, that person has very sensitive feelings and strong *vibrations*. If he can communicate wordlessly, imagine what he could do with words if they incorporated that great sensitivity and those positive vibrations, and transmitted them into a lyric and/or composition.

Again, it's all a matter of identifying with someone or something else's feelings. Walking in their shoes, horseshoes, or paws, as the case may be.

Every great songwriter I know personally has a love for animals. Somehow their sensitivity to creatures, which are so totally vulnerable to our dispositions and depend on us for all their needs, overlaps into their great songs. Regardless of what the subject of their songs may be, the sensitivity is there.

I sincerely believe that sensitivity to all creatures, great and small, that depend on us and sensitivity to children and sensitivity to the elderly is within all great writers.

I further feel this applies to greatness in all the arts, sculpting, painting, sketching, dancing, acting, etc. The more sensitive the performer, the better the performance. We are all performers. Shakespeare once said, "The world is but a stage and we each must play our part."

If you don't have *empathy* for others, how can you possibly communicate with them or even begin to understand their feelings.

Many times actions are involved with feelings, and oftentimes negative actions can be exhibited. While no one has the right to hurt anyone through vengeful or jealous actions, this does, unfortunately, happen every day. And, at times, such actions need to be written about in songs. These issues should be written about as being a wrong way to handle a situation. For instance, if you're writing about love and you want to write about the wrong way to handle a situation, you might write, "you tore up the love letters I once wrote you, and left the pieces of my heart there on the floor." Then you will want to let the listener know these emotions hurt you. So you may write, "when you broke my heart and a love we once shared, you should have taken the mem'ries that still make me care."

Other Lyrical Devices

Some lyrical devices are as follows: assonance, consonance, alliteration, metaphors, similes, cadence, inflection, universal content, illusion, allegory, circumlocution, the proper use of cliches and adages, and the proper use of colloquialisms, idioms, and vernacular speech. You need to understand how to smoothly use opposites, comparing and contrasting, diphthongs, irony (must be used with care), and personification. You need to understand the differences between poems, prose, and lyrics. You need to understand prosody, rhetorical questions, rhyme patterns, and the proper use of slang. You need to understand symmetry, synonyms, antonyms, syntax, tenses, diagraph, coda, foot, meter, harmony, intro's, measures, the minor scale, modulation, pitch, rhythm, timbre, tempo, turnarounds, instrumental breaks, and wraps and tags (both musically and lyrically).

You should try to understand: accidentals, bar, beat, bridges (both lyrically and musically), the chromatic scale, the diatonic chords, enharmonic key centers, chord progressions, number charts (so you and your musicians won't have to transpose keys).

Then, you need to "sleep on it." Look at your lyric again and again, be sure there is nothing more you can do to make it tighter, more cohesive. Be as sure as you can be that you wasted no words. You need to understand many words, then use as few as possible. Look and see if perhaps your last verse would be better as your first verse, or if your second verse might make a better flow for your song if it were your third verse. This is part of the *polishing* process. Polishing is very important. It is the last step before you go in the studio to have your demos done. Get your songs out there and try to find some "ears" to appreciate your songs and believe in your ability as a great hit songwriter.

Summary

Keep the world in mind when you write. Write universally. Be in touch with the feelings and emotions of others, in order for them to identify with your songs. And, never dictate to another person how they should feel or be feeling.

You can write about any situation you choose to write about, so long as you are either writing from the first person, or are allowing, the person perhaps, through a "duet" or a "he said/she said" device, to state their own feelings. You need to transmit your feelings and emotions to others, in a universal way. You need to have empathy (walk a mile in my shoes) to whatever subject, content, or situation you are writing about. Remember, there is no right or wrong to a feeling. But, bad actions are a different matter, and should be shown to be an incorrect way to handle hurt feelings in your songs.

Finally, you must handle heavy situations in a very soft manner.

Insights of
ROGER SOVINE
BMI, Nashville

I've been around the music business most of my life. My dad, Red Sovine, was a country music singer. I started work in the business 20 some years ago, and have never regretted it. The music business, especially in Nashville, is a very close-knit community and therefore we see each other on a regular basis. I have built a lot of very strong friendships in the business. It's almost like being in a second family.

Every day is different and always exciting. You never know who the next person walking through your door will be. Maybe the next great songwriter or the next major superstar. And if I am able to contribute in some small way to helping these people realize their dreams, that's my reward. I love this business and look forward to going to work every day.

Roger Sovine has been around the music business all his life. The son of country music entertainer Red Sovine, Roger served a four-year stint in the Marine Corps before making his professional entry into the music industry.

In 1965, he joined Cedarwood Publishing Company, where he learned the business from every aspect. After leaving Cedarwood, he worked with Show-Biz Publishing and South Publishing Productions. In 1969, he was the recipient of the Spotlight Award from the Junior Chamber of Commerce.

Sovine joined BMI in 1972 as director, Writer Administration, and was promoted to assistant vice president in 1976. He remained with BMI until 1979, when he accepted the position of vice president, Professional Services at the Welk Music Group. Three years later, he became vice president of Tree International (now Sony/Tree). He returned to BMI in 1985 to assume his current role as vice president, Nashville, directing all writer/publisher relations activities from the Music Row office of the world's largest performing rights organization.

Actively involved in the music industry and throughout the Nashville community, Sovine is vice president and a member of the Board of Country Music Foundation; a board member of the Nashville chapter of the National Academy of Recording Arts and Sciences, where he served three terms as president; and past president and chairman of the Board of Country Music Association. He is also an honorary lifetime board member and a past president of the Nashville Entertainment Association; a Commissioner of the Tennessee Film, Entertainment and Music Commission; and a charter organizer and board member of Leadership Music. In addition, he has been involved in Leadership Nashville and has been a member of the Campaign Cabinet of the United Way of Middle Tennessee.

Roger Sovine *(Photo by BMI/Alan Messer)*

Part 2

♦ ♦ ♦

The Business Ending

Chapter 9

Music Is a Business

Terms Used in This Chapter

Business: 1. One's work, occupation, or profession. 2. A special task, duty, or function. 3. Rightful concern or responsibility [no one's business but his own]. 4. A matter, affair, activity, etc. [the business of packing for a trip]. 5. The buying and selling of commodities and services; commerce, trade. 6. A commercial or industrial establishment; store, factory, etc. 7. The trade or patronage of customers. 8. Commercial practice or policy. 9. Action in a drama, especially for a particular effect, to take up a pause in dialogue, etc. (of or for business; business is business sentiment; friendship, etc., cannot be allowed to interfere with profit making; doing business with). *(Webster's Dictionary)*

Money (monetarism): A theory which holds that economic stability and growth result from maintaining a steady rate of growth in the supply of money.

This chapter presents—in an oversimplified and brief scenario—some of the very complex entities in the music industry.

The lengthy definition of business is presented in this chapter to help you understand that we are all in a business of one kind or another. However, in describing the music business "commercial practice or policy. . . , business is business sentiment; friendship, etc., cannot be allowed to interfere with profit making" are the most appropriate definitions.

While that may sound harsh, it is true. It's why this book was originally *The Bottom Line Is Money*. That's not to say that there are not many good-hearted, ethical people in the music industry. There certainly are. However, everyone has someone over them, and, usually at the top is (pardon the pun) "where the buck starts." Therefore, corporate policy dictates the "nature of the beast," in most cases.

Generally, attitudes in any given company or corporation are similar: likes hire likes. There are a great variety of attitudes in the music industry, but within each office attitudes seem to gravitate down, even to the receptionists. Some are warm, sincere, and genuine, while others are the opposite. The adage "birds of a feather flock together" seems to be very true in the music industry.

Money, of and by itself, is a fairly harmless commodity. In the right hands it can do a great deal of good. In the wrong hands it can do a great deal of harm. It depends very much on who is in power, and who has control, as to how money is used in distributing power and control.

There are very few record companies that are owned by Americans. Most of the large labels are owned by foreigners (e.g., Japanese and Swedish). Having foreign companies controlling American interests makes matters more complicated due to interlocking corporate entanglements.

The following is a brief breakdown of who does what, and various ways in which money is made.

Managers

Managers guide and direct the career of their artist(s). Managers often are part of the decision-making process, along with producers and the artist in deciding what material the artist should select to be recorded.

Managers and their staffs carry out all matters relating to the artist's public relations, publicity, and advertising. They decide what bookings the artist should take or turn down. And, management routes the artist on his tours.

Managers decide what public appearances the artist should make, and whether or not the artist should do certain interviews. Managers decide, along with the artist, depending on contracts signed, how to follow through with publicity (i.e., whether or not the publicity would be in the artist's best interests to further his career).

Managers also decide what charitable contributions—in the way of free public performances—the artist should make to further the artist's career and to place the artist in the most positive setting for public appeal.

Managers always want their artist to be in the most "favorable" light, to shine for the public. Managers usually decide what "gimmick" would be in the artist's best interest to make him stand out and be very visible.

It is the manager's job to advance the artist's career. The manager and his staff decide what photos should be presented on behalf of the artist to the public. They also tell the artist's fan club precisely what to charge for autograph photos and other artist paraphernalia. The fan clubs receive a portion of the proceeds, and the balance is sent back by the fan club treasurer to the management offices.

Mangers also help in the selection of *road managers* for the artist. Road managers handle transportation, lodging, etc. Road managers usually are employed and paid by the artist's management company for engaging people to set lights and sound when the artist is on the road.

Managers wear the "black hat" on behalf of the artist and run interference for him should there be a disgruntled fan, disc jockey, road manager, musician, etc. Managers protect the artist, at times, from his closest friends and sometimes even from his family. If management believes that anyone could hurt the artist's career, in any way, the manager and his staff do their best to prevent any and all negative publicity.

Managers make their money in several different ways. Some managers either make some of their money from the gross receipts and travel reimbursements or from net receipts, after taxes have been paid (if the latter is true, the manager usually receives a lesser percentage of the artist's receipts) and monies from performances and publishing rights have all been tallied. Usually, their percentage is between 15 and 25 percent of the artist's receipts (either gross or net depending on their contract). From this money, managers take their parts (whatever their individual management/artist contract stipulates), and pay their staffs (e.g., road managers, secretaries, publicists, road musicians, wardrobe people, sound and light men, etc.).

Managers may receive as much as 20 to 30 percent of the artist's record royalties, if the manager was the one who got his artist the record deal.

Management contracts usually run for a term of from one to three years, with options up to five years. Then, they may be renewed or terminated. If the contract is terminated, the manager may, retroactively, be entitled to commissions long after he and the artist have ended their relationship. Built into many management contracts are clauses which provide for the manager, who obtained certain releases for the artist, certain bookings, record contracts for the artist, etc., to continue to receive commissions from the origination of said record deals, releases, bookings, publishing, etc., which the manager originally obtained for the artist.

Therefore, managers make their money from gross or net receipts from all of their artist's earnings, unless the contract provides for some "special performance rights," such as Las Vegas bookings, which will then be paid to different sources.

Music Attorneys

Music attorneys negotiate the complex contract mechanisms between the artist, record labels, agents, business managers, managers, producers, etc., and draw up all necessary contracts. He "divides up the pie;" that is, he disperses all monies earned by the artist. The music attorney uses his expertise to make sure everything is clear and nothing overlaps in such a way as to confuse issues between so many different entities in the music industry.

Artists

How an artist becomes an artist is complex. Usually a person or group desiring or wanting to become a "star," or "stars" as the case may be, will struggle along, seeking advice from friends, making demos of original songs, putting a band together. They might also play at clubs during the various writer's nights, which enable writers to play and sing their original material.

When the artist feels he has achieved enough visibility, he may then begin knocking on the doors of various record labels, in hopes of securing a spec (speculation) deal. A record label is cautious not to overextend its financial resources until they believe the artist will yield the label a return on their investment.

Labels sign artists to exclusive agreements, so there will not be conflicts with other record labels. Once signed, the record label pays for all recording sessions, which they hope to recoup at a later time when the artist is making money. Record labels working with a new artist usually have a large say in the selection of material their artist will record. Sometimes labels work along with the advice from the artist's managers (if the artist has a manager at that time), and/or producer, if the artist has attracted the interest of a producer. The label usually always makes the final decision of what a new artist will record.

An artist may find an interested producer or manager as his first contact. In that event, the producer or manager will make record company contacts on behalf of the artist.

The artist makes money from live performances, television, videos, and songwriting royalties (if that artist is a writer). Many artists retain a portion of the publishing on songs they have written or co-written. When an artist becomes well established, he usually opens his own publishing company, and receives royalties from all songs his company obtains releases on.

The artist receives money from proceeds from fan clubs, record label contracts, mechanical licensing (units sold), etc. A very major artist may receive as much as $5,000 to $10,000 for one live performance, depending on the type and size of the performance. Many artists book certain club dates for a week's run and are highly paid for those performances.

It should be noted that artists pay a lot of dues by being on the road. They are very well paid for their efforts, once they have made it.

Sometimes artists fall, and when they do, they fall fast. However, most major artists are truly sincere, hardworking, and extremely talented people.

Record Labels

Record labels (companies) make their money in various ways. Usually, contracts provide for an escalating scale of the artist's proceeds in units sold. The more units sold, the greater the percentage for the record label.

Artists receive a percentage of album units sold. Artists also receive money from performances. Record labels also make money from taking a percentage of the artist's revenues, whatever the source of said revenues may be. Usually the label receives some percentage.

In artist recording contracts, unless otherwise stipulated, all the proceeds from the artist's services belong to the record label (Recording Agreement). The label usually also owns a portion, if not all of the copyrights in sound recordings.

Record labels may receive as much as 80 to 85 percent of the proceeds for each unit sold (e.g., cassettes and discs).

Labels also have the exclusive right, unless otherwise stated contractually, to sell their copyright ownership in masters and sound recordings.

Producers

Many producers look for new artists and act as their own talent scouts. The producer also decides how much the budget should be for recording costs for his artists.

The producer usually selects the studios, session musicians, studio engineers, arrangers, background vocalists, etc., for his artists. The producer may also help his artist(s) get a record deal if that producer's property (the artist) is someone the record label considers to be a "hot property." The producer's name will appear on the record label, as that artist's producer, which is great publicity for both the producer and his artist.

The producer makes money from the record labels, if he secured a record deal for his artist, in the form of royalty payments on album units sold or from the label for a pre-recorded master session.

If the producer gets his artist a distribution deal, then the producer receives a profit margin from the distribution fee from the record label, instead of a percentage or royalty payment on units sold. However, everything depends on individual contracts between all entities involved.

The producer receives a percentage of royalty payments, if he is hired by the record label to produce that label's artist(s). The royalty payments are paid out of the artist's royalties and are not separate and apart (as in an individual producer/label contract).

The producer usually always receives fees from labels before he will accept artist production. This payment is regarded as an advance against monies or royalties to be earned.

Many times the producer receives part of the publishing royalties on songs recorded and released by his artist(s). He may receive a percentage of performance royalties and a percentage of mechanical payments on units sold.

Publishers

Publishers always belong to the American Society of Composers, Authors and Publishers (ASCAP), Broadcast Music Incorporated (BMI), and the Society of European Stage Authors and Composers (SESAC) because publishers work with writers who are affiliated with one of the above affiliations. A writer may only belong to one affiliation. Publishers must have companies with all affiliations in order to receive their royalty payments from the different affiliations, if they obtain a recording for their writer(s).

The publisher pays the writer(s) mechanicals on units sold and must account to its writers every six months, or as publisher/writer contracts stipulate. Performance is paid out by the affiliation every three months. Or, a publisher may hire an administrator, especially where the business of collecting foreign royalties is concerned. Then, the administrator takes a percentage off the top of mechanical monies received (usually about 15 percent), and sends the balance to the publisher. The publisher then sends the writer(s) their share of the mechanical payments.

If a publisher is the sole publisher on a song release and the writer is the sole writer, the publisher/writer check amounts will be the same; it is a 50-50 split. However, this is rare. In order to secure a cut for their writer, the publisher usually splits publishing with various entities (i.e., artist managers, producers, record labels, record promoters, etc.). If there is more than one writer on a song, the writers split the writers' portion of performance and mechanicals also. Song royalties from both performances and mechanical payments are split with all respective entities (e.g., publishers, writers, etc.) unless otherwise stipulated by contracts.

It is the publisher's job to plug the writer's material and get into the doors the writer may not be able to get into (e.g., label doors, management and producer doors, etc.). Some record labels will only accept material through a publisher and will not deal with writers, regardless of that writer's stature in the industry. This policy is for two reasons: (1) publishers are supposed to understand how to negotiate splits to their advantage and to the advantage of their writers; and (2) labels have staff writers and do not want a conflict of interest by taking outside material.

I have had the unfortunate experience of dealing with some non-major, independent publishers, who asked me to sign publishing contracts with no reversion clause. I have since learned never to sign such a contract.

Some publishers request a no reversion clause contract so they can build their catalog and perhaps sell it to a major label later on. After the writer has done all the work and gotten in the doors himself, and gets his songs recorded and released, some publishers sit back and get the checks. Also, these publishers' catalogs continue to build over the years—the years the writer does not have—so that they may sell their entire catalog to a major company in the future.

An ethical publisher will always stay in touch with his writers and advise them as to who their material has been pitched to and the status of the writer's material. For the most part, the independent publishers never stay in touch. Deal only with the most reputable publishers and song pluggers in the industry. Do not sign a contract unless you have been assured, to the best ability of the publisher, that you will have not just a recording, but a release.

I have seen so many new writers overjoyed that a publisher has signed their material to a contract or contracts. All that usually means is that the writer's material is tied up. And, if that publisher is not ethical and does not do his job to earn his money from the material, then the writer has lost 50 percent of the incentive to pitch his material elsewhere.

Remember, everyone wants and needs a part of the publishing on your material. If it is tied up and unworked, where does that leave you?

In major publishing houses, staff writers receive "tip" sheets letting them know exactly what artist is about to go in the studio and what kind of material they are looking for and how many sides (cuts) are left open on that artist's project (album).

Be very cautious in signing publishing contracts with non-major, independent publishers. If you are a new writer and have no choice, make sure you get a reversion clause in your contract. If that publisher has done a good job for you (kept in touch with you and worked your material), then renew your contract with that publisher after a one- or two-year term.

I have signed contracts with major publishing houses with no reversion clauses because I believe that the major publishing houses will work my material. Usually the major houses have no reversion clauses in their contracts because they are working with their signed staff writers, whereby the publishing of the signed staff writers belongs to the company they are signed with, unless otherwise stipulated by contract.

Remember, independent, non-major publishers, including those who got lucky and have had a few major cuts, should stay in touch with their writers and help pay for demos. If they don't or won't, find another publisher.

Songwriters

"Songwriter"
Written by Jennifer Ember Pierce

IT'S WHO DO YOU KNOW, AND PAY WHAT YOU OWE
AND, KEEP WATCHIN' YOUR BACK ALL THE WAY
IT'S YEARS OF HARD DUES, AND TWIST THE WORD BLUE
AND, KEEP THANKIN' THE LORD FOR EACH DAY

IT'S A TOUGH GIG, TO GIVE AND LET LIVE
PITCHIN' OUT TO THE POWERS THAT BE
YOU'RE WRITIN' YOUR BEST, KNOW YOU'RE UP WITH THE REST
THEY SAY, THAT SONG DOES NOTHIN' FOR ME

SONGWRITER, YOU'RE WRITIN' YOUR LIFE WITH A PEN AND A KNIFE
FIGHTIN' TO KEEP YOURSELF SANE
WHEN YOU'VE SPENT YOUR LAST BUCK AND YOU'RE DOWN ON
    YOUR LUCK
SONGWRITER, YOU'RE LEARNIN' THE GAME

IT'S ONE MORE REWRITE, NO SLEEP THE THIRD NIGHT
AND, THEY'LL TURN YOU DOWN ALL THE SAME
IT'S KEEP A FIXED GRIN, AND MAYBE YOU'LL WIN
AND, BE VINYL ONE OF THESE DAYS

Bridge

IF YOU DON'T GIVE A DAMN WHEN THEY ALL TURN AWAY
WHEN YOU KNOW YOU HAVE SOMETHIN' TO SAY
IF YOU KEEP YOUR CHOPS UP AND HOCK YOUR OLD TRUCK
    FOR DEMOS AND STUDIO TIME
AND, IF YOU FACE THE TRUTH AND GIVE UP YOUR YOUTH
ALL FOR THE WORDS ON A PAGE
A SONGWRITER YOU MIGHT BE ONE DAY

[Don't concern yourselves with the structure of the bridge; this was not written as a commercial song. I just wrote it because I felt like writing it. I used the word vinyl in the above lyric, of course, there is no more vinyl to speak of. The saying used to be, "It's not final 'til it's vinyl," now I'll say, "It's not a disc, 'til it's in your fist."]

Many issues concerning songwriters are addressed in the publisher section. A songwriter is paid through his affiliation for performance, every three months, and through his publisher or publisher's administrator on mechanicals every six months. A songwriter is paid on foreign royalties every six months also.

You probably won't receive any foreign payment for two years. And, your first performance money usually takes about nine months to get to you. The reason for all this slowness is because ASCAP and BMI have to wait until their surveys are in on new songs. Once you get that first check, you will receive them regularly.

Be cautious if a major publishing house wants to sign you. It will be for one of four reasons.

1. You're not quite there, but they like your attitude and will ask their major writers to help you along. In this case you will probably receive a very small draw, if any.

2. You are a great writer, and they'll sign you to keep your songs from getting cut because they have so much money poured into their major writers. Then, your songs won't see the light of day, unless, of course, you get with one of their major writers and he can legitimately earn writer credit with you. Wherever you are signed your publishing belongs to "the company store."

3. You're writing is not there, and may never be there, however, they still like your voice, your playing ability (either on guitar or keys), or you have something they can use you for. And, if you are on a draw, you can be taken as a tax write-off.

4. Even though you are a beginner, you show talent of being one of the best writers in the country. You will be put on a good draw (around $150 or more per week). That

company will work very hard to get you cuts, and make money for you and for themselves off of your publishing. (Draws for staff writers in Nashville are from $0 to $800 a week.)

While this sounds harsh, remember, the bottom line is money. If you are a semi-great writer, also be wary you are not buried underneath 60 to 70 staff writers who are signed with the major publishing houses. The major houses do not have nearly enough song pluggers to work on all those writers. So, they work only their top-of-the-line writers. They physically do not have the time to listen to that many songs. It is not possible for three or four song pluggers to listen to the songs of 60 to 70 writers. Think about it. And, working with their top writers, they are still overburdened, sometimes listening to as many as 200 songs on their listening days.

If you sign with a major publishing house, get a good music attorney to help you negotiate your contract. And do all you can to make sure that your material will be plugged.

However, after you have gotten some major cuts on your own, you may be asked to sign with a major house for totally legitimate reasons. If the draw is right, if you feel good with the people there, then sign. It's great working with a team, having a home, so to speak.

The ASCAP Survey and Your Royalties

The goal of the ASCAP survey and distribution system is the fair and sensible allocation of license fees to the society's members and the members of foreign societies who license through ASCAP.

ASCAP currently licenses:

- 900 local commercial television stations;
- 8,500 local commercial radio stations;
- 35 cable program services and the major cable system operators having the majority of cable subscribers;

- 300 non-commercial television broadcasters;
- 1,500 non-commercial radio broadcasters;
- hundreds of background music services (including airlines) representing some 200,000 background/foreground music users;
- 2,000 colleges and universities;
- 2,100 symphony orchestras and concert promoters; and
- tens of thousands of "general" licensees: bars, restaurants, hotels, ice- and roller-skating rinks, circuses, theme parks, and veterans and fraternal organizations.

Over 1 billion ASCAP-licensed performances take place each year.

Following the collection of ASCAP's revenues, operating costs are deducted and the remainder is distributed. About 80 cents of every dollar received is paid out each year.

Revenues from each group of ASCAP licensees are segregated and distribution of royalties is made on the basis of performances by licensees within each group.

Thus, local radio revenues are distributed on the basis of local radio performances, local television revenues on the basis of local television performances, and so on. One exception is in the "serious" or "standard" music field. ASCAP multiplies by five the license fees received for live serious concert performances to increase the fund from which composers and publishers of serious music are paid.

Every performance picked up in ASCAP's survey generates a certain number of credits, the number varying with the medium in which the performance takes place (e.g., local radio, network television), the type of use (e.g., feature, theme, background), and, in the case of radio and television, the station weight of the station airing the performance.

For network television performances the number of stations carrying the show also affects the credits generated by a performance. The length of the work is not a factor except in the case of background music (i.e., music used as underscoring in films and television programs), certain feature performances of less than 45 seconds on television, and performances of serious music, where the duration of a performance, and, in the case of live concerts, instrumentation also affect the number of credits a particular performance will generate.

The ASCAP survey is the product of long experience and reflects the views of independent survey experts as well as the U.S. government. The survey is monitored by two special distribution advisors, whose semi-annual reports to a U.S. District Court are also sent to members.

The survey may be divided into two components: those performances counted on a census basis, and those included on a sample basis. A census, or full count, is taken of all performances on network television and the Home Box Office (HBO) cable service, and of performances of serious music in concert and symphony halls. Also included on a census basis are certain background/foreground music services and a group of non-broadcast, non-concert licensees. ASCAP can do a complete count of the performances on these licensees because the universe to be sampled is relatively small and performance information relatively simple to process. A sample of performances is relied on for all other media.

The Census Network Television

ASCAP is able to count all network television music performances because there are only three networks. Program logs and cue sheets are provided by the networks and program producers. The fees involved are substantial.

In addition to the logs and cue sheets, ASCAP makes audio and video tapes of network television performances to verify the accuracy of information furnished by the networks and program producers.

Symphony and Concert Halls and Educational Institutions

This census operates by means of programs submitted by symphony orchestras, promoters of serious music concerts, and colleges and universities.

One exception to this census is for those performances in educational institutions where the artist is paid less than $1,500. These performances are included in the survey on a sample basis.

Background/Foreground Music Services

Customusic, Magnetronics, and Tape-Athon are all included on a census basis, using reports submitted by these services. ASCAP's survey of performances by Audio Environments, Inc., (AEI) captures a complete count of AEI foreground performances and a sample of AEI background performances. ASCAP has now doubled its samples of performances by two major users: MUZAK and airlines.

General Licensees

ASCAP conducts a census of performances on the two units of Disney on Ice and the two units of the Ringling Brothers' circus.

The Sample

ASCAP finds sampling performances necessary because it is not possible, as a practical and economic matter, to count each of the millions of music performances in the United States. Even if ASCAP could obtain data concerning all music performances, the cost of researching and processing that data would be so prohibitive that it would have little, if anything, left to distribute.

ASCAP's sample is random, stratified, and disproportionate. A random sample is scientific by definition. It is determined solely by mathematical probability and leaves no room for personal discretion. The randomness extends to the time periods of the day, and the days of the year. Under this system, every performance has a chance of coming into the survey.

ASCAP's sample is stratified because licensees are classified into groups that have significant common characteristics. This enhances sampling precision. ASCAP's samples are stratified by media (e.g., local radio, local television); by type of community (e.g., New England, Middle Atlantic, Pacific); and by size of the licensee in terms of annual fees to ASCAP (e.g., $1,000 to $10,000, $10,000 to $20,000, and so on).

Thus, rather than draw a random sample for local radio from the entire United States and Puerto Rico, ASCAP draws a random sample simultaneously from each of 432 "stratified cells." In other words, it might sample a radio station in a rural area in the $5,000 to $10,000 license fee range. At the same time, it might also be sampling a radio station in the metropolitan Chicago area in the $300,000 to $400,000 license fee range. A similar procedure is followed for the random sample of local TV stations.

The sample is disproportionate because the depth of the sample varies with the amount of the fees paid by licensees within each stratified cell. A station which pays ASCAP $20,000 in license fees is sampled twice as much as a station which pays ASCAP only $10,000. The greater the license fees, the greater the sampling depth. All radio and television stations that pay $10,000 or more per year are included in the sample.

Local Radio

Local radio stations in the United States broadcast an average of 18 hours per day, or some 53 million hours per year. ASCAP samples 60,000 of these hours each year, including both commercial and college/university stations. This amount, considered statistically representative by independent survey experts, was reviewed by the Bureau of the Census, U.S. Department of Commerce, and approved by the U.S. Department of Justice.

ASCAP obtains its performance information by taping local radio. Its system of identifying works by means of its taping procedures has less than a 2 percent margin of error. Moreover, taping is carried out with absolute confidentiality. Neither the stations, the ASCAP board, nor ASCAP management have prior knowledge as to which stations are being taped. Because ASCAP relies on tape recordings of broadcasts, it employs a large staff of specialists in music identification to analyze the tapes and prepare lists of all works performed. Feature works which cannot be identified through the usual process are referred to a special group called "solfeggists" who maintain a file of such works according to the do-re-mi scale. This enables ASCAP to credit these performances when the works are identified subsequently.

The completed list of identified words, along with similar lists from other media, are the basic data used to determine royalty distributions.

Local Television

There are approximately 900 local television stations in the United States. ASCAP's television sample consists of 30,000 hours of local programming. To determine what works are being performed, a combination of cue sheets, tapes, and various regional issues of *TV Guide* (a weekly publication containing comprehensive listings of all TV stations and programs in the country) is used.

Public Broadcasting Service

ASCAP samples 1,530 hours of public television per year and 690 hours of national public radio. The procedures followed in conducting these surveys are similar to those followed in commercial broadcasting. Fewer hours are sampled because the fees paid are much lower than those paid by commercial broadcasters.

Background/Foreground Music Services

ASCAP receives about 90 percent of its background/foreground music license fees from MUZAK and AEI.

These significant users provide music performance information via computer file delivery compatible with ASCAP's computer system, which enables ASCAP to efficiently process these performances.

As indicated above, there are other background music performances that are processed on a complete count (or census) basis.

The airlines provide copies of the program listings in their in-flight magazines.

Sums received from other, unsurveyed, background music licensees are distributed on the basis of feature performances on radio and television.

General Licensing

The majority of general licensees are not surveyed. This is because surveying the tens of thousands of users would cost more than ASCAP could possibly collect. Therefore, following the advice of independent survey experts, and with the exceptions noted above, ASCAP uses feature performances or radio and TV as "proxies" for the distribution of the monies received from these users. The society believes its extensive survey of radio and television performances fairly reflects the many kinds of music performed by its general licensees.

Cable

Cable television connotes "secondary transmissions" and cable originations. These are two different sources of music and two different surveys of performances. Secondary transmissions originate as over-the-air broadcasts that cable systems pick up and retransmit to their subscribers. They are licensed by virtue of a compulsory license provision of the copyright act that also sets the fee. The Copyright Royalty Tribunal determines how that fee is to be allocated among the various claimants (including non-music as well as music copyright proprietors). ASCAP's share of these fees is distributed based on a sample of performances by those local television stations which are re-transmitted by cable systems.

Cable originators are not subject to the compulsory license. Fees are arrived at by negotiation or by court determination. At this time, virtually all program services and most cable systems are licensed by ASCAP, but interim license fees set by the court are paid only by the services and not yet by the cable systems. Distributions are being made on a census basis for HBO and on a sample basis for the following: American Movie Classics, Arts and Entertainment, Black Entertainment Television, Bravo, Cinemax, CNN, CNN Headline News, Country Music Television, Discovery Channel, The Disney Channel, Family Channel, HBO, Lifetime, The Movie Channel, MTV, The Nashville Network, Nickelodeon, Playboy, Prism, Showtime, Turner Network Television, and USA Network.

Performances on all the foregoing cable program services appear on members' statements under the "Cable" heading. Table 9 provides contact information for ASCAP headquarters and membership offices.

Table 8. ASCAP Credit Values

Survey Year	Publisher Credit Value
1990 (4th quarter 1989–3rd quarter 1990)	$3.33
1989 (4th quarter 1988–3rd quarter 1989)	$3.10
1988 (4th quarter 1987–3rd quarter 1988)	$2.79
1987 (4th quarter 1986–3rd quarter 1987)	$2.78
1986 (4th quarter 1985–3rd quarter 1986)	$2.36

Table 9. Headquarters and Membership Offices

ASCAP Headquarters
New York ASCAP Building 1 Lincoln Plaza New York NY 10023 (212) 621-6000

Membership Offices
Los Angeles 6430 Sunset Blvd. Los Angeles, CA 90028 (213) 883-1000
Nashville 2 Music Square West Nashville, TN 37203 (615) 742-5000
Chicago Kingsbury Center 350 West Hubbard Street Chicago, IL 60610 (312) 527-9775
London 52 Haymarket Suites 10 and 11 London, England SW1Y4RP 011-44-71-973-0069
Puerto Rico Office 505 First Federal Savings Condominium 1519 Ponce de Leon Avenue Santurce, PR (809) 725-1688

Insights of
CONNIE BRADLEY
Southern Regional Executive Director
ASCAP/Nashville

There is no doubt about it, Nashville is a songwriters' town. That's why ASCAP, a membership society made up of songwriters and music publishers, plays such an important role in the Nashville music scene.

Music has always had the ability to bring people together and nowhere is that more evident than at ASCAP's Nashville office. Whether attending to the needs of its many composer, lyricist, and publisher members, supporting and encouraging new talent through songwriter workshops and showcases, or working with other area music organizations, ASCAP is committed to the Nashville music community.

In addition to writing great music, many of ASCAP's Nashville songwriters take an active role in the activities of the society by serving on the Writers Advisory Committee and by joining legislative efforts in Washington to protect the rights of all music creators. Nashville is also represented on the ASCAP Board of Directors both on the writer and publisher side, making it the only performing rights organization on which ASCAP has a voice.

ASCAP never loses sight of its original goal: to protect the rights of members by making sure they are compensated for performances of their music. This is why the society actively licenses more music users and negotiates the best license fees for members. Because American music is so popular abroad, ASCAP also places great emphasis on making sure its members are compensated properly for performances of their music around the world.

Connie Bradley is the Southern Executive Director of ASCAP and has been with the firm for 17 years. At ASCAP she is in charge of a 20-state area where her main objective is not only to sign the new up-and-coming writers and publishers who will be the future hit makers, but also to watch the ASCAP percentages grow in the country charts.

A native of Shelbyville, Tennessee, Bradley attended Middle Tennessee State University. Prior to joining ASCAP, her experience in the music industry included positions with RCA Records and Famous Music/Dot Records.

Bradley was named "Lady Executive of the Year" (1985) by the National Women Executives and was featured in *Nashville* magazine as one of the seven leading ladies in Nashville. Bradley was chosen as one of the eight professional women honored by the Nashville Women's Political Caucus in October 1987, and in the 1991 *Sourcebook*, she was chosen as the most successful woman in Nashville.

Active in local civic as well as industry organizations, Bradley was chairman of the Nashville Area Chamber of Commerce Music Industry Relations Committee. She currently serves on the Board of the Country Music Association, the Country Music Foundation, the Copyright Society of the South, the W.O. Smith Nashville Music Community School, the Alabama Hall of Fame, and the Georgia Music Hall of Fame. She is also an Advisory Council member of the Tennessee Film, Entertainment and Music Commission and is an alumni of Leadership Music.

Connie Bradley

Insights of
MERLIN LITTLEFIELD
Associate Director
ASCAP/Nashville

If life is a carnival, then the music business is the state fair. It's the biggest . . . more like Texas or Illinois or wild and crazy like Cheyenne frontier days. It's filled with a giant roller coaster, a shooting gallery, lots of games, and lost children.

After 27 years I'm happy to say I'm still on the midway, having ridden most all the rides and played all of the games. Fortunately, I'm here with some friends—you just can't have fun or survive here without your pals. Most of us come through the main gate paying our dues as admission while others walked through the back gate with an all-access pass around their neck. Those were the ones who had the "right" last name or knew somebody. A lot of these folks create instant jealousy even though most of them do a good job. This is mainly because of their family's reputation, plus Daddy and friends in the business will kick their a_ _ if they don't. Then there are the gate-crashers—those people who try to buy their way in the business. They're always thrown out.

But everyday is not fun at the fair. There are those who lose everything by playing a game and sometimes even their life on a bad ride. Let's not forget lost children who can't find their way home.

However, if you want to take chances, ride the roller coaster. Come to the fair! Possibly, you might even be on top of the Ferris wheel when it stops.

Littlefield was born in Ft. Worth, Texas. He graduated from Texas Christian University with majors in radio-TV-film and sociology.

His music business career began in Texas in 1967 with Capitol Records where he became division promotion manager. He was subsequently division promotion manger for RCA Records before forming his own management and publishing companies, with such acts as Bloodrock, B.W. Stevenson, and Michael Martin Murphy.

Following his personal venture, Littlefield became national promotion manager for Stax and Capricorn Records, respectively. Littlefield moved to Nashville in 1974 and has been employed by ASCAP since that time, except for one year when he was general manager of Peer-Southern Publishing Company.

Littlefield serves on the board of the National Academy of Recording Arts and Sciences and is also past president of the Nashville Chapter. He is a board member of the Country Music Association, and serves as chairman of the Legislative Committee. Littlefield is vice-president of the Academy of Country Music, is on the board of the Better Business Bureau, and the Advisory Board of the Atlanta Songwriters Association. He is a member of the Gospel Music Association (GMA), Nashville Songwriters Association International, and the Copyright Society of the South.

A recipient of a Dove Award, presented by the GMA, Littlefield is credited with finding the Grammy and country music award-winning song, "The Gambler" by Don Schlitz, which was an international hit by Kenny Rogers.

Merlin Littlefield

Chapter 10

◆ ◆ ◆

The Music Industry

In the music business, the highs are slow and the lows are low!

The competition is stiff. Very stiff. Approximately 316 country music singles chart in *Billboard* per year, according to computer statistics—while hundreds of thousands of songs are pitched. It's even tougher in New York and Los Angeles. And, those pitches are from the best writers in the country.

One of my singles was put on hold for a year and a half; that's about standard. The industry has many delays. There are so many involved in a "project" (cutting an album). So many decisions must be made by labels, producers, managers, and artists. For my single that was on hold for one and a half years, over 2,000 songs were listened to by the artist, the artist's producer, and the artist's manager, and ultimately by the record label's A&R (artists and repertoire staff). Those 2,000 songs were from the finest writers in the country. Then, out of those, the final 10 sides were selected. And, out of those 10, the three singles were selected. The final decision was with the label. However, the producer, artist, and manager all gave the label their input.

The two largest publishing houses in the world are Tree International/Publishing and Warner Chappell/Publishing. Approximately 40 to 60 staff writers are signed to Tree, and the number is even higher at Warner Chappell.

Every major producer has staff or "in-house" writers. Most managers have in-house writers. Artists write. There are signed writers working for every entity in the music business, including the record labels. To make the competition even stiffer all the major labels have subsidiary or secondary labels with their staff of writers. That's a lot of writers all trying to get one or more of those 316 singles per year.

The major doors are closed to outside writers, unless you know someone on the inside. Most of the smaller doors are closed too. One top artist is pitched over 1,500 cassettes (with at least three songs on each cassette) per month from the outside world. They cannot and will not take unsolicited material. They hardly have the time to listen to the songs their own staff writers are writing. "Highly competitive," is putting it mildly.

I wrote "That Old Wheel" in 1984. It was rejected 22 times. In 1988–89, it was finally cut by Johnny Cash along with Hank

Williams, Jr., on the duet album, "Water from the Wells of Home," and it was released as the A-side single from the album. "That Old Wheel" was released again as an album cut in 1991 on "The Best of Johnny Cash" (one-and-only series), Curb Records, Burbank, California, and on "The Best of Hank Williams, Jr." (one-and-only series), Curb Records, Burbank, California. There were no singles released on those two projects.

If you don't have a thick skin and a great sense of humor, this business could easily drive you "nuts." To be creative a writer has to shed that thick skin—but, when the demos are finished, put that armor back on. It's all business.

Producers write, even some managers write. Everyone, it seems, wants to be a songwriter. This makes it even tougher for the writers who do nothing but write. Their only source of income is from their writing.

Greed, fear, and ego enter into the music industry, just as they do in any other business. What is so sad about the music business is that it's supposed to be all about creativity, sensitivity, and fragile emotions.

Staff writers on the highest draws usually get their material worked the hardest, because the label needs to recoup the large draws paid out to those writers. When their performance checks come in, their draws are deducted, and the writer receives the balance. The label and the publishing houses work hard, because if those writers on high draws don't get cuts over a certain period of time, their contracts are terminated and everyone loses.

This is a quiet business for many reasons. The main reason is competition. Your best friend will try to beat you out of a cut if you tell them you know of a major artist going in the studio. I don't blame the friend. I suggest you keep information to yourself, knowing how difficult singles are to come by, even album cuts are extremely difficult to get.

Everyone wants and needs those singles. It is the only way a writer becomes known. An album cut is great, but no one will ever hear your song on the radio. You'll make money off of sales (mechanicals) only, no performance. Performance is how songwriters make the money that matters.

If you are the only writer of a number one song by a number one artist your performance checks could easily be $100,000 the first year alone. If that song goes on his "greatest hits" album, relax, you can retire if you want to. Writers never stop writing. They live to write and have their songs heard through the artist's performances throughout the world. And, it has been my experience that money is not the number one priority with great writers. Writing is the number one priority with the great writers.

However, money is the number one priority for labels and other entities in the music industry. They need to keep the machine wheels greased and turning. They need lots and lots of money to do that.

An artist and his producer usually go in the studio with 30 to 50 (last-pick songs). From those the final 10 are selected during studio time. And, sadly, sometimes great songs get bumped at the last minute after long holds, when favors are owed. If an artist's best friend or family member brings them a song in the studio (where you and I can't go), your song may get bumped, out of that artist's friendship with another person, whether that person is a writer or not. Families of artists suddenly become writers too. There is so much pressure on the artist, it's no small wonder the artist needs the insulation they get from their producers, managers, agents, and labels.

Hit songs make artists. The song always comes first! A good way for a writer to break into major circles is to work and to write with an up-and-coming artist. Even then, if and when that artist gets signed, staff writers' songs will be pushed on the new artist instead of yours, even though it was your song that broke the artist in the first place.

Some artist/writers may become so busy with road work, they can't write great songs because writing a great song takes a great deal of thought and energy. Some artists continue to write when they are worn out, but still have the contractual power to cut their own material. This is one of the reasons we hear bad songs on the radio.

Powerful publishing houses also get cuts for so-so writers, and pay record promoters very highly to push those songs up the charts so they can recoup the large layouts of draws they have in their primary writers, even when those writers are no longer writing great songs.

This is part of the reality of the music industry. No one wants to lose, everyone wants to win.

The music industry is basically still a man's world. There are many great female writers and artists. But, it is much harder for a woman to make it. Male egos (or the lack of egos) are involved. Some men, in places of power, still believe that women belong in the kitchen. Some men don't like to "get bested" by females. However, many men in the industry are secure and helpful to females.

Even those artists and writers with gold and platinum to their credit can fall if they fail to continue to make money for the labels. Their contracts will be terminated. It's all in the songs.

When the public stops buying, everyone loses. That is why I believe the writing should be left to the writers. It is their songs that keep everyone under contract.

I feel managers should manage, producers should produce, artists (who are not writers first and foremost) should stick to entertaining and singing—*and leave the writing to the writers.* Egos may even get in the way of making money and helping artists stay on top. The artist's own ego can deliver him to the land of "the great music void" if he insists on continuing to write and release his own "bad" songs.

To be a gifted writer you must be intelligent, imaginative, sensitive, empathic, have a mastery of words and illusion, and be humble all at the same time. There are only a handful of truly great songwriters, in my opinion.

Great writers can become great artists, like Nelson, Kristofferson, and Croce. However, a great singer/entertainer may not necessarily become a great writer. That is why more secure and less greedy artists get their material from the songwriters.

I am honored that the quotes in this book are from some of the greats—not only great writers, but great managers, producers, and industry people, who are secure, and do their jobs extremely well. They don't try to spread themselves too thin by trying to be all things to all people.

You must be very disciplined to be a writer. I've been asked if writing is first in my life. My answer is: it's not a matter of writing being first, writing is part of my life, part of me. I not only want to write, I need to write.

Songwriting can be harmful to interpersonal relationships. Writing does not come before someone I love. I just can't separate my writing from myself. When a writer is "on a roll," they can't quit to go out to dinner or a show. They could lose the entire feeling they are involved with.

Writers' friends are very patient people. This is also true of producers, artists, musicians, managers, etc. They need to do what they do. It is part of them, not separate from them.

This business is tough. But, great competition in any area makes all of us better at whatever we strive to achieve in life. So, don't fear competition, learn to welcome it. It will make you work that much harder.

Summary

The personal characteristics needed in order "not to go nuts" in the music business are: a love for what you do, a lot of patience, a great sense of humor, and a large amount of talent. And, if you are a songwriter, the ability to do a quick change from the sensitive, imaginative, disciplined writer, to rubbing a lot of oil on your back, will help because you're going to have to let a lot of "stuff" slide off. If you have a good understanding of the business and know everyone's only human, and keep cool, you'll get by and be able to hang in there.

However, if you grow bitter, get a case of "sour grapes," become impatient, or get an attitude, you won't make it. At least you won't make it in a very good "frame of mind." It's nice to be around positive people, people who don't put others down. Negative people use up so much energy on negative thoughts and feelings that could and should be used to improve their art.

Remember, writers don't manage. Writers don't produce. Writers don't tell session players how to play or think they can play as well as those great players. Writers don't sing to make money or entertain. Writers *write.*

Insights of
GILLES GODARD
Songwriter, Producer, Publisher

Mr. Webster defines the word *industry* as: "1. Diligence in an employment or pursuit. 2. Systematic labor for the creation of value. A distinct group of productive or profit-making enterprises."

The music industry encompasses both of these definitions of industry. Whether you are an artist, writer, producer, publisher, musician, engineer, record executive, manager, publicist, promoter, radio programmer, club owner, graphic artist, and the list goes on, you are all part of the industry, and you need to remember that you can only expect to get out of it what you are committed to put into it.

This is the world of show business. There are only four letters in *show*; however, there are eight letters in the word *business*. Which could lead us to believe that the business end of things is more important than the show. . . . Not far from true. One thing is certain, if you have the best show in the world, but your business affairs are not together, it's just not going to work. That's why you need a team of good players to work with you.

Whether you are a beginner or an established player in this industry, there are two things you need to remember: (1) always be professional in your work (perception is reality), and (2) be a team player—you are an important link in the chain (network, share, and compare notes).

It's not an easy business, and, like any business, success and failure are close relatives. "Success is the ability to go from failure to failure without loss of enthusiasm."

Work smart, study those who are already successful in your field, learn from their work. Set your goals, keep a positive attitude, and learn from your mistakes but never lose your enthusiasm.

Enjoy yourself along the way. Being on top of the mountain is a great feeling, but it's the climb that's exhilarating!

Born and raised in Cornwall, Ontario, Gilles Godard studied steel guitar throughout his teenage years. It was in Nashville,

Tennessee, where he studied steel guitar, that Godard decided to record some of his own compositions in 1979, and released his first album in 1980.

In 1986, Godard received four Pro Canada Awards for "Hold on to What You Got" and "Nothing Good About Goodbye," as a writer and publisher. In 1987, he received a Pro Canada Award for "No Holiday in L.A.," written for Ronnie Prophet. In 1986, he received Big Country's Producer of the Year Award. In 1987, he received a Felix Award for Best French Country Album, which was released on RCA Records in Quebec. And, in September 1990, he was voted Record Industry Person of the Year by the Canadian CMA.

His nominations include a Juno Award (three times); in 1985 for Top Country Duo or Group with Kelita Haverland for their duet "Nothing Good About Goodbye"; in 1987, for Best Country Male Vocalist; and, in 1989, for Top Country Duo or Group with Colleen Peterson for their duet "I Still Think of You."

Godard has produced records for artists such as Tommy Hunter, Janie Frickie, Ronnie Prophet, Eddie Eastman, Kelita Haverland, "Hee Haws" Hager Twins, Terry Kelly, Bobby Lalonde, Hal Bruce, Bruce Golden, Royce Ryan, and the list goes on.

Gilles Godard

Chapter 11

♦ ♦ ♦

The Professional/Artist/Writer/Composer

Terms Used in This Chapter

Artist: Craftsman, artisan. 1. A person who works in or is skilled in any of the fine arts, especially in painting, drawing, sculpture, etc. 2. A person who does anything very well, with imagination and a feeling for form, effect, etc. *(Webster's Dictionary)*

Composer: 1. To create (a musical or literary work). 2. To create musical or literary works—a person who composes, especially one who composes music. *(Webster's Dictionary)*

Entertain(er): 1. To keep the interest of and give pleasure to; divert; amuse. 2. To give hospitality to; have as a guest. 3. To allow oneself to think about; have in mind, consider [to entertain an idea]. 4. To keep up, to maintain. 5. A person who entertains; especially a popular singer, dancer, comedian, etc. *(Webster's Dictionary)*

Professional: 1. Of, engaged in, or worthy of the high standards of, a profession. 2. Designating or of a school, especially a graduate school, offering instruction in a profession. 3. Earning one's living from an activity, such as a sport, not normally thought of as an occupation. 4. Engaged in the professional players [professional hockey]. 5. Engaged in a specified occupation for pay or as a means of livelihood [a professional writer]. 6. Being such in a manner of one practicing a profession [a professional hatemonger]. 7. A person practicing a profession. 8a. A person who engages in some art, sport, etc., for money, especially, for his livelihood, rather than as a hobby. 8b. A golfer, tennis player, etc., affiliated with a particular club as a contestant, teacher, and the like: usually clipped to pro. 9. A person who does something with great skill. *(Webster's Dictionary)*

Writer: 1. To be the author or composer of (literary or musical material). 2. A person who writes. 3. A person whose work or occupation is writing; specifically an author, journalist, or the like. *(Webster's Dictionary)*

The Professional Artist

Any *professional* does his job to the very best of his ability. The professional artist has several jobs in one: He must entertain. He must be up when he's feeling down. He must smile when he feels like crying. He must move around on the stage when he's too tired to sleep. He must sign autographs until he can hardly play his guitar. The professional artist knows "the show must go on."

The professional artist needs to have his head on real straight. He must be bigger than life and at the same time, be true to life. He must be humble with his friends, fans, family, road manager, business manager, musicians, management, producer, record label, receptionist, secretaries, etc. If he begins to buy his own publicity, he can become quite obnoxious, at least to the people in the music industry who know him well. He may become too busy to spend even five minutes with those who originally were there for him when he first started out. The public may never know, but the industry people know about the change in his attitude.

No label signs an artist with an attitude, but that does not mean that artist won't develop an attitude later on.

With thousands, sometimes hundreds of thousands of fans, all screaming for his attention, the artist must keep a solid grasp on the fact that he did not get to where he is alone. It took a team effort. He should never forget those who helped him achieve his success.

If an artist is very young and does not have a secure sense of who he is, he usually won't be able to maintain the proper attitude and will start believing that he is bigger than life.

There is a big difference between an artist and a professional artist. The pro will not develop an attitude. Every artist realizes, at one point or another in his career, how difficult it is to be a major artist. That is why they need to be insulated by their managers.

The professional artist has to have had something to offer in order to have been signed by a major label. He usually has a very definitive way of delivering his material (or the material supplied to him by the songwriters) which makes him stand out in a crowd. An artist must be different in order to make it.

He must be dedicated to what he does. He must not complain about it privately. He should never become sour about his fans or the amount of work he has to do. He is being very well paid for what he does, and he is the one who chose to become an artist in the first place.

From time to time stories circulate about artists who on stage pretended to be drug free, Christians, etc. Then, eventually news gets out that those artists who have so blatantly made public statements against drugs (or whatever) are found to be using drugs themselves. Even though those artists may still have a good living off of the past royalties, their careers are virtually over. Again, the public is not stupid. The public will only accept so much pretense. The public does not like to be duped. They have a right to believe in the image the artist represents.

Most professional artists are sincere people who work very hard at what they do. They are always trying to improve themselves and they remain humble throughout their careers.

The professional artist pays his dues without complaint, without hypocrisy, and without buying his own publicity. Unfortunately, some artists become secure with the wrong kinds of things. They may win awards. They may be on many national television programs. But, it is their integrity that must hold up throughout the years.

The professional artist should get along with everyone. He should try to do as much as possible to help others once he has made it. He has a true humility about the fact that he is so popular. The professional artist will become more humble with each step he takes up the ladder of success.

The professional artist must have some very special qualities. He must be very strong, both physically and mentally, in order to endure the incredible amount of "road work" he must put in and in order to promote his projects. He usually is a great vocalist and/or guitarist, and is able to communicate on any level, with anyone, and make them feel comfortable.

Singing Tips

At some point during the career of the professional artist, he will probably engage in some form of vocal training.

The following list of "tips" on singing professionally should be carefully studied and practiced by the aspiring artist.

1.   Singing is talking on key.

2.   Talk the lyric lines clearly. Singing is clear speech.

3.   Take your breath from your pelvic area, very low in your body. Imagine yourself swallowing an apple. Let the entire apple go all the way down and stop between your legs, in your pelvic area.

4.   Do not use any breath when you are singing. Control your breathing as you need the breath for each note and/or phrase. When you are singing, place a candle in front of you. You should not blow the flame out. The flame should waver, but it should not go out. The candle should be placed approximately 10 to 12 inches directly in front of your mouth.

5.   Keep tension out of your body. Keep your shoulders pushed down. Keep your entire body pushed down. Your chest should not visibly move when you are singing. If your chest moves, you are not utilizing proper breath control. Breath should be taken from the area of your diaphragm, not your chest. Of course, between phrasing, as you draw in a deep breath, your chest may move slightly, but there is a great difference in chest movement if you take the breath from the pelvic area as opposed to taking a breath from the chest area.

6.   Keep your back straight. Your breath must flow upward smoothly.

7.   The focal point of your sound should be coming from the area of your upper molars. Keep your palate up. Force your mouth into an overbite, forcing your upper teeth forward. Imagine yourself biting into an apple. When your palate is up, you will not go flat. Flatness is caused by not having enough breath behind the note. When the palate is up, your breath will not be obstructed as it flows upward. Many singers smile while singing. They know a smile forces the palate up.

8. Do not try to use your throat when singing. Your throat is only a passageway for your instrument. Your voice is your instrument. Learn to depersonalize your voice to the extent that you think of it as an instrument. Then, you will learn the mechanics of proper use for your instrument.

9. Keep all tension out of your face. Consciously think about being in a relaxed position when you sing.

10. When you hold a note, think of that note as coming out of your mouth on a horizontal line. This will help you to hold the note smoothly.

11. Do not hold consonants. Do not hold harsh sounding words. They are not pleasing to the ear.

12. Get off all *H*s and go to the next vowel sound. Vowels are pleasing to the ear. *H*s are not pleasing and are breathy.

13. Keep the sound small. Learn to focus on the vowel sounds by picturing a small circle surrounding the vowel. Allow your focus to grow as the phrasing calls for more sound. This is another method of controlling or saving breath. The vowel sound should begin from behind the nose. Keep the sound low. Keep the sound small. Your controlled breath will push the sound over your vocal chords naturally.

14. At the end of a lyric line, hold vowels and soft notes with a low sound. Think low, even if the sound is soprano. This method helps keep the harshness out of your instrument.

15. Think of your breath as going behind and through the back of your head, flowing underneath your upper molars and out of your mouth. Imagine a focal point in the back of your head the size of a small silver pin. Focus your sound in this area and bring it forward.

16. Your vocal chords are an instrument just as much as a piano or guitar is an instrument. Vocal chords must be taken care of and used properly.

17. Your breath will flow naturally from your nasal passages, not from the focus of your mouth.

18. Power singing comes from singing with no breath. This is called vocal control. Every professional understands and utilizes vocal control.

19. Phrase and sing the lyric just as you would talk the lyric. Place the power behind important words and phrases.

20. Never forget the emotion in the lyric. For example, if it is a sad song, think sad. If it is a happy song, think happy. Sing the lyric just as you would say the words. Use proper emotion and feeling.

Your breath intake comes from your pelvic area. It then flows up a straight back, through a relaxed body, through your throat. The sound is focused at a small point in the back of your head. It then flows naturally through your nasal passages, under your upper molars, and out. The power comes from the pelvic area, not the chest area. When you are controlling your breath from the low place of this area, you will find you will be able to use your breath as you need it. You cannot control breath in your chest. If you try to control your breath from your lungs (your chest area), your breath will become shortened and gaspy. Also, you will not be able to keep your palate up if you are taking breath from the chest area.

Here's a good exercise to do in order to keep your palate up. Wrap masking tape around the eraser ends of two wooden pencils. No metal should be showing. Take the pencils in your hands and slip the taped ends into your mouth so that the taped ends are pushed underneath your upper molars. This position causes your mouth to form an overbite and keeps your palate up. Practice vocalizing with the pencils in your mouth. Practice the vocal scale this way.

When you remove the pencils try to keep your mouth in the same position as when the pencils were in place.

These tips are by no means all you need to know about singing professionally. Even if you have a great natural talent, take vocal lessons, if for no other reason than to save your instrument and protect if from damage from improper use.

The professional artist must be an "actor," but not to the extent that he maintains that role off stage. Professional artists are the ones who bring life and feeling to the writer's songs.

Writers

All that mankind has done, thought, gained or been: it is lying as in magic preservation in the pages of books.
                                                    Thomas Carlyle

This book is all about writers, the people who express themselves by putting their feelings, their hearts and souls, their emotions all in words. Their words are strong and true, and need to be heard, digested, and remembered.

The world cannot do without the professional songwriter. Even though their names may be small and they achieve the least amount of fame and glory, many are gratified, just because they write.

The only glory the writer usually wants is to have his material heard. The writer has the desire to give something, something he believes is important, something that perhaps can make the world a little brighter, a bit more fun, something that can bring lovers back together again, or words that pay tribute to loved ones no longer with us. The power of the pen is the mightiest power of all. The writer seems to have a deep understanding of what may become immortal. A life-and-death understanding that goes beyond words and settles somewhere deep within the heart, soul, and mind of the writer.

Without writers no one would ever learn anything. Everything comes from the written word. Songs, movies, screen plays, Broadway shows—everything and anything we learn—originates from the written word.

Writers usually read a great deal because they want and need to be learning all the time. Words are their tools.

God be thanked for books. They are the voices of the distant and the dead, and make us heirs of the spiritual life of past ages.
                                                William Ellery Channing

Composers

Music is the only language in which you cannot say a mean or sarcastic thing.

John Erskine

The professional composer has a gift, like the writer, that comes from deep within his heart, mind, and soul. He is filled with feelings and he needs to express those feelings through his great music—music so great it stands alone. Brahms, Bach, and Beethoven were some of the great composers, but there are many more. Composers have an "ear" that most of us do not have.

Nothing pleases me more than when a great composer asks me to put lyrics to his music. Great music touches me deeply, as do great lyrics. They hit an emotional chord. They strike at the heart. A great composition can take us all away to distant places. It can make us see new horizons, as we look over mountaintops and become lost in clear streams.

The professional composer must have a very unique kind of freedom within himself in order for us to feel and see so much when we listen to his great music.

Not only does a professional composer have a great amount of knowledge to be able to fully understand music theory, and be able to translate notes into the softest or the most uplifting feelings we have ever felt, he also has a "seventh" sense about him. This sense enables him to paint fantastic pictures through his music. Sometimes they make you see a great eagle flying, a small child crying, or an army marching. Professional composers have a great talent.

Where words fail, music speaks.

Hans Christian Andersen

Insights of
BARRY BECKETT

Barry Beckett's life in music started in Birmingham, Alabama, when he was learning Floyd Cramer piano licks as a teenager. This led him to Muscle Shoals, Alabama, in the late 1960s where he eventually became part of the Muscle Shoals Rhythm Section. During the 1970s and early 1980s he played keyboards on projects ranging from Paul Simon, Joe Cocker, and Aretha Franklin to Joan Baez and The Oak Ridge Boys. He began his production career with acts like Bob Dylan (Slow Train Coming), Dire Straits (Communique), Delbert McClinton (Jealous Kind), and many others including Glenn Frey and Bob Seger. Beckett's first hit came with the Sanford Townsend Band's "Smoke from a Distant Fire." Mary McGregor's "Torn Between Two Lovers" was his first number one country record, after being number one in the pop charts.

Beckett began working in Nashville in 1984, eventually moving there in 1985. He became Director of Arts and Repertoire at Warner Bros. Records, Nashville Division. While working at Warner Bros., Beckett began co-producing Hank Williams, Jr., with Jim Ed Norman. "Montana Cafe" and "Hank Live" both went gold and "Born to Boogie" went platinum, winning the Country Music Association's Album of the Year in 1988.

Beckett left Warner Bros. in 1987 to concentrate on his production career. He continued to produce Hank Williams, Jr., and in 1989 "There's a Tear in My Beer" won CMA Vocal Event of the Year. Beckett has had number one records with Eddy Raven, Lorrie Morgan, Alabama, Lionel Cartwright, and Lee Roy Parnell. He also has produced K.T. Oslin, T. Graham Brown, and Asleep at the Wheel.

Beckett got back into the rock-'n'-roll world producing Grammy-nominated Etta James ("Seven Year Itch" and "Stickin' To My Guns"). He also produced Delbert McClinton ("I'm With You"), Jason and the Scorchers, and Bob Seger ("The Fire Inside"). In the early 1990s, Beckett began producing many international acts including The Waterboys, Doro, Brendan Croker, Feargal Sharkey, J.P. Capdevielle, and Anne Haigis. His current productions include the newly released Lynyrd Skynyrd album ("The Last Rebel"), Phish, Ian Moore, and Confederate Railroad.

Barry Beckett *(Photo by M.J. Morris)*

Barry Beckett—Credits

1. Paul Simon, "There Goes Rhymin'"/Simon, Muscle Shoals Rhythm Section/Barry Beckett, 1973.
2. Bob Seger, "Beautiful Loser," Muscle Shoals Rhythm Section/Barry Beckett, 1975.
3. Bob Seger, "Night Moves," Muscle Shoals Rhythm Section/Barry Beckett, 1976.
4. Mary McGregor, "Torn Between Two Lovers," Peter Yarrow/Barry Beckett, 1976.
5. Joe Cocker, "Luxury You Can Afford," Allen Toussaint/Barry Beckett, 1978.
6. Bob Seger, "Stranger In Town," Muscle Shoals Rhythm Section/Barry Beckett, 1978.
7. Dire Straits, "Communique," Jerry Wexler/Barry Beckett, 1979.
8. Bob Dylan, "Slow Train Coming," Jerry Wexler/Barry Beckett, 1979.
9. Bob Dylan, "Saved," Jerry Wexler/Barry Beckett, 1980.
10. Delbert McClinton, "The Jealous Kind," Muscle Shoals Rhythm Section/Barry Beckett, 1980.
11. Bob Seger, "Against The Wind," Muscle Shoals Rhythm Section/Barry Beckett, 1980.
12. Delbert McClinton, "Plain From The Heart," Muscle Shoals Rhythm Section/Barry Beckett, 1981.
13. Glenn Frey, "The All Nighter," Glenn Frey/Allen Blazek/Barry Beckett, 1984.
14. Hank Williams, Jr., "Montana Cafe," Jim Ed Norman/Hank Williams, Jr./Barry Beckett, 1986.
15. Hank Williams, Jr., "Hank Live," Jim Ed Norman/Hank Williams, Jr./Barry Beckett, 1987.
16. Hank Williams, Jr., "Born to Boogie," Jim Ed Norman/Hank Williams, Jr./Barry Beckett, 1987.
17. Etta James, "Seven Year Itch," Rob Fraboni/Ricky Fataar/Barry Beckett, 1988.
18. Lorrie Morgan, "Leave The Light On," Barry Beckett, 1989.
19. Jason & The Scorchers, "Thunder and Fire," Barry Beckett, 1989.

20. Alabama, "Southern Star," Josh Leo/Barry Beckett, 1989.
21. T. Graham Brown, "Bumper to Bumper," Barry Beckett/T. Graham Brown, 1990.
22. Kris McKay, "What Love Endures," Barry Beckett, 1990.
23. Delbert McClinton, "I'm With You," Barry Beckett/Delbert McClinton, 1990.
24. Hank Williams, Jr., "Lone Wolf," Jim Ed Norman/Hank Williams, Jr./Barry Beckett, 1990.
25. Etta James, "Stickin' To My Guns," Barry Beckett/Etta James/Kim Buie, 1990.
26. Asleep At The Wheel, "Keepin' Me Up Nights," Barry Beckett/Ray Benson/Tim DuBois/Scott Hendricks, 1990.
27. K.T. Oslin, "Love In A Small Town," Barry Beckett/Josh Leo/Jim Cotton/Joe Scaife, 1990.
28. Waterboys, "Room To Roam," Barry Beckett/Mike Scott, 1990.
29. Feargal Sharkey, "Songs From The Mardi Gras," Barry Beckett, 1991.
30. Hank Williams, Jr., "Pure Hank," Barry Beckett/Jim Ed Norman/Hank Williams, Jr., 1991.
31. T. Graham Brown, "You Can't Take It With You," Barry Beckett/T. Graham Brown, 1991.
32. Brendan Croker, "The Great Indoors," Barry Beckett, 1991.
33. Bob Seger, "The Fire Inside," Don Was/Barry Beckett/Bob Seger, 1991.
34. Doro, "True at Heart," Barry Beckett, 1991.

Chapter 12

◆ ◆ ◆

Review

Terms Used in This Chapter

Ambivalence: Simultaneous conflicting feelings toward a person or thing, as love and hate. *(Webster's Dictionary)*

Childish: 1. Of, like, or characteristic of a child. 2. Not fit for an adult; immature, silly. *(Webster's Dictionary)*

Deceive: 1. To make (a person) believe what is not true; delude; mislead. 2. To be false to; betray—*deceive* implies deliberate misrepresentation of facts by words, actions, etc., generally to further one's ends [deceived into buying fraudulent stocks]; to *mislead* is to cause to follow the wrong course or to err in conduct or action, although not always by deliberate deception [misled by the sign into going to the wrong floor]; *beguile* implies the use of wiles and enticing prospects in deceiving or misleading [beguiled by promises of a fortune]; to *delude* is to fool someone so completely that he accepts what is false as true; *betray* implies a breaking of faith while appearing to be loyal. *(Webster's Dictionary)*

Deceit: 1. The act of representing as true what is known to be false; a deceiving or lying. 2. A dishonest action or trick; fraud or lie. 3. The quality of being deceitful. 4. Tending to deceive; apt to lie or cheat. 5. Intended to deceive; deceptive; false, dishonest. *(Webster's Dictionary)*

Immature: Not finished or perfected; incomplete. *(Webster's Dictionary)*

Influence: The power of persons or things (whether or not exerted consciously or overtly) to affect others [he owed his position to influence]; *authority* implies the power to command acceptance, belief obedience, etc., based on strength of character, expertness of knowledge, etc. [a statement made on good authority]; *prestige* implies the power to command esteem or admiration, based on brilliance of achievement or outstanding superiority; *weight* implies influence that is more or less preponderant in its effect [he threw his weight to the opposition]. *(Webster's Dictionary)*

Introspection: To look within. To look into (one's own mind, feelings, etc.). A looking into one's own mind, feelings, etc.; observation and analysis of oneself. *(Webster's Dictionary)*

Terms Used in This Chapter *(cont.)*

Love: To be fond of, desire. 1. A deep and tender feeling of affection for or attachment or devotion to a person or persons. 2. An expression of one's love or affection [give Mary my love]. 3. A feeling of brotherhood and good will toward other people. 4a. A strong liking for or interet in something [a love of music]. b. The object of such liking. 5a. A strong, usually passionate, affection of one person for another, based in part on sexual attraction. b. The person who is the object of such an affection; sweetheart, lover. 6a. God's benevolent concern for mankind. b. Man's devout attachment to God. 7. To feel love for. 8. To show love for by embracing, kissing, etc. 9. To delight in; take pleasure in [to love books]. To gain benefit for [a plant that loves shade]—to feel the emotion of love; be in love—fall in love (with) to begin to feel love (for)—in love, feeling love; enamored—make love. Love implies intense fondness or deep devotion and may apply to various relationships or objects [sexual love, brotherly love, love of one's work, etc.]; *attachment* implies connection by ties of affection, attraction, devotion, etc. and may be felt for inanimate things as well as for people [an attachment to an old hat]; *infatuation* implies a foolish or unreasoning passion or affection, often a transient (passing) (not permanent) one [an elderly man's infatuation for a young girl]. *(Webster's Dictionary)*

Mature: 1. Fully developed, as a person, a mind, etc. *(Webster's Dictionary)*

Sad: 1. Having, expressing, or showing low spirits or sorrow; unhappy; mournful; sorrowful. 2. Causing or characterized by dejection, melancholy, or sorrow. 3. Dark or dull in color; drab. 4. [Colloq.] Very bad; deplorable. 5. [Dial.] Heavy or soggy [a sad cake]—sad is the simple, general term, ranging in implication from a mild, momentary unhappiness to a feeling of intense grief; *sorrowful* implies a sadness caused by some specific loss, disappointment, etc. [her death left him sorrowful]; *melancholy* suggests a more or less chronic mournfulness or gloominess, or, often merely a wistful pensiveness [melancholy thoughts about the future]; *dejected* implies discouragement or a sinking of spirits, as because of frustration; *depressed* suggests a mood of brooding despondency, as because of fatigue or a sense of futility [the novel left him feeling depressed]; *doleful* implies a mournful, often lugubrious, sadness [the doleful look on a lost child's face]. *(Webster's Dictionary)*

Terms Used in This Chapter *(cont.)*

Truth: The quality or state of being true; specifically: a. Loyalty; trustworthiness. b. Sincerity; genuineness; honesty. c. The quality of being in accordance with experience, facts, or reality; conformity with fact. d. Reality; actual existence. e. Agreement with a standard, rule etc.; correctness; accuracy. 2. That which is true; statement, etc. that accords with fact or reality. 3. An established or verified fact, principle, etc. 4. a particular belief or teaching regarded by the speaker as the true one (often with the)—in truth, truly; in fact—*truth* suggests conformity with the facts or with reality, either as an idealized abstraction ["What is truth?" said jesting Pilate] or in actual application to statements, ideas, acts, etc. [there is no truth in that rumor]; *veracity*, as applied to persons or to their utterances, connotes habitual adherence to the truth [I cannot doubt his veracity]; *verify*, as applied to things, connotes correspondence with fact or with reality [the verity of his thesis]; *verisimilitude*, as applied to literary or artistic representations, connotes correspondence with actual, especially universal, truths [the verisimilitude of the characterizations in a novel. *(Webster's Dictionary)*

Vacillate: 1. To sway to and fro; waver; totter; stagger. 2. To fluctuate or oscillate. 3. To waver in mind; show indecision—wavering or tending to waver in motion, opinion, etc. *(Webster's Dictionary)*

Weak: 1. Lacking in moral strength or will power; yielding easily to temptation, the influence of others, etc. 2. Lacking in mental power, or in the ability to think, judge, decide, for yourself, etc. 3. Indicating or suggesting moral or physical weakness [weak features]—weak, the broadest in application of these words, basically implies a lack or inferiority of physical, mental or moral strength [weak muscle, mind, character, foundation, excuse, etc.]. *(Webster's Dictionary)*

Weakminded: 1. Not firm of mind; indecisive; unable to refuse or deny. 2. Mentally deficient. 3. Showing weakness of resolve or thought [a weakminded decision]. *(Webster's Dictionary)*

Weakness: 1. The state or quality of being weak. 2. A weak point; fault or defect, as in one's character. 3a. A liking; especially an unreasonable fondness (for something). b. Something of which one is unreasonably fond [candy is his one weakness]. *(Webster's Dictionary)*

To be a "hit" songwriter, you need knowledge of lyrics and music, you need to understand feelings and emotions, and you need to write universally. This book has attempted to teach and show a myriad of technical devices used in songwriting. It has also explained content in order to help you write a "hit" lyric. However, the most important thing to remember is your lyric must also "hit" people in their universal hearts! The true emotions in your song should make people cry, laugh, dance, sing, think, and even pray. Your songs need to touch universal emotions.

I'm not only addressing country music in this book. Croce certainly was not a country writer. There are all kinds of music and lyric formats. Whether they be rhythm and blues, pop, rock, or hard rock, they all use the same devices, as are adhered to in country music. They all must be written with a universal content message. The format changes and everything else remains the same.

Rock music can be much more aggressive and esoteric lyrically than country music. It has longer verses and choruses. Pop music is usually more "middle of the road." It also may have longer choruses and verses. Rhythm and blues has many more repeats, especially in the chorus, than country music. And hard rock can be very harsh, hard, esoteric, and philosophical. The formats change. The devices remain the same. You can write to any format. If you write rhythm and blues, pop, rock, or hard rock, all you need to do is listen to the format changes on a cassette, CD, or on your own radio. Buy the sheet music, if necessary. Writers are intelligent people, who usually have great "ears" and a quick ability to learn, especially what comes naturally, which is the feel, "pocket," or "groove."

The best lyricists are those most sensitive and deeply and closely in touch with their own feelings. How else could they get in touch with the feelings of others? They must be empathetic, they must walk a mile in your shoes after having walked many, many miles in their own shoes. They must have sensitivity to all living things. Professional lyricists feel vibrations very strongly.

Anyone who is willing to spend two to three years understanding lyrical devices can write a pretty perfect lyric. But, no one can give you sensitivity, empathy, and understanding for how others feel, anymore than anyone can make you taller or shorter.

If you are in touch with your own feelings enough to know whether or not you are a truly sensitive person and you discover you are not as sensitive as you need to be, a great deal of introspection may help you to become more sensitive.

You should be able to clearly define how you feel, and your feelings need to be consistent. Your lyric can't be cold one day and hot the next. While we have good days and bad days, ups and downs, the core of your lyric should be consistent in its values, beliefs, ethics, and morals.

Don't change emotional positions in your lyric. Don't *vacillate*.

Consistent feelings make for consistent songwriting. Consistently positive feelings make for consistently positive songwriting. Positive does not mean you should never cry or feel sad. We all cry, we all feel sad, and we all get temporarily confused; but we pull out of it, and get back to being who we are. Being positive implies trying to be positively in touch with whatever and however you are feeling.

Humans are very complex. The songwriter, however, must be able to focus on a specific feeling and remain true and consistent to that feeling throughout his entire song, never losing sight of the emotional content. Even when a pro is having a bad day, they can become actors. They can put themselves in the little mini-motion picture they are writing, where they can identify with the ideas, ideals, images, and emotions they are writing about.

We are all influenced to some degree. But we should not be so influenced that we do not know what we might have achieved but for the influence of another person.

You may be asking yourself, "What has all of this got to do with songwriting?" A great deal. It is the job of the professional songwriter to clarify, to show, to explain the full range of human emotions to the world. When those in the world feel lost, it is the songwriter's job to help them find themselves. That is why all of the above has merit. A professional songwriter needs to get inside the hearts and minds of others and help them understand their own feelings and emotions. This cannot be done if the writer is not sure of his own emotions and feelings.

A confused person, who allows that confusion about life and what he wants to carry over into his songs, cannot write a clear or universally identifiable song.

Writers need to have their heads on pretty straight and have their hearts in the right place, a place of understanding and consideration for the feelings of others. Great writers don't usually invent their songs, they write from true life experiences. To do that, they must have those experiences defined. Next, they get in touch with the emotions and feelings of those specific experiences and/or situations. Then, they turn that experience or situation around from the *personal* to the *universal*. They take from the innermost part of themselves, their hearts, and give that part to the world.

Great lyricists also say things without saying them (e.g., *six string* instead of guitar, Buffett; *something in my eye* instead of tears, Croce. They also make use of similes (like) and metaphors (as).

Many writers are readers. Croce was an English literature major; Kristofferson also majored in English.

Words are your tools. Without them you can't write. The more words you understand, the better equipped you will be to work on your lyrics. The more tools you have to fix your car or the more quality tools a mechanic has, the better your chances of having your car properly repaired. However, that mechanic also needs to have learned a skill. He needs to have the ability to understand what needs to be done and why and how. So, too, the songwriter. You need to have special skills and abilities, with the added ingredient of *feelings*, and you must love to write. You also need to know the *whys* and *how*.

Remember, if you don't know where you're going, chances are you will never get there. You also need to know why you are going there, what your destination is, and what you believe you will find once you arrive. You need to visualize the beginning, the middle, and the end of your journey. If you are not sure, wait until you are sure. When in doubt, don't . . . If you don't know you're in love, you're not. If you don't know where you are going in a song, don't try to write it.

Great race car drivers must "focus." They must have all the technical knowledge and they must have a feel for high-speed driving. Great athletes must have all the technical knowledge to perform their *skills*. They must love what they do and be *disciplined* and *dedicated* to their art. The race car driver or the gymnast on the balance beam could be permanently injured or even killed if they don't have a clear and precise knowledge of what abilities are necessary to perform in their areas of expertise. The worst thing that can happen to a songwriter (besides hurt feelings) is his songs will never be recorded and released.

However, there are politics and power plays involved in the music industry. So, even when you've done everything right, you still may get bumped or turned down for a lesser song. You will know if you are a great writer because great writers never quit. Your time will come. The best cannot be denied.

There is always more to learn. The one thing that's constant is change. Stay well tuned-in to what is going on in your area of expertise, whether you are a writer, artist/writer, artist, manager, or producer. Always try to work with those who know more than you do. You can't learn anything from those who don't know as much as you do. You'll always learn something from everyone. There is nourishment in "milk," but there is more nourishment in "meat."

Life is all about many emotions. Take *love* as an example. Pick up your pen and write down how you feel about (1) love of life, (2) family love, (3) love for spouse, (4) love for children, (5) love for animals, (6) love for nature, (7) love for freedom, (8) love for God, (9) love for beauty, and (10) love for art and writing.

Sadness is another universal emotion. Write down how you feel about being (1) sad about a lost love, (2) sad about loss of income, (3) sad about homeless people, (4) sad about people in prison, (5) sad for people who are victims of crimes, (6) sadness for abused animals, (7) sadness for abused woman and children, (8) sad about morality, and (9) sad about greed. Do these situations make you feel sad?

I wrote the following lyric when I was feeling very low and very lost and the terrible situations in the world were getting to me. I expressed my feelings, at that time, in the following lyric.

"Hello God"
Written by Jennifer Pierce (lyric) J.R. Bevers (music)

(HE SAID)
HELLO GOD IT'S JUST ME
YOU KNOW MORE THAN I DO WHAT I NEED
I KNOW YOU HAVE A MILLION THINGS TO DO
AND THERE'RE MORE IMPORTANT PEOPLE TRYIN' TO GET THRU
BUT I'M OUT HERE ON THE STREETS WITHOUT ENOUGH TO EAT
AND ALL I HAVE FOR SHOES IS CARDBOARD ON MY FEET

    HELLO GOD HEAR MY PRAYER
    I FEEL LIKE YOU'RE THE ONLY ONE WHO CARES
    I KNOW YOU WON'T BURDEN ME WITH MORE THAN I CAN BEAR
    HELLO GOD HEAR MY PRAYER

(HE SAID)
HELLO GOD IT'S JUST ME
I'M ONLY TEN YEARS OLD AS YOU CAN SEE
I HAVEN'T BEEN PRAYIN' VERY LONG
AND I'M HOPIN' THAT I DON'T GET THIS WRONG
BUT MY MOM AND DAD ARE FIGHTIN' EV'RY NIGHT
I KNOW IT'S ALL MY FAULT, THEY SAY, I DON'T DO NOTHIN' RIGHT

(Optional Verse)

(SHE SAID)
HELLO GOD IT'S JUST ME
I KNOW YOU CAN SEE THINGS I CAN'T SEE
BUT LATELY I'VE BEEN FEELIN' SO ALONE
I'VE BEEN PRAYIN' LORD THAT YOU WILL CALL ME HOME
MY DADDY'S DOIN' THINGS TO ME I KNOW HE SHOULDN'T DO
AND THE ONLY ONE I HAVE TO TELL IT TO IS YOU

Bridge

WITH A LITTLE FAITH IN YOU ANY MOUNTAIN CAN BE MOVED
HELLO GOD, HELLO GOD, HEAR MY PRAYER

(Modulate)

(Repeat chorus)

Write to your emotional feelings first. Select a given situation, real or imagined. Write about your feelings, putting yourself in the lead role. See your surroundings. Make every word count. Make every line flow easily and seamlessly right into the next line. Always leave hope at the end. Never presume how someone else feels. State how *you* feel, not how others feel. Write about what you see, feel, smell, taste, touch, and hear. Write from your heart.

You are unique. No one can write like you do because no one shares your personal insights, experiences, and feelings.

The words *truth, deceive, deceit, mature, immature, childish, weakminded, weakness,* and *weak* are more words that contain emotional implications. They are presented and defined in this chapter to give you a better understanding of your own feelings and emotions and the feelings and emotions of others.

All of these emotions and feelings are addressed in songwriting. Hopefully you will have a clearer understanding of exactly what they mean, and, therefore, be able to write about them in more accurate terms.

There are many, many more emotionally forceful words that are used in songwriting (e.g., *lie, broken, heartbroken, ache, memories, touch, feel*). There are far too many to define in this book. Look them up yourself to enable you to understand their meanings so you can effectively use their emotional impact in your songs.

Remember when you are "pitching" your material and you know your songs are there but you are still turned down by the listeners, whomever they may be (e.g., song pluggers, producers, publishers, managers, artists, co-writers, co-authors, musicians) they have feelings too. Perhaps you will have "hit" an emotional chord with them on that particular day that they did not want to feel.

Don't get discouraged. Pitch those songs again, perhaps in about six months or so, back to the same listener. He may be in a different frame of mind at that time. Every listener will have some kind of emotional response to your material.

Writers write true to life. For example, Steven Crane wrote *The Red Badge of Courage,* a book considered by experts to be the most accurate book ever written on the Civil War. Crane was born in 1871, six years after the war's end. He wrote the book in 1895 in New York. He had never been near a battlefield or even in a fight.

If you have that great a knowledge of history, feelings, emotions, life, and death, then you will be the one in a million who can write songs without ever having experienced, felt, or been in the situations of your songs.

Bringing Lyric and Music Together

A lyric is professionally written when music, cadence, and inflection almost write themselves. In professional writing you should be able to tell when your song is completed if you have written in 2/4, 4/4, or 3/4 time.

Some songwriters may believe they are writing lyrics and music at the same time. In my opinion, one or the other always leads the writer. Either the *words* or the *music* were in his head first. Furthermore, it is according to experts, impossible to have two thoughts going through your head at precisely the same time. One thought always comes first.

When your lyric and music finally come together, hopefully you will have created a masterpiece. How many times have you seen an eclipse (solar or lunar)? Separately there is beauty. But when passing across the other's identity there is a greater beauty. Lyrics with music are expressions of love, beauty, passion (all universal emotions). Then, when they flow one into the other, there is a togetherness, an equality, and the depth of the colors double in their intensity.

When the music comes first, the composer must find the exact feeling to marry that mood, tone, and specific emotional identity to the lyric.

A completed composition has an identity all its own. Many musicians and artists get into a "pocket" or "groove" and sincerely believe the music and lyric were written simultaneously. However, I would suggest one was definitely in his mind first. Even if it were only for an instant. One came first.

When you think your lyric is complete, read your lyric to see if just by reading it by itself, it moves you. Next, play your music by itself. It must also stir your universal emotions (give you chills) just as the lyric did when you read it. Each must be whole even when apart.

When the marriage between your music and your lyric are as perfect as is humanly possible, your song will be like a beautiful sunrise, blending night into day. Or like an evening sunset, blending the day into night. Each separately beautiful and filled with its own emotions, then becoming greater by becoming one.

How many times have you listened to words that made you emotional, that gave you "chills" because they stirred your heart. They put you in a certain mood, perhaps to dream, laugh, cry, love, drift away, dance, or remember. Those words found a place in your heart and became a part of you. How many times have you listened to great music and that music put you in a certain mood, causing you to dream, drift away, or want to dance, fall in love, or even cry.

The lyric must stand alone. The music must stand alone.

Neil Diamond's words say it all: "You are the sun, I am the moon, you are the words, I am the tune Play Me."

Summary

Much has been discussed throughout these pages regarding songwriting. This section summarizes the salient points of this art.

Always keep your lyrics totally conversational. If you wouldn't say it, don't sing it. Write as though you are ending your lines with commas instead of periods. Lyric lines should run seamlessly one into the next one, and so on. Stick to your subject. Stay with the lines before and after just as though you were talking with someone. Pauses in speaking are delays in lyric writing (diamonds) or (half-diamonds).

Never jump from one subject to the next. In university English classes, it is called restricting your subject. Be succinct. Clearly and briefly state what needs to be said, or in songwriting shown.

Don't be redundant. Don't say the same thing over and over again. However, don't jump from subject to subject. Say different things about the same subject.

Never use punctuation, grammatical marks such as exclamation points, questions marks, or periods in lyric writing. Commas may be used. A lyric is not poetry. Lyrics flow easily and naturally. There is no need for punctuation marks, or other grammatical devices which are necessary in learning proper writing in school. This is a *brand new school*. Your musical delays on your demos are your punctuation marks.

For example:

(Right Way) No Easy Horses

Entire first verse stays with the bicycle
Entire pattern stays the same
Entire second verse stays with the young man leaving home
Entire pattern stays exactly the same as it was in verse one

And, remember, show it, don't tell it. Even if you are writing a great philosophical song, keep the pictures very clear, as was done in "No Easy Horses."

Be sure the feelings and emotions in your song are universal. People from New York, California, Texas, Wyoming, Georgia, Chicago, Germany, Africa, the former Soviet Union, and Japan need to be able to relate to the feelings and emotions in your song.

Don't waste words. Make every word count. Don't get lazy and use fillers.

Never reach for a rhyme. Change the line before you do that. The content of your lyric is much more important than the ending rhyme word.

Hook it. Hook it several times in your chorus, especially your first and last chorus lines. If you can hook the last line of each verse, that's fine too. This should not be done all the time, but if that's the way your lyric works out, that's great.

Keep your lyric fresh and different. Don't overuse cliches and old expressions. Don't try to be too clever.

Always leave hope at the end of your song or, at least leave hope in your chorus, which will be repeated at the end of your song, and tagged.

Count your line-by-line syllables. Line 1, verse 1 should be close to line 1, verse 2; line 2, verse 1 should be close to line 2, verse 2, etc.

Follow a tight pattern *aabb, abba, abcb,* etc. Stay with that pattern in each verse, line for line. A Quad A chorus is the most commercial. Nothing is written in stone. Although your chorus may be different form your verse pattern, your chorus pattern still must be cohesive—super glued.

Keep your song simple and at the same time say all you need to say to get your message across. Just as though you were talking to someone. You can write in the first person dialogue; that is, talking directly to someone right there. They may or may not answer you. If it is a duet, they will. For instance in "The Chair" the singer is making rhetorical statements so no one responds. You can use internal monologue (talking to yourself); third person dialogue (talking to the world or a group) as in "That Old Wheel"; second person dialogue (talking to someone else directly, with *you* not *I* as in "Yesterday's Wine."

Stay with the tense you start with. If you are in first person *(I)*, second person *(you)*, or third person *(they)*, stay there.

If you are writing from a flashback point of view, stay there, unless you can bring it to the present without changing too abruptly.

Keep your lyric smooth and flowing all the way through your entire song. Don't make the listener *think*, make them *feel*.

Try to keep your hook and title short and memorable and at the same time fresh and different.

Use specific images in your verses. Keep your chorus general. The chorus is usually the only part of a song most of the public remembers and sings along with. The chorus makes it memorable and easily learnable.

Don't use a bridge unless your lyric calls for one in order to bridge back to chorus.

Don't use the same rhyme word more than once at the end of verse lines. Don't use the same rhyme word more than once at the end of your chorus lines, unless it is your hook.

Don't use the same words over again in your song (i.e., don't use love, feelings, heart, or leaving more than once). Use a thesaurus if you need to find a word that is different, but has the same or nearly the same meaning as a word you have previously used.

Stay away from words like *just, but, well,* and *so.*

Don't be poetic.

Don't get too far out there. Write for everyone's feelings, unless you want a very small buyer's market.

Polish your song. Once you are finished with all your 10 to 20 rewrites, then polish it. Look and see if any lines would be stronger if they were switched around, or even entire verses may make your song stronger, if they were moved around. Sleep on it (not literally), and look again and again, until you feel there is nothing more that can possibly be done to make your song stronger. Make your song as strong as it can possibly be. Remember who your competition is.

Write great songs, not good songs. Don't think what you hear on the radio is always great. That is not always the case. Remember there are artists who insist on writing, even when they are too tired to write, or they may feel they owe a friend or someone else a favor, maybe a band member. Who knows? Who cares! That's politics! (I did this for you, so now, you do this for me—even if the song is lousy.) Don't grow bitter about things you cannot change.

Write the greatest songs you can write. Don't quit. Study. Study the lyrics of the truly great writers. Learn and you'll make it.

Remember, "The pen is mightier than the sword." (From "Richelieu" by Edward Bulwer-Lytton.)

Insights of
DAN WILSON
Creative Director
Sony/Tree Publishing Company

Being one of the few people in the music business to grow up in the Nashville area, I was able to follow its changes from up close.

I come from a musical family. Several years before we had a TV, my dad and I would go to the Goodyear store in Lebanon, Tennessee, where they had a little round television set up in the window. On certain nights they would broadcast a show featuring Grand Ole Opry stars. I remember the first time I saw Little Jimmy Dickens singing "Sleepin' at the Foot of the Bed." I was hooked.

I love songs and those who create them. I love to write and I wish I had more time to do that. However, I deal with the best talent in the world of music: Curly Putman, Harlan Howard, Robert Miller, and so many more at Tree International. Just being associated with such rare talent is my career's finest reward.

We call it the "music business." These two words are somewhat mutually exclusive. Music is fun; business, well, is business.

My philosophy is have fun but always remember that the word *business* is attached and in the real world, the "B" word is the more important of the two.

Dan Wilson's credits include: former professional manager, Jim Reeves Entertainment; director, Creative Service, Sony/Tree Publishing Company, Inc.; member, Country Music Association; Wrote "Good Ol' Girls" (artist Sonny Curtis); co-wrote with T.G. Sheppard "War Is Hell on the Homefront Too"; co-wrote with Ricky Skaggs "Life's Too Long To Live Like This."

Dan Wilson

Appendix 1

Radio in the Large Market

Interview with Kevin O'Neal

Kevin O'Neal

The following is an interview with Kevin O'Neal, former operations manager, Nashville 95 WSM-FM, AM 650 WSM, WSM AM-FM.

Author: Where are you from? What brought you to Nashville? How did you get started in radio?

O'Neal: I've been in the radio business for 21 years. I started in 1972, in a little 1,000-watt daytime radio station in Wilson, North Carolina.

My dad owned radio stations. He had one in Wilson and another one in the mountains of Virginia. So I grew up in the business. I've been in it all of my life.

My dad, Ray Frazier, was a disc jockey back in the 1950s. He had his top 10 published in *Cashbox* magazine back in the late 1950s. He was a big DJ at WXGI in Richmond, Virginia, back in the mid-1950s when it was one of the powerhouses of country music. So, I grew up in it and have been doing it all my life.

I went on the air at a very young age. In the next four to five years I became a program director. I did everything on the air from sign-on to sign-off. I cut spots, sold spots. I basically did a little GM. It was a great learning experience to learn the industry from that point of view.

Author: What do you mean by cut spots? And, what does a general manager do?

O'Neal: Basically, cutting spots is actually writing commercials. Going into the production room and studio and actually voicing and cutting the commercial. Then calling the client back and letting him hear the commercial to see if he liked it. Then getting it on the air. Basically, doing everything for a sponsor. In the little operation we had, there were only about three or four people, so you pretty much had to do it all.

The little town I lived in had bout 30,000 people. They had three radio stations. I worked at all three of them while I was in town. I did that through high school. Then I became a program director for a top-40 station for a year or so. I still did country because I worked with my dad's station quite a bit. Then when I was about 21 years old I moved from North Carolina and went to Panama City, Florida. We had an "in" with the country station WPAP. It's a big 100,000-watt FM. We went to number one for the first time in that market with a country station two years after I arrived. We had almost 25 percent of the market listening to our station at that time. It was great because country had just gotten over the "Urban Cowboy" craze and had begun to slip a little bit. We still were able to be very successful.

Author: What finally brought you to Nashville?

O'Neal: After WPAP, I went to work for several other companies. I worked for the Beasley Broadcast Group for three or four years. I was in Milwaukee, Wisconsin, at the time. I was operations manager and program director for WMIL and WOKY which is AM and FM. Their FM is a country station. Their AM is big band. I'd been there for about a year and a half when the general manager at WSM-FM called me because the station had slipped to second in the market. It had slipped at times to third. They were looking for someone to come in and get really aggressive and get some young, new ideas involved in what WSM was doing and to attack our competitor. I came in about two and a half years ago. And five months after getting here we were number one and have been ever since. We're the number one AM and FM in Nashville and continue to dominate revenue money-wise and radio-wise, here in town.

But this town's very different as far as programming. I know because I've worked outside of town in four or five other markets.

Author: In what way is Nashville different?

O'Neal: It's real different because you see the artists all the time. You run into Garth Brooks in the grocery store. I have many chances to play golf with the artists and it gives you an opportunity to build a relationship with them other than just being a radio station somewhere that just plays their music. You get to know them on a personal level, and that helps.

On the other hand, the backside of that is, an artist puts a record out that you don't want to play for whatever reason.

Then, you hear from mom and dad and sister and brother and aunts and uncles and friends and managers and publicists and booking agents.

I mean, being here in town, everybody hears what you do, everybody knows what you're doing and you really have got to be fair. You really have got to be on the up-and-up from an ethics point of view. You really have to play your cards right. You've got to stay right there because you're really under a magnifying glass.

Needless to say, over about a period of a year just about every country programmer that programs a station in the medium or major market comes to town. Your peers hear your station all the time. When you're in another market your peers very seldom hear your station unless you send them a tape. So it's real different.

Author: On your rotation, do you play top-20 rotation, top-10 rotation?

O'Neal: No, we play a lot more than that. Country music in the last year has changed. We've gone from an "oldie"-based format where you heard a lot of the gold, the Merle Haggard's and the Conway's, to where now we've become a current-based format and a song-based format.

We're now playing about 50 currents. About 70 percent of what you hear in any given hour will be current music. And that is just unheard of for country radio. It's never been that way. It reminds me of the top-40 days. We're seeing country radio take the play of the top 40. If you remember WLS radio and John Leyendecker and some of those guys, that type of radio is what we're doing today. That's what's working with country. It's really gone full circle.

Author: How have videos effected radio?

O'Neal: It's been a little bit effective. Videos have not had the impact on radio that they have had on sales. Videos directly impacted sales. From a radio-directed point of view, I've only seen, in the last couple of years, maybe four or five singles that radio had not jumped on that video created. One of those was "The Dance" for Garth Brooks, the video made that record. Video did a lot for Billy Dean's "Only Here for a Little While" record and Travis Tritt's "Anymore" record. As a general rule, videos have not forced radio really to make any reactionary moves to video.

Author: You said you feel videos have effected sales. By sales do you mean mechanical payments to the songwriters?

O'Neal: Exactly. Songwriters make more money with videos because videos stimulate the emotion in people, therefore, making them react, go to the counter and spend $9.99 to buy a CD or a tape. Videos have been very good for the industry.

Author: Then, videos have helped the writer?

O'Neal: It's definitely helped the industry beyond a shadow of a doubt. Videos have made people aware that this music has "mass appeal." It has made people realize that country music is not country and western music. And, that it is not very nasal, very "twang" oriented. People had felt it was still "hick" music (which we haven't played, seen, or heard of in at least 15 years). Many people feel it is more refreshing to listen to, easier to listen to, and more comfortable to listen to than they ever imagined it would be. I think it's been great. It's helped to open many eyes. I think video has had a lot to do with the "craze" we're seeing today in country music.

Author: Do you feel that country music, in the last three years, has appealed to a broader based market? Are there more college people listening to country radio now?

O'Neal: I think so. We're definitely showing up in our ratings research and we're seeing it in the buying habits. We call this "qualitative." We find out how much money the audience spends, what they make, what they earn, what they drive. That has definitely gotten better.

The one thing that I do feel though is that we've had a lot of people like that for a long time. The kind who didn't want to admit that they listened to country radio. Those people have been "closet country listeners." When Arbitron would call or when Neilsen would call or whoever would call and do a ratings survey to find out who's listening to what, they would never "fess up" that they were listening to a county station. If you went out in their car and looked at what was on the button that was pushed, it was probably the country station. So, I think it's become a "hip" term now. It's no longer stigmatized, that if you listen to country you have to wear a country hat and boots. Now, country's become "cool." I guess if that's the term to use for it.

Author: What do *Billboard, Radio and Records (R&R), Gavin,* and *Cashbox* have to do with radio? How do they effect the writer? The artist? The radio station?

O'Neal: Well, all four are different. The four trade magazines are very important to the industry. They all carry their own weight and they all serve their own need. I think particularly the two major trades have done a very good job of finding their niche. *Billboard* actually has computers in markets around the country that listen to your radio station and track what you play. We don't turn our list in to *Billboard* anymore. They automatically hear what we play. They have a computer where they have encoded certain parts of songs so when that part of the song plays, the computer hears it and picks it up. We don't know what part of the song that is. We have no idea. The computer just tracks us.

I can call *Billboard* and they can tell me in the last seven days every record I've played and how many times I've played it. So we don't give them a chart at all. *Billboard*'s chart is extremely accurate. It's what's being played on the radio. The negative side of the *Billboard* system is only the medium and major markets are on this system. Your starter stations are not there. It's an accurate barometer of what markets of 100,000 people or more are playing, that is for sure.

For *R&R* we do turn in our rotations. Rotations meaning the songs we play very heavy. We also turn in the songs we play sometimes and some we play very seldom. *R&R* does have the opportunity for promotional "hype" for the record companies to call us up and ask us to help them out with an upward rotation—meaning giving them more airplay. That in turn, helps them with *Billboard*.

In *R&R* they want the report there. *R&R* serves a need because it's helping record companies know how their records are being played. It also gives them an opportunity to help them get their records played more. *R&R* fills that void.

Cashbox and *Gavin* are the biggest "panels." *R&R*'s panel is 200 or so stations. *Billboard*'s, I think, is in the neighborhood of 170. *Cashbox* and *Gavin* are 300 and 400.

Author: Would you define "panels"?

O'Neal: Panels are the group of stations that actually report to the trade magazine. *R&R* has 200 or so stations. These are the only stations they track. The public thinks that all 2,000 country stations are what make up a *Billboard* chart or an *R&R* chart. That's not true. It's only the stations that the magazine has subscribed to that become a reporting station on their reporting panel.

Author: What is the criteria to be a *Billboard* reporting station?

O'Neal: I think ratings success. You've got to have enough listeners. They're looking for the most popular radio stations because those are the ones that are the most successful and those are the ones with the most listeners. They track the stations that have more people listening because that, of course, turns into buyers for the singers and the songwriters.

From a singer and a songwriter's point of view, I think *Billboard*'s probably very important for them to see because that's actual airplay. Airplay is what ASCAP, BMI, and SESAC are going to turn around and pay their songwriters off of. You've got to have success in *R&R* because that's what keeps you on the radio. The radio stations follow *R&R*. They look at it. They look at *Billboard* but *R&R* became an industry standard in the last year or so. So you've got to have a number one in *R&R* for the publicity—to be able to say you've had a number one record for the industry to recognize you. Radio stations do follow what *R&R* does.

Author: How do record promoters fit into all of this? People are paid to promote records. Is that contingent upon radio? How does that effect radio?

O'Neal: Their job is to get us to play records. We've seen more promoters come into the business in the last couple of years than ever. They're intense. They work hard. There's a lot of them. And how it effects us is it helps us be aware of what records we need to know about.

I've always had a saying, and I don't mean this to be disrespectful to record promoters, but the sign of a good record promoter is the guy that can get a radio station to play a record that's not a "hit." Because we're going to play the "hits." I've been real fortunate the years that I've been in the business. Country radio particularly is unlike "rock" radio. In "rock" radio and other pop formats, there seems to be more, I guess you'd say "shadiness," going on in the record community. Country radio is very much above board. I've never been offered anything. I wouldn't take anything. I wouldn't accept anything. It's unethical. I'm happy to work in an industry where it's not even on the table. That's good to know.

The record promoters here have been very good. They help us recognize records, particularly in the Nashville market. We're not in the position to be a "starter" station—that is, a new song by a new artist and the song is so-so. We don't have the airtime to devote to those records. Smaller markets do. Where record people come in handy for me is letting me know what small city in Alabama and Panama City, Florida, and Kingston, North Carolina, and Augusta, Georgia, and Des Moines, Iowa, are doing. They let me know if starter stations can play these brand new records by brand new artists. If they get some success there, the record promoters let me know. We, in turn, can then calculate our chances on a record being a success and a "hit" for us. Reliable record people, folks you can trust out there, that can give you some honest answers are worth their weight in gold. They're great. They can really help make your decision process much better.

Author: How would you define a "hit"?

O'Neal: A "hit" is a record that the public wants to hear. I mean that they want to hear and want to hear and want to hear. It's tough, in the beginning, to give you a reason for why you add a record or do not add a record. We do a tremendous amount of research in Nashville. We go out and ask people what songs they want to hear. What artists they want to hear. What they are tired of hearing. Or do they want to hear more.

In the beginning to get a record on, it's really a "gut call" by myself, my music director, and other people in the building. If we feel that it's a record that fits our radio station, what we're trying to do, what we want to sound like, then we'll take a chance and get on it. From that point we do "call-out" research, which means we call people and actually play short portions of a song for them. We ask them if they like it, dislike it, are tired of it, want to hear it more, whatever.

Author: Like the Gallup Poll?

O'Neal: Exactly. After a record is on a station and we do the research, the research dictates what we do at that point. We do not let the record industry dictate our rotations. If a record is testing well, if the audience likes it, and they want to hear it more, and we're getting requests for it, and the research looks good, it's going to be played more. Because our job is to please the listener. My customer is the listener.

Author: So there's no favoritism toward the powerful record labels?

O'Neal: No. Not at WSM. At WSM we play a lot of independent products from people who are not on major labels. For example, Step One Records, here in town, is considered an independent.

I consider them a major label. They're a major force in the marketplace. They have Ray Price. They have many of their own artists. They have an artist called Clinton Gregory. Clint is a product that some radio stations say: "We don't play. He's an independent product. He's not on a major label. We're not going to play it." I don't believe in that. WSM was built on giving people breaks, jumping out there and taking chances, and building careers. We've been behind this guy all along. If we hear a great record, we're going to play it.

Author: I've heard K-TEL is now changing its format. K-TEL will now be for sale in the major record stores. Will radio get involved with K-TEL?

O'Neal: I would get involved with them from a promotional standpoint, to promote some of the products that they have. Most of what K-TEL sells though is the "oldies." It's just the grouped albums of different "oldies." Our format's become so current and intensive I'm not sure how successful that would be right now. The appetite out there for new music by the new "hot" artists, Clint Black, Garth Brooks, Alan Jackson, Mark Chestnut, Joe Diffie, is huge. I would be kind of skittish to jump out on a limb putting a lot of "oldies" out there in the marketplace. What we're seeing in our research is the appetite's not there.

Author: What would you think if K-TEL changed their format and went to more updated material?

O'Neal: I think they'd do real well.

Author: Do record promoters make somewhere around $1,500 a week for a five-week run?

O'Neal: Somewhere in that neighborhood.

Author: With promoters there's a certain time slot during each day where *Billboard*-reporting, *Cashbox*-reporting promoters are allowed to call the major stations. How do your people work

236 Radio in the Large Market

with the promoters and how do you decide what calls to take
and what calls not to take?

O'Neal: Being here in town, in Nashville, makes it more
interesting. Garth Brooks walks in the front door and brings
you his new single. Then Hank, Jr., comes in the door. These
people *walk in* and see us.

We have tried to have a very open door policy in dealing
with record labels. It's good and it's bad. The good part is
we've built some very good relationships; the bad part is you
get "hammered" a lot. We try to position ourselves. My music
director takes one day a week for about three hours and we
don't restrict any phone calls. If you want to promote a record,
no matter how big, no matter how small, or whatever the case
may be, you get in the "window" of those three hours and we'll
take your call. The rest of the week we deal with the people we
know. That's just because of the relationships that we've built.

At this radio station we're not looking for "attitudes." We're
not looking for anybody here to get "cocky" or for anybody here
to say, "I don't have time to talk to them because they're a little
guy." Let me tell you we all were little guys. We all still are
little guys. We're all just people and you got to give people a
break out there.

I heard a great story. I was at the Grand Ole Opry House last
night, and I was talking to Steve Wariner about the Academy
of Country Music Awards show in which Garth Brooks said,
"You know there're nice guys out there, like Steve Wariner and
Chris LeDoux, and a few other people." I said to Steve, "I guess
you've had that mentioned to you many times." And he said,
"Yeah. Let me tell you something. I used to play Oklahoma
four, five, six years ago. Garth Brooks' band opened for Steve
Wariner. He did it a lot in bars in Oklahoma. This kid would
come on my bus and we'd sit there and talk about the business.
I never told him no. I never would not see him. You never
know who's going to be who. Now you turn the tables, and
Garth Brooks is the biggest thing in the industry out there. So,
you know, I believe in that as well."

When the program directors and disc jockeys come to
Nashville, and if I've got time when they call, I'm really glad to

show them the radio station and show them what we do. I'm a fan of WSM as much as anybody. I grew up in awe of this radio station. I want as many people to have a chance to see it and see what we do and experience what this radio station is all about. Some of the guys that I took time with 10 years ago are now major market program directors and they're friends of mine. So I just don't believe in that pretentious thing that we just don't have time to spend with the little people anymore. We've got to do that. That's what America's all about. We try to do that here.

Author: Why do you suppose "rock-'n'-roll" artists don't have to tour as much as country artists? Do rock-'n'-roll artists make more money than country artists?

O'Neal: Yes. No question. The touring schedules are changing. Garth's now touring six months on, six months off. Most of the other acts are trying to get into the same mode.

Back to the beginning of country music. When I say the beginning I mean going back to the 1950s and 1960s and the early 1970s. Country did not have the popularity of rock-'n'-roll. You didn't have the record sales. You didn't make the money. The concert dates didn't sell 10,000 tickets so you didn't make the gross dollars. An artist would go into a market, sell a thousand tickets and have a great show. Therefore, you had to tour 50 weeks a year to make any substantial amount of money in the entertainment business being a country entertainer, if you weren't a songwriter.

Nowadays it's become much more big business. Garth Brooks and The Judds' tour was the biggest grossing tour of any music tour last year, anywhere. I mean they did more business than anybody else. Garth had the people but he didn't draw the amount of dollars because he kept his ticket prices down. I think we're seeing that. Garth is here deciding whether or not he's going to play stadiums or coliseums. Country acts have never had that decision to make. Thank goodness for Alabama and other artists who have broken through and done that. I think we're seeing much more big business. Five years ago you'd come to Nashville on a special invitation to a Gold

Record Party, it happened twice a year, it was a rare thing then. And Music Row shut down. We've had 16 so far this year. So we're still taking just a huge jump in record sales. Total dollars make it (it used to be a family, a very small minute bunch of people) big, big business.

Author: If you see room for improvement in any single area for mega radio, what would you say that would be?

O'Neal: I think just getting out there and working really hard to expose the music to as many people as you possibly can. I think some radio stations, and there's very few now, because many have seen that getting aggressive really pays off, but some stations are very comfortable with what they have. They feel like they've been doing what they've been doing for 15 years. They say, "It put my kids through school. I don't want to change. I don't want to break what is here."

I think country programmers have got to have vision. They've got to look to tomorrow. We've got to get out there and create possibilities and not become complacent. I'd say don't rest on your laurels. We've got an opportunity for this format to be the format of the 1990s, to be the mass appeal format.

We're already the number one music format in popularity. So we've got an opportunity to really go after it if we don't get scared and get complacent and get to "don't test the water." We didn't get to where we are, and WSM and the Grand Ole Opry didn't become a multi-million dollar conglomerate here at Opryland USA, by people saying, "let's keep what we have." Everybody worked and you've got to move forward.

Vision is the big thing. I'm a big believer in that. Let's try to figure out tomorrow what the other guy hasn't thought about yet. If we can do that, we'll beat him and be successful.

Author: Does your station ever do test runs for records?

O'Neal: We do a couple of things. We have a one-hour show on Sunday nights that is devoted to new music. Robert Orrman, a great free-lance music columnist and critic, who is the entertainment reporter for the *Tennessean*, and a writer for *Music Row Magazine*, does the show for us. It's nothing but an hour of brand new stuff. This is not stuff that we've added to regular rotation. This is just stuff that has come out this week and you'll hear it in that one hour. That's something new for us. And, it's the only show that I know of its kind.

Author: How would you say you differ with your large competitors here in Nashville?

O'Neal: The two country stations are way out in front of everybody. Our competitor WSIX is one and two in the market. We're five shares, six shares in front of everybody else. It's a two-station battle. The differences between us is that we built our station on music. They built their station on personalities and they've got some good personalities. So that's the difference in the two. We've become very similar simply because the format's become so explosive that there's an opportunity for two stations to do extremely well in the very same type of format. So for both of us, things are just going real well.

Author: With Garth crossing over into the pop market, do you see that as a wave of the future?

O'Neal: No I don't. Every act I've seen that's gone after crossover, I've seen it fail. And when I say fail, I mean they tried to spread themselves to broad. You've got to appeal to certain people.

I'll give you my feeling on that. I'll go to a restaurant mentality. When you go to McDonald's you know what you're going to get. If you walk into McDonald's and they try to serve you a pizza burger, you probably would freak out.

So when you come to a country radio station and you come to Alabama, you've got to know it's a country act. I give Alabama and guys like Garth a lot of credit. They may have crossover airplay that happened coincidentally because adult contemporary (AC) programmers wanted it. It's not because they went out there and serviced it and went after it. Country radio and country listeners are a very loyal bunch of people and they expect that loyalty back in return. Whether it's right or whether it's wrong is not my place to say. But they do feel a little bit betrayed, I think, when they try to reach out to that pop audience, when they feel you're a country act.

Author: It seems that country is using more pop melodies and pop structure. It's like a cycle. I hear some of the things on the radio now very much like I heard in the 1970s. How do you feel about that?

O'Neal: What's happened is a lot of producers and a lot of songwriters have come from LA and New York to Nashville. We now have pop divisions in the labels in town here. We've got Christian divisions. We've got jazz alternative divisions. We didn't have this years ago. This town was made up of nothing but country songwriters, country pickers, country bands. Everything was country, country, country. Now when you go hang out at a bar downtown on Music Row and start talking to a songwriter, you might be talking to a guy that writes jazz music and a guy that writes country songs. And you might talk to somebody who says, "I just write songs. I don't care where they go. I'm not locked into a format."

If anything, there has been a tremendous influx of talent into this market. Garth Brooks, is not your "stereotypical" country show. A lot of people are getting away from the stereotypical thing. There's no question that we're beginning to see a lot of rock influences in country music, the country productions, the concerts, the songs, everything. We have, I understand, a studio right here in town that just recently put in a new digital computer system of which there are only three in this whole country. There's one in LA, one in New York, and one in Nashville. And that's it. Who would have ever thought that Nashville would have been on a par with others like that.

Author: We really are a "music city."

O'Neal: It's a "music city." It's a "music centerpiece." I think you're going to find in the 1990s we're going to become the number one "music city center" in America. The problem in LA and the problem in New York is that they're so big. They say that Nashville's a big city but it's just a small town. Everybody's real and comfortable to deal with. They're good people. I don't see the back-stabbing going on here that I see in the other cities and things like that. It's just a good place to be and the people are enjoying it.

When you come to this town and you're a songwriter or an artist, and you do make it, you get about 10 miles out of town and buy yourself about a hundred acres of land. You'll feel like your living in heaven. It's just beautiful here in middle Tennessee.

Author: Is one state more important, like in presidential elections with the electoral votes, as far as country music and radio are concerned?

O'Neal: I don't think there's a state, I think there's a region. I think that's the Southeast and the Southwest.

Author: Do you have to have Texas to get the nation?

O'Neal: You've got to have Texas. You've got to have the Southwest—Arizona through that area of New Mexico. And you've got to have the Southeast. If you don't have Georgia, Alabama, Mississippi, Tennessee, Texas, Oklahoma, and Arkansas, you're really going to have trouble. The problem that you run into is many artists feel like that's all they need to do, if they can do the Texas Swing sound.

Unfortunately in New York, Philadelphia, Baltimore, Milwaukee, and Chicago, that Texas Swing doesn't work as well. You've got to find a real balance. You've got to have those major metropolitan areas for massive record sales, for airplay, the whole bit. There's a real fine line there as to what you can do because there are some radio stations in the North where a real strong Texas fiddle scares them to death, even today.

Author: What do you say to people when they complain about hearing "lousy" songs on the radio?

O'Neal: I would tell them to call the radio station, be heard. The worst thing you can do is be unhappy and be quiet. I love to get input from listeners. I spend a good part of my day responding to every letter and every phone call that I get from my listeners. If it's a complaint, so be it, I want to hear it. If it's a compliment I want to hear it. The worst thing you can do is keep quiet.

To me the worst thing you can do is switch radio stations. I'd rather have someone call me and say, "Look, I don't like what you do." "I like this but I don't like that," and give me a chance to be a radio station. It's very difficult sometimes when the public wants us to know what they want without them telling us. That's almost impossible to do. So we want the feedback.

If you're a listener out there and there are songs you want to hear; if you travel across country and you hear a song on a station, and you get home and it's not on your favorite station; or you come to Nashville for a vacation and you hear us play a song and you go back to Washington, DC, and WMZQ's not playing it, call them. Call the program director. Call the music director. Be persistent. Tell him, "Hey, I don't understand. What are you doing." Call a week later and tell him, "Hey, have you listened to this record I told you about? Where are you at?" I like that input.

Author: Who is the main man at this station that calls the rotations shots?

O'Neal: Me. I do all that. My job is product manager, basically that is what it comes down to. Everything you hear coming out of the radio station is my responsibility. It's like if I was in charge of the product at McDonald's, and my responsibility was every hamburger that went across that table. I'm going to make sure of what's in every hamburger. How it's doing, what the bun looks like, the whole "nine yards."

Author: Does a song have to strike an emotional chord with you, regardless of how big that song is, or how big that writer's name is? Does it have to be a great song?

O'Neal: It has to be a song that we feel (and I say we, not only myself but other people that I have confidence in) we need to play.

In our research we build what we call a "marketing model" for our radio station. We know what type of person we're trying to talk to and what type of music they want to hear. Country music has about six or seven different sounds. There's old traditional, new traditional, rock, pop, modern, middle of the road, and crossover. So we break it down and we know what we want. To tell you the truth, if I personally don't like a record, it doesn't matter. I'm listening with my ears to what the radio station needs. That's what we're supposed to do. I've played a lot of records I didn't like. I just didn't like them. There have been records and there have also been songs that I have loved and wanted to play but weren't fit, so I didn't play them. It comes down to what's best for WSM, not what's best for me.

Author: I've talked with some professional writers about what would happen if we "pitched" our songs and didn't put our names on the lyric sheets. Names do matter.

O'Neal: It's a label town. I agree with you. It's a town of who you know, and what doors you can open. Unfortunately that's the American way. That's just the way this old supply and demand has worked and "the buddy-buddy system" has been in place longer than we've been here and will be here long after we're gone. It's unfortunate, but, you know, it's kind of like fighting "city hall." I'm not really concerned about who does it as long as it's good. If you've got a great record that can help my radio station be more successful in the ratings, if you've got a song that the public wants to hear, I'm going to play it. It doesn't matter if Randy Travis cut it or Joe Jones or the Joneses cut it. Hell, we're going to play it.

Author: If Kevin O'Neal had something to say to the songwriters, what would he tell them?

O'Neal: When I spoke at the Nashville Songwriters Symposium recently, one of the things I said was that we have been very blessed to have gotten some great songwriters in town in the last four or five years. There's still only *x* number of slots on a radio station. Don't quit. Don't give up. If you're writing good material, it's going to get through. By golly keep poundin' away. There's a lot of doors out there. They didn't get opened by people walking away from them. They got opened when somebody stood there and beat on them until they opened. Get to know people and get out and talk to people. Come by the radio stations. Go see the people that are out there.

My whole staff, my disc jockeys, go to all the parties. They go to the number one parties. They know the artists. They know the producers. They know the label people. My night guy, Rich Miller, is a songwriter. He writes. He spends a lot of time during the day pitchin' songs on Music Row.

Just don't quit. Keep at it because that's the life blood of the format. If songwriting stops, well you know, I'm out of work.

Author: Tell the people from Canada to Germany to Africa to New York to LA to South Texas what you feel is the most important role radio plays for the listener?

O'Neal: That's a bagful. The one thing that comes back in a nutshell is that radio is intended for the listener. It's out there as an entertainment medium to make people happy, to make their days brighter. I think that country radio stations out there lose vision. Just get out there and do things and make things happen. Don't be scared to take chances. This is America. This country wasn't built on people just sitting back and waiting. I don't think we would be here if that had happened with the forefathers of our country.

So get out there and get after it. Don't feel because you're a country radio station or a country programmer that you're in a minority. Nowadays we finally have become the majority and it's fun to be there and seize the opportunity. Go after it. Make things happen. Do what the listeners want from your radio station.

A good friend of mine programs a station in another market, that will go unnamed. To listen to it from a programming point of view it's not the best you've heard. But if you go into that town and you talk to those people that have listened to it for 15 years, they think it's the greatest thing they've every heard in their life. That radio station has become their best friend. And regardless of what the industry says or what anybody else says, appeal to those people that listen to that radio station because that's the lifeblood of the format. That's the record buyer. That's the concert ticket buyer. That's the listener of the radio station. The bottom line is appealing to them. Just because we do it in Nashville, does not mean it needs to be done in San Antonio, Texas. Because they do it in Austin, which is another country music capital, doesn't mean we do it in Nashville. We do what we do because the people of Nashville have said, "Here's what we want WSM to sound like" and that's what we deliver. And even if I don't like it, then that's the way it is. Don't give up. Stay after it and let's keep movin' forward—that's the thing I'm anxious to see.

Author: It's great to know that you are for the heart and the soul of the music.

O'Neal: It makes a difference you know. I love this place. Growing up as a kid I listened to AM for years and coming to Nashville and taking over WSM-FM was the highlight of my career. The scariest point in my career was when I was told the AM was also under my direction because that's the "mother church" of country music. That AM is the to 50,000-watt Grand Ole Opry radio station. To me it carried a lot of weight and it does, I think, to many country music listeners out there. This is a great place to work. It's a great company. I'm glad to see their foresight in country music because of the growth of TNN, the growth of CMT (Country Music Television), Opryland Theme Park, the General Jackson, the Opryland Hotel, and now our company has just invested in Fiesta Texas which, of course, is just outside of San Antonio.

We're growing in the area where we know country music needs to make things happen. I'm glad to see this company becoming aggressive in doing these types of things with the video opportunities that are there. Our radio stations are tops in our market and it's a great company to work for.

Appendix 2

◆ ◆ ◆

Radio in the Small Market

Synopsis by Ron Twist

Ron Twist (*Photo by Lehman Studio*)

Though there are others more qualified than I to express the radio side of the industry, I have seen it from the writers', producers', and DJs' end of the industry.

I am the morning "jock" and program director for KTAK Radio, 93.9 FM in Riverton, Wyoming. I have been asked several times why I would want to work in a market of less than 25,000 listeners after working in the San Antonio, Texas, market. The answer is simple. In a market the size of Riverton, you have the freedom to promote the artists that a market the size of San Antonio cannot. In a large market like San Antonio, LA, San Francisco, Houston, Nashville, and such, the competition for superiority is fierce. The trend is to play only the proven artists. The Dwight Yoakams, Garth Brooks, Clint Blacks, etc.

I went to San Antonio from a market of about 50,000 in Gallup, New Mexico. As the music director for KGAK, as in Gallup, I made it my own personal policy to listen to all the small label cuts that came in. Though many of them were, to be honest, pretty bad, there were a lot of cuts that were, in my opinion, as good as any major label cuts that I had heard. For instance, I recall a record on an independent label that I could not stop playing. It was a remake of the old song "Runaway." It was, in my opinion, better than the original, and the artist was a girl named Robin Lee, who went on to do the song "Black Velvet," which made a name for her in every market. This is just an example of the freedom one has in smaller markets to "discover" new talent.

The pressure in larger markets to stay with the well-known artists is so great that artists on independent labels stand little or no chance of exposure in these larger markets. They could play these artists if they wanted to, but many of them won't due to the policy of playing only "tried-and-true" and proven artists.

As a writer and publisher, I relate to the smaller artist. I know the work and the time that go into that session are just as important to them as it is to the major labels who spend hundreds of thousands of dollars on their artists. These lesser known artists live on hopes and dreams of being heard in the markets that count. They are usually running on a limited budget, and cannot afford the promotional "big gunning" that the majors can afford. Thus, there are artists out there that are as good or better than your top 20, but may never be heard in a major market because they have never had a top-40 hit.

This is not only true for new artists, but there is a trend to stay away from older artists as well. I worked off and on for two years in San Antonio, and with the exception of "The Highwaymen," never played a cut by Johnny Cash, and never played a cut by Marty Robbins or Patsy Cline. This is not because my program director didn't think they were great, but because the consultants told them that to do a top-40 contemporary country format, you had to stay with the currents. Artists like Johnny Cash (a personal favorite of mine, whom I play a lot of here in Riverton) were not selling records like they used to. This is also due to the label's pumping most of their promotional budget into their new artists, and letting the Johnny Cashes ride on their reputation. I feel as though they sell the "standards" short. When John released "That Old Wheel" in 1988, I was working for an FM outlet in San Antonio. I received a call from a lady one night who asked if I had the latest Johnny Cash/Hank Jr., single, "That Old Wheel." In school, we were taught that if you don't have it, tell them you do and can't get to it. I told this listener that I didn't think it was released yet. She assured me that it was, and went on to tell me that she had written it. (I don't try to B.S. my way out of requests anymore.) The caller was Jennifer Pierce, and the song didn't get much play on that station in San Antonio. The shame about it is, that if it was done by George Strait or Clint Black, the song would have been on super-heavy rotation. The good that came out of it was that Jennifer and I went on to write some great songs together.

Many stations say they care about what the listener thinks, or what the listener wants, but it's not altogether true. If I had a nickel for each one of the times that in that major market, listeners called wanting to hear artists like Johnny Cash, Merle Haggard, Patsy Cline, I could have my house paid for by now. So, the stations tell the listeners that this is what they want to hear, and the listeners are at their mercy. Kind of like the "Old Jedi Mind Trick." "You don't want to hear 'oldies,' you want to hear Garth Brooks 74 times today. . . ." What a crock!

My own personal philosophy of radio programming is somewhat different and would possibly be construed in larger markets as insane and too much of a chance to take, though I can assure you that there isn't a program director on the planet who has not at one time or another wished they had free reign over the way the station presents itself. They are too often at the mercy of the general manager or worse, those damned consultants who are the "know-all-be-all" of the radio industry. Granted, every market is different, and has different needs. What works in one market may not, and sometimes *will not*, work in other markets.

Take for instance the market I worked in, in Gallup. There was a large population of Native Americans, mostly Navajo and Hopi Indians. KGAK was geared toward the Native American, and was a free-form type of outlet. I told the program director that I would like freedom to program my show my way. There was much hesitation, but eventually the program director gave in and let me do my thing. I did a morning show that was more like a "rock-'n'-roll" zoo format, and geared it toward a country listenership. Lots and lots of request music and lots of live listener response to things on the air. It was a "seat of my pants" show, no liners, no structure, and "no holds barred" within the realm of good taste. It was billed as "Crazy Ronnie in the Morning" and it was the likes of which that market had never seen. It was a hell of a lot of fun, and became the most popular show in the area for four years, until I left.

The point here is not to tell you how great I am. I'm not. There are jocks out there that I think are "super talents" . . . Rick Dees, Dr. Don Rose in San Francisco, John Waylon who I grew up listening to in Oakland, California (who is, by the way, the person I pattern myself after the most), and Jerry House in Nashville, just to name a few. My point is that I went into a small little market and did something totally different than what they were used to hearing. I played the new artists and made a very big deal out of them. I played the "demo from hell," where I took one of those bad records and played it just because it was so bad . . . but . . . it got played. (Sometimes it would get added to the play list.) I tried to make radio fun. Not just for me, but for my listeners.

If we were running a station that was only going to play top-40 country, we could have just automated and all gone home. The listeners don't want to hear the same old thing day after day. The same old artist every hour. I don't care if you are Garth or Clint or Reba . . . there comes a time when the station just needs to give it a rest.

Let me give you an example. At the time of this writing, the song "Achy Breaky Heart" by Billy Ray Cyrus is the hot thing on the charts. There are rumors flying around that Garth Brooks is going to be dethroned as the "grand poobah" of the whole world. For the last four weeks I have been getting about a zillion requests for this song every day. (I swear every other phone call is for this song.) So, I have been playing the song on a heavy (once every two hours) rotation. Something happens after about four weeks of this song being played every time I turn around. All of a sudden people are calling in and saying "If I have to hear that song again, I am going to go kick a wall." I find then that it's not just me. My afternoon jock says he's been getting death threats from his listeners regarding playing "Achy Breaky Heart." As I go out on the streets, people are saying they are tuning in to the "other" station because they are so tired of that song. What we have done here is offended our listeners.

So, where are the consultants when we need them? They are in the large markets telling the powerhouse stations to play "Achy Breaky Heart" because people love it. Now, I may be wrong, but I have noticed that in a small market, the cross section of listeners seems to be more accurate in the trends than large markets. Though the large markets get the new releases first, and break all the new songs, and do all the reporting to people like *Billboard*, it's the small markets that know when the song is dead. I called two major markets recently and asked them about "Achy Breaky Heart." I was told, "It's the hottest song we have, and we are playing the hell out of it." So what does my station do? The reporting stations say the song is hot. The small markets (of which there are many more) say the song was fun the first 17,000 times we heard it, but now the dance is over, let's hear some Patsy Cline. This has nothing to do with the song or the artist. It has to do with actually playing a song to death. As a writer, I would love to have a hit like "Achy Breaky Heart," but I would start to worry when the disc was being used as a shuffleboard puck and no one seemed to care.

That brings us to an interesting point: the reporting stations. The "powers that be" seem to think that just because we are small, we don't really matter. It's not that we don't want to, it just seems as though no one has time to really worry about markets of less than 10,000. It's these markets that will actually play the requests. When I worked in San Antonio, our request policy was to write it down and never get to it. If the song happened to be coming up on the play list, the listener was happy and the song would have played if they had called or not. My wife was the first to ask me why we even do a request line if we know we won't play it unless it's coming up. We go back to the Old Jedi Mind Trick again. The listener tells us what they want to hear, and the trends and consultants tell us what to tell them they want to hear. What is wrong with this picture? The wrong is that what we are hearing is controlled by the record companies, and the statisticians, and no one gives a damn about what the listener wants.

We are under the impression that the listeners make the stars. That's true to a certain extent, and was very true a long time ago. Today it's not the listeners but the public relations people who make the stars. For instance, Garth Brooks is a talented human being. He would have made it with or without the "big guns" and mega-million-dollar marketing campaign. I think though, that if left to just his voice and airplay without buying all the "hype," Garth would be just another very good country artist.

It's hard to market just a good voice without a gimmick. A prime example is Gary Morris. Gary's voice is among those that are classified in my book as awe-inspiring. No gimmick, no mega marketing, no deity status. (I still think Gary could sing Garth, Clint, George, and, yes, even Mr. Cyrus under the table.) I'm not trying to put anyone down, or say that our superstars don't deserve the recognition they have. My only point is that there is a load of talent out there, and access to give them the exposure they so well deserve. If more music and program directors would take the time to listen to some of the smaller label cuts, they might be surprised at what they hear. *The bottom line is money.* The majors have it, and go by the Golden Rule: "The ones with the gold make the rules."

I urge all small labels to keep sending your best stuff to small markets. As long a there are program directors who will listen, there are potential stars on small labels who will get airplay. And remember, you never know who's out there listening.

Appendix 3

Writers' Organizations

American Society of Composers, Authors and Publishers (ASCAP)

The American Society of Composers, Authors and Publishers (ASCAP) was founded in 1914 with the goal of safeguarding the rights of songwriters and music publishers by making certain that they would be fairly compensated for the public performance of their work. The story of ASCAP is the story of its members and their efforts to attain that goal.

During its first year, ASCAP had 192 members, a one-room office in New York, and licensed only 85 hotels and restaurants to perform music in the ASCAP repertory. Today, ASCAP has over 48,000 members, membership offices in New York, Los Angeles, Nashville, Chicago, London, and Puerto Rico, and licensing offices in 24 cities across the United States, including Nashville. ASCAP now licenses over 10,000 radio stations, 1,200 television stations, and hundreds of thousands of other music users, including nightclubs, retail stores, background/foreground music services, conventions, expositions, trade shows, airlines, concert promoters, and colleges and universities. The ASCAP repertory embraces every kind of music imaginable, from soul to symphonic, jazz to country, gospel to film, and theater to rock.

ASCAP is the only U.S. performing rights organization governed by a board of directors made up solely of composers, lyricists, and music publishers elected by the membership. That is why ASCAP has always been at the forefront of efforts in the courts and in Congress to protect the rights of its members. ASCAP is also the only performing rights organization to provide financial reports to its members and the only one to hold annual membership meetings in Nashville, New York, and Los Angeles. ASCAP is the voice of music and, at ASCAP, its members have a voice.

ASCAP's Nashville songwriters and music publishers play an important role in the activities of the society. Serving on the ASCAP board of directors as of September 1993 are: Stanley Adams, Martin Bandier, Jack Beeson, Marilyn Bergman, Leon Brettler, Arnold Broido, John Cacavas, Cy Coleman, Hal David, Ron Freed, Morton Gould, Arthur Hamilton, Waylon Holyfield, Dean Kay, Burton Lane, Leeds Levy, Johnny Mandel, Keith

Mardak, John McKellen, Jane Morgenstern, Stephen Paulus, Ralph Peer II, Erwin Z. Robinson, and Lester Sill.

Many of these writers and publishers have taken an active role in ASCAP's efforts to defend the rights of music creators in the legislative arena. They have traveled to Washington, DC, as part of ASCAP delegations to educate members of Congress on issues affecting songwriters and to urge them to support the society's positions. In 1990, Waylon Holyfield convincingly testified at a Senate hearing on behalf of his songwriter colleagues on a digital audio tape bill that did not adequately protect the interests of music creators.

ASCAP has a dedicated staff of 16 in its Nashville membership office headed by Connie Bradley, Southern Regional executive director. The staff is responsible for recruiting new writer and publisher members, attending to the needs of current members, representing the society at industry functions and community events, and organizing the annual ASCAP Country Music Awards—where the writers and publishers of ASCAP's most performed country songs are honored. Every year the awards dinner is attended by over 1,000 country music stars, songwriters, music publishers, and Nashville music executives.

The achievements of the society's country members are also honored through the ASCAP No. 1 Club for songwriters and music publishers that have number one hits on the *Billboard* Country Singles Chart and/or the *Radio & Records* National Airplay Chart. Their success is commemorated with a reception at which they are presented with a special certificate.

ASCAP is also committed to helping new and aspiring songwriters develop their craft and make the contacts they need to break into the business. The Nashville office offers annual songwriter workshops in country and Gospel music to all writers, whether or not they are members of ASCAP. With the influx of artists to Nashville representing all genres of music, ASCAP is developing pop and theater music workshops as well. In addition, ASCAP has on-premises writer's rooms furnished with pianos for the convenience of its members. Seminars and monthly showcases are also held throughout the year to assist and encourage new talent.

ASCAP goes a step further by supporting local music organizations such as the Country Music Association, Gospel Music Association, Nashville Songwriters Association International, Tennessee Repertory Theatre, W.O. Smith Music Community School, Nashville Entertainment Association, and the National Academy of Arts and Sciences, to name just a few. Connie Bradley and other members of the executive staff serve as advisors to some of these organizations and others, and are on their boards.

In its efforts to reach as many songwriters as possible, ASCAP sponsors events in Nashville and other parts of the Southern region, such as the Nashville Entertainment Extravaganza, Alabama Music Hall of Fame Awards in Birmingham, Copyright Society of the South/USA, Country Radio Seminar, South by Southwest in Austin, Texas, Memphis Producers Showcase, North Carolina Music Seminar, Chapel Hill, Birmingham City Stages, Alabama, Athens Seminar and Showcase in Georgia, Georgia Music Hall of Fame, and the New South Music Seminar in Atlanta.

Writer/artists are also an important part of ASCAP's membership. Among the many country artists who are current members of ASCAP are Clint Black, Garth Brooks, T. Graham Brown, Johnny Cash, Alan Jackson, Kentucky HeadHunters, Kathy Mattea, Reba McEntire, Restless Heart, Oak Ridge Boys, Kenny Rogers, Billy Joe Royal, Ronnie Milsap, Ricky Van Shelton, Shenandoah, George Strait, Randy Travis, and Don Williams.

ASCAP Nashville's 25,000 square-foot building serves its membership most effectively and stands as a symbol of ASCAP's ongoing commitment to the Nashville music community and to the writers and publishers that make up the society. ASCAP, the voice of music, where members have a voice.

Contact Information

For further information regarding ASCAP's Southern region, contact: ASCAP, Two Music Square West, Nashville, TN 37203, (615) 742-5000.

(Source: Eve Vaupel, ASCAP Nashville Public Relations)

Eve Vaupel *(Photo by Alan Mayor)*

EVE VAUPEL
Nashville Public Relations, America Society of Composers, Authors and Publishers

Eve Vaupel was born in Nashville, Tennessee. She graduated from Vanderbilt University with a Bachelor of Arts degree in Fine Arts.

Vaupel began her career with ASCAP in 1983 as receptionist and was promoted to Public Relations Assistant in 1985. In 1986, she was promoted to Public Relations Liaison and in 1989, Nashville Public Relations. Vaupel is responsible for all press relations and advertising activities, promotion and marketing for special events including ASCAP's GMA Luncheon, ASCAP's Country Music Association (CMA) Week activities, and ASCAP's Nashville annual membership meeting.

Vaupel is active in local community affairs, music business and sporting events. Her professional activities include membership in the CMA, Academy of Country Music, and the Nashville Songwriters Association International. She is a board member of the Mayor's Sister Cities and works with Vanderbilt University community affairs.

Broadcast Music Incorporated (BMI)

One of the most amazing stories in the vivid history of American music is that of the growth of Broadcast Music Incorporated (BMI) during a period of five decades. Starting with little more than the determination to provide competition and opportunity, BMI today represents the largest group of composers, songwriters, and music publishers in the world: more than 120,000 American creators of music with a repertoire of over 2 million music works. In this growth, BMI has been abetted by a number of factors—technological, social, political, and economic—which have changed the scope and character of popular music around the world.

A far different music world than the one we know today existed in the later summer of 1939 when attorney Sydney M. Kaye unveiled plans for a new music licensing body to be known as Broadcast Music, Inc. At the time, three companies dominated the recording industry. They provided virtually all records bought by the public, used by those of the 800 existing radio stations that were permitted to broadcast recorded music, and in the 400,000 machines of the burgeoning jukebox industry. Fewer than 150 music publishers and slightly more than 1,000 songwriters shared in an annual performing rights income of about $6 million. Most of that money was distributed only on the basis of live performance during evening hours on four radio networks. Recorded performances did not count, nor did those on independent radio stations.

Although there were thousands of composers and music publishers who could not share in this source of revenue, it was impractical for these individuals to negotiate performing rights licenses with the thousands of establishments that utilized music commercially. Forms of music that are widely popular today were generally unknown, except to small and isolated audiences. Country music was referred to as "hillbilly," rhythm and blues as "race." These and other manifestations of the great American musical genius were frustrated by the lack of economic encouragement and cultural acceptance. Such a state of affairs could be resolved only by the creation and development of meaningful competition and economic opportunity which would lead to the democratization of American music.

In 1940 about 600 enterprises, many of them engaged in broadcasting, others maintaining radio stations as part of their business portfolios, formed BMI with the understanding that the company would not operate for profit. Pledging 50 percent of their 1937 payments to ASCAP as funding, they paid, $300,000 for stock, and the remaining total of $1.2 million as initial license fees. Original investments averaged around $500. No dividends were expected and none has ever been paid. All BMI income is distributed except minimal operating expenses and a small general reserve.

By achieving the classical feature of competition—a free and unrestricted market for intellectual property—BMI opened its doors to all creators of music, including those who had previously been denied an opportunity to share in performing rights income. It adopted a method share of compensating these writers and publishers which would equitably credit them with actual performances—whether live or recorded, whether national, regional, or local. It offered non-discriminatory licenses to all users. Most significantly, it served the public by encouraging every kind of music.

In the classic American tradition, BMI began by grubstaking; that is, financially assisting small, independent music publishing ventures.

An initial statement of BMI policy addressed to the American public said:

> *BMI is a complete new force in American music. It is also a means of giving you who make up the musical public an opportunity to hear its music and most significant of all, an opportunity to grow familiar with the work of composers who previously have not been privileged to put their music before you. BMI has dropped the bars and now the new writers, the younger writers, those you may not have heard, can bring you their music.*

The past decades have seen a dramatic realization of that goal. Because of BMI's existence and because of its concern, the many sounds of American music have been heard, accepted, and acclaimed. New writers have been successful internationally. New music publishers, most of them starting as small businesses, have made a cultural contribution. Together they have brought the public country, rhythm and blues, Latin, jazz, rock-'n'-roll, gospel, contemporary, popular, concert music, and electronic and experimental sounds. It is their work that makes up the majority of America's contemporary musical tradition.

Because of its open door policy, BMI was able to pioneer in the encouragement and development of the music that has gained the greatest international popularity in history. The first and most important creators of country, rhythm and blues, rock-'n'-roll, and other manifestations of contemporary music licensed their works through BMI. As a result, both the BMI repertoire and its writers and publishers were able to grow in a manner without precedent. Evidence of BMI's contribution to musical history is found in these facts: over 75 percent of the writers inducted into the Country Music Hall of Fame and the Rock-'n'-Roll Hall of Fame, and 90 percent of the Rhythm & Blues Foundation Pioneer Awards honorees are represented by BMI. Additionally, 75 of *Rolling Stone* magazine's Top 100 Singles of the Rock Era claim BMI creators.

Integral to the explosion of American music is BMI's southern strength. BMI Nashville, headquarters for the Central Regional Territory, presently boasts approximately 25,000 writers and 12,000 publishers throughout 15 states. The Writer/Publisher Relations office has been a forceful presence on Music Row since its 1958 founding by Frances W. Preston, now BMI president and CEO. BMI was the first performing rights organization to open an office in Nashville to support the careers of country music makers. BMI was also the first to honor publicly country songwriters and publishers; the annual BMI Country Awards, saluting the creators of the year's most performed songs, is a highlight of October's Country Music Week.

Currently under the direction of Vice President Roger Sovine, the Nashville performing rights office oversees the distribution of royalties, assists writers and publishers in the administration of their musical works and in networking within the music industry. BMI's role in the music business has always gone far beyond its royalty function to include participation in organizations such as the Country Music Association, the Country Music Foundation, the Gospel Music Association, the Nashville Songwriters Association International, and the Nashville Entertainment Association, among others. BMI continues its commitment to nurturing the development of new music centers through associations, seminars, workshops, and showcases. Sponsorship of events such as Austin's South by Southwest, New Orleans' Delta Music Conference, the Memphis Producers Showcase, Nashville's Extravaganza and Country Radio Seminar, and Atlanta's NewSouth Showcase are representative of the company's leadership nationwide. BMI Nashville also makes major contributions to educating and encouraging new writers and industry members, as well as to strengthening the craft and business of songwriting, in such cities as Dallas, Louisville, Ft. Lauderdale, Miami, and Birmingham.

Over the last few years, Nashville has proven to be a place of increasing importance to BMI's national operation. The departments that oversee network television, cable, and film royalty accounting payments have recently moved to Nashville. Nashville has also been chosen as the site of one of the three regional "mega-centers" for BMI's licensing department, which is responsible for signing agreements with clubs, hotels, and other businesses that offer music. With the inclusion of special projects, the department that produces songwriter awards and other events hosted by BMI in New York, Nashville, Los Angeles, and London (Pop Awards, Country Awards, Motion Picture and Television Awards, PRS/BMI Awards), the staff in Nashville numbers in excess of 100 people, testament to BMI's long-term positive relationship with the city.

Now in its sixth decade of existence, BMI can look back on an unparalleled record of accomplishment. Many of the innovations and trade practices it introduced to music licensing have become internationally accepted, and its commitment to technological excellence is unsurpassed. The open door continues to attract the majority of those who produce the music preferred by audiences the world over. A sampling of BMI's repertoire surveys The Beatles, Michael Bolton, Alabama, Elvis Presley, Michael and Janet Jackson, Little Richard, Billy Joel, Hank Williams, Jr. and Sr., Woody Guthrie, Willie Nelson, REM, Holland-Dozier-Holland, Paul Simon, The Judds, Warrant, Ray Charles, Dave Grusin, Harlan Howard, Gloria Estefan, Bo Diddley, Paul Overstreet, Take 6, Dolly Parton, Goffin and King, Rosanne Cash, The Who, Sandi Patti, Miles Davis, and Dave Brubeck.

Vice President Roger Sovine believes, "That promise made in 1940 to create 'a complete new force in American music' has become a reality far beyond the hopes of BMI's founders. The opportunity and competition it has introduced into music licensing have been of benefit to both citizens of the United States and those of the countries represented by the 40 societies with which it has forged reciprocal agreements."

Contact Information

For further information regarding BMI, contact: BMI, 10 Music Square East, Nashville, TN 37203, (615) 291-6700.

Society of European Stage Authors and Composers (SESAC)

Founded in 1930 by Paul Heinecke, SESAC (originally known as the Society of European Stage Authors and Composers) is one of the three music performing rights organizations identified in the Copyright Act of 1976, Title 17, U.S.C. 116 (e) (3), definition:

> *"A 'performing rights society' is an association or corporation that licenses the public performance of nondramatic musical works on behalf of the copyright owners, such as the American Society of Composers, Authors and Publishers, Broadcast Music, Inc., and SESAC, Inc."*

Without a performing rights organization writers and publishers would find it too costly and time consuming to locate and license every music user. Music users would have similar problems keeping track of thousands of copyright owners and negotiating individual licenses to authorize the performance of each copyrighted work. SESAC offers an economical and practical solution to these problems. Utilizing computer technology, SESAC provides three valuable services to its writer and publisher affiliates: licensing of music users, collection of license fees, and distribution of royalties.

Rights Granted Songwriters by Law

You, as the copyright owner of the songs you write and/or publish, are given certain exclusive rights by law. Among these rights are: the right to reproduce your work (commonly known as a mechanical and/or synchronization right); the right to prepare derivative works from your work; the right to distribute your work; the right to publicly display your work; an the right to publicly perform your work.

The performing right, the right to perform publicly a copyrighted work, is granted to owners of musical compositions under U.S. copyright law. Generally, authorization must be granted before the public performance of a copyrighted musical work can legally occur on radio, broadcast and cable television, and in nightclubs, hotels, colleges, universities, theme parks, theaters, auditoriums, country clubs, skating rinks, restaurants, and dance schools—in short, just about anywhere music is performed publicly.

How Does SESAC Differ from ASCAP and BMI?

SESAC, by design, is the smallest of the three performing rights organizations. Selective in its affiliation of writers and publishers, SESAC is able to provide efficient and personalized service to every affiliate. This personalized service spans many areas, including catalog consultation and collaboration recommendations.

SESAC uses sophisticated computer technology to tract performance activity on independently maintained databases such as *Billboard*'s Information Network and *Radio and Records*' Esi Street, individual radio playlists, syndicated television, network television, cable television and pay television music cue sheets, and popularity charts that appear in national publications (*Billboard, Cashbox,* and *Radio and Records*). This unique system is based on publicly disseminated, industry-accepted information—information not within SESAC's control. Therefore, it is a fair means to be used in determining an equitable royalty distribution.

Additionally, all SESAC affiliates have the opportunity to directly report performance activity.

Under SESAC's unique distribution system, affiliates can closely estimate their actual performance earning from a payment rate schedule based on chart activity.

Kinds of Music Represented by SESAC

During its early days SESAC was best known for its representation of American and European classics, along with religious and country music. Today, however, every category of music is contained in the widely diversified SESAC repertory, including adult contemporary, black/urban, jazz, Hispanic, big band, country, gospel, dance, educational, Latin, classical, polka, rock, marching band, new age, film scores, television theme music, and advertising jingles.

Other SESAC Services

SESAC is deeply committed to the continuing development of its affiliates. The benefit of its size allows for personal services unique within the industry. SESAC's legal and affiliation departments provide consultations with its songwriters and publishers.

SESAC's trained staff explores placement opportunities of copyrighted works with publishers and record labels. The organization promotes, in conjunction with its affiliates and/or record companies, suitable material for radio and TV programming.

Where feasible, SESAC arranges for showcasing opportunities. In addition, information regarding current copyright legislation is provided on a regular basis. SESAC is an active participant in all legislative groups dealing with matters pertaining to the protection of its affiliates' rights.

Contact Information

For further information regrading SESAC, contact: SESAC, Inc., 156 West 56th Street, New York, NY 10019, (212) 586-3450; or 55 Music Square East, Nashville, TN 37203, (615) 320-0055.

Appendix 4

◆ ◆ ◆

Songwriters' Organizations

Academy of Country Music (ACM)

The first and foremost purpose of the Academy of Country Music is to "enhance and promote country music throughout the world." The quote is from the academy's original non-profit charter issued by the state of California in 1964.

As a member of the academy, you will share in the dream of its founders, Tommy Wiggins, Eddie Miller, and Mickey and Chris Christensen. They wanted the music and its performers to be shared with more people and then to be publicly recognized by their peers for outstanding achievement.

Country music's very first awards presentation was held by the Academy of Country Music in 1965 when Roger Miller was proclaimed "Man of the Year" and the "Most Promising Male Vocalist" was Merle Haggard. This event has become an annual tradition where the entire country music industry gathers to honor musicians, singers, producers, songwriters, publishers, record companies, radio stations, disc jockeys, and night clubs of America's music. Although the gathering for the awards show night is much like a reunion of close friends, it has also become a major event where the spontaneity of live television invites the world to share individual excitement when the results of secret ballots are made known for the first time.

Television plays an important role in the growth of country music and the academy. The awards presentation is one of television's most successful and highest rated specials and has been nationally televised since 1974. The live, two-hour event airs in early spring on the NBC television network.

Publications featuring country music are a significant part of the industry. The ACM supplies information about the activities of members and special events.

Radio stations around the world give vital support to country music and the academy. The ACM supports country radio by providing historical facts and information on artists and events. The "Country Radio Station" and "Disc Jockey of the Year" are saluted by the ACM during the televised awards presentation. The academy also supports and participates in the Country Radio Broadcasters Seminar in Nashville each year. One of the highlights every year is the ACM "Super Faces Show" which, in the past, has featured Hank Williams, Jr., Alabama, The Judds, and George Strait performing special shows for the CRBS attendees.

The academy is involved year round in activities important to the country music community. Some of these activities include charity fund raisers, participation in country music seminars, talent contests, artist showcases, assistance to producers in placing country music on television and in motion pictures and backing legislation that benefits the interests of the country music community. The academy is governed by a board of directors with elected officers, elected by the professional membership, overseeing the daily activities of the ACM office.

One of the major events sponsored by the ACM is the annual Celebrity Golf Classic and Dinner. Held at a Los Angeles area golf club, the classic has benefited national charities such as the American Heart Association, the T.J. Martell Foundation, and the Neil Bogart Memorial Laboratory.

The academy periodically allots monies for national research of the country listener and viewer. This includes likes and dislikes about the media, details about music purchases, what motivates concert attendance, and what and why they, as consumers, buy. The research includes statistical information that serves to provide academy members with an accurate profile of the country consumer.

Music and its lyrics are a reflection of people's feelings about their lives. This is as true today as it was in the past. Country music, the true art form of the country setting, has been called western, bluegrass, hillbilly, blues, rock-'n'-roll, and country. What better way could the music of this country be described than to call it "America's music."

Protection

The academy was in part responsible for the anti-piracy laws enacted by the state of California against the unauthorized reproduction of records and tapes. A concerted effort to lobby, along with other record industry groups, has helped to protect the rights of musicians and others associated with this industry and to prosecute those who would illegally take advantage of talent and hard work.

Newsletter

The *Chronicles of Country Music* is published monthly by the academy and mailed to members. This vital bulletin keeps the activities of members before the industry by direct mail to radio stations, music and magazine publishers, talent bookers, record companies, television producers, and the news media. International relations are maintained by distribution to many of the world's newspapers through the cooperation of the foreign press.

Voting Privileges

Professional members have the opportunity to vote for directors, officers, and the annual awards, which include top male and female vocalists, vocal group, duet, top new male and female vocalists, new vocal duet or group, album, single record, song, entertainer of the year, and all bylaw changes.

Contact Information

The academy is a ready source of information about country music bookers, artists, radio stations, record labels, night clubs, publishers, and many other facets of the industry. For further information, contact: Academy of Country Music, 6255 Sunset Blvd., Suite 915, Hollywood, CA 90028, (213) 462-2351.

Country Music Association (CMA)

The late 1950s were booming years for rock-'n'-roll. With fewer country radio stations and dwindling record sales, country music was taking a back seat to the sounds of Elvis Presley, Buddy Holly, and Bill Haley. That's when a group of country music heavyweights decided an organization was needed to rejuvenate the country music industry.

In 1958, Connie B. Gay, Dee Kilpatrick, and Wesley Rose, among others, founded the Country Music Association (CMA). It was the first organization ever formed to promote a type of music. A little over 230 people joined that first year with a spirit of putting personal interests aside to pull for the common good.

Strength in Numbers

Today, CMA boasts a membership of almost 7,000 country music industry professionals in 45 countries. Artists, musicians, artist managers, producers, songwriters, record companies, radio stations, concert promoters, and publishers are among the groups represented in CMA's 15 individual membership categories. CMA's membership also includes some 737 organization members. Member support and involvement makes a vital contribution to CMA's promotion and development of the country music industry.

CMA is guided by a board of directors which is comprised of 62 top music industry executives who serve gratis and pay their own expenses. This group of dedicated volunteer leaders is CMA's number one asset. The association's day-to-day activities are executed by a professional staff of fewer than 40 people.

CMA, headquartered in Nashville, with an office in London, is a not-for-profit corporation tax-exempt under IRS Code Section 501(c)6.

America's Premier Music Awards Telecast

The first music awards on network television, the CMA Awards Show has long been considered the most prestigious and spectacular awards evening in country music. Since its first telecast in 1968, the CMA Awards Show has consistently captured top ratings and expanded the audience for country music. Televised on the CBS network, the show is sponsored by top national advertisers such as Kraft, McDonald's, General Motors, and Kellogg's.

International Country Music Fan Fair

Each June the Tennessee State Fairgrounds resounds with the best of country music, the cheers of 24,000 sunburned country fans, and a million camera clicks. Since 1972, Fan Fair has played host to such acts as Alabama, Johnny Cash, Reba McEntire, Randy Travis, The Judds, Garth Brooks, Vince Gill, Barbara Mandrell, Clint Black, k.d. lang, Gary Morris, Tammy Wynette, Patty Loveless, Dwight Yoakam, and Ricky Skaggs. Fans from Jackson to Japan and Denver to Denmark experience more than 30 hours of concerts and hundreds of country stars offering photo and autograph sessions. Fan Fair is co-sponsored by CMA and the Grand Ole Opry. Proceeds are put into a special fund and used to market and promote country music.

Spreading the News

Two specific areas in which CMA is promoting country music are the European market and college students.

European Market Development. Since CMA established a European Market Development office in London in 1982, country music has become increasingly popular in Europe. CMA's presence provides a forum to stimulate European music industry involvement with country music. IN 1986, CMA funded the first U.K. country album chart compiled by Gallup. That same year, CMA and the U.K. divisions of the major record labels jointly organized the first country music promotion and marketing campaign to expand the market for country records. The campaign met with notable success in the 1980s and continues into the 1990s as CMA strives for more media attention and a larger market share in the emerging European community.

Developing a Younger Audience. In the late 1980s, CMA took to the road with its Lost Highway Tour, a series of college concerts/workshops aimed at educating and exposing college students to the new genre of country artists who have youth audience appeal. From the campus of Boston's Berklee College of music to UCLA, from the College Media Journal (CMJ) National conventions in New York to the National Association of Campus Activities (NACA) conventions, the Lost Highway Tour has continued to make inroads with the college-aged consumer. CMA's demonstrated success at attracting a younger demographic to country music yielded a tie-in since 1989 with the NACA Services Corporation (NSC).

Tackling Tough Issues

Through a host of conventions, seminars, and meetings, CMA exposes members to technological changes and issues-related topics. In addition, CMA is active in the political issues affecting the country music industry.

Networking and Professional Growth. Buyers and sellers of live entertainment are the target group at CMA's annual SRO Convention, successor of the Talent Buyers Entertainment Marketplace. Marrying talent showcases, an expo marketplace, and educational sessions, SRO brings those who book talent for fairs, auditoriums, parks, theaters, and other venues together with the movers and shakers of the industry. SRO is traditionally held in conjunction with the CMA Awards Show in October.

A hotbed of topics are discussed at the CMA-sponsored Music Industry Professional Seminar. MIPS sessions are held each March as part of the Country Radio Seminar—the country radio industry's biggest get-together. CMA also coordinates the Artist/Radio Tape Sessions, a unique opportunity for stations to get customized liners from top-name country artists.

CMA also hosts periodic town meetings, inviting representatives from all areas of the industry. The town meeting serves as an opportunity for country music professionals to explore how changes in the business will affect their jobs and the industry's future.

Legislative Affairs. CMA has always taken an active role in political issues which affect the music industry, including tape piracy, copyright revision, home taping, and product labeling. CMA's main focus is to protect the rights of those who create and perform the music.

Recognizing Professional Excellence

Each year millions of viewers see the winners of the coveted CMA Awards. But CMA recognizes excellence in other areas as well. It established the Country Music Hall of Fame in 1961 and bestows this highest honor every year as a part of the CMA Awards Show. CMA also honors outstanding achievements in radio with six broadcast awards.

The annual Founding President's Award is given to the person who has rendered exemplary service on CMA's behalf, and the Media Achievement Award and the Wesley Rose Foreign Media Achievement Award recognize journalists who have broadened the visibility of country music. SRO Awards are given to recognize excellence in the touring industry.

In 1983, the CMA board inaugurated the Irving Waugh Award of Excellence. Named for its first recipient, the award is intended to highlight singular achievements having a profound impact on the state of the industry.

Information, Marketing, and Research Materials

Among the materials disseminated by CMA are the country radio list, reference guides, and audience profile.

Country Radio Station List. Annually, CMA surveys all broadcasters in the United States and Canada to compile a complete listing of the more than 2,100 full-time country radio stations. The CMA listing is the most extensive and detailed available for any radio format.

Reference Guides. Hundreds of industry personnel are included in this handy cross-reference guide of artists, managers, record labels, talent agents, producers, publishers, etc.

Country Music Audience Profiles. CMA consistently commissions research information on country music consumers, their attitudes, their demographic characteristics, and their listening and purchasing habits.

Getting the Facts Straight

CMA's publishing efforts include *Close-Up* magazine, ad agency reports, and *New from CMA*.

Close-Up Magazine. CMA's monthly publication *Close-Up*, gives CMA members an up-close look at informative new stories, perspectives, and columns affecting the country music industry.

Ad Agency Presentations. Since 1963, CMA has continued to take country music's story to the advertising community, providing research data on the scope and quality of country music's audience. CMA's ad agency efforts are intended to keep dollars flowing into country radio, television, and other media. In 1989 CMA initiated a landmark series of in-house presentations to major agencies in New York, Chicago, Detroit, Los Angeles, Dallas, Houston, and Atlanta. The presentations illustrate that the country music audience represents a large consumer segment which would not be overlooked in media planning.

New from CMA. In addition, CMA also publishes *New from CMA* to give advertisers, radio stations, and the press a quick overview of the latest news about country music.

Poised for the Future

For more than three decades, CMA has been open to the challenges dictated by the ever-changing music world. More than any other force, CMA has helped propel country music to an unprecedented worldwide popularity. Touted as an organization by which others are measured, CMA stands poised to prove that even greater success lies ahead.

CMA Benefits for Member Songwriters

Number One Song Certificate. A special certificate is given to CMA member songwriters who have a number one song in either *Billboard, Radio & Records, Gavin Report,* or *Cashbox.*

Triple Play Award. The Triple Play Award is an exclusive CMA plaque for those songwriters who achieve the unique accomplishment of having three number one songs in a 12-month period.

Close-Up *Magazine. Close-Up* is CMA's trade publication. It is filled with information on the country music industry and spotlights member songwriters in the special feature section, "I Write the Songs."

CMA Awards Show. The CMA Awards Show is the hottest ticket in country music and the tickets are only available to CMA members. Songwriters are recognized on the highly rated show, as they receive the CMA crystal trophy for Song of the Year.

Sir Discount. CMA members are entitled to a 10 percent discount on instrument rentals and studio time from Studio Instrument Rentals. The CMA discount applies to all four locations: New York, Los Angeles, San Francisco, and Nashville.

Major Medical Coverage. CMA offers its members special group insurance rates on major medical plans.

Contact Information

For further information regarding CMA, contact: Country Music Association, One Music Circle South, Nashville, TN 37203, (615) 244-2840.

Nashville Songwriters Association International (NSAI)

Established in 1967 by professional songwriters in Nashville, NSAI is a non-profit trade organization, chartered under the laws of the state of Tennessee, to advance, promote and benefit composers and authors of musical compositions. Over the years NSAI has grown to a membership of more than 2,600. Members reside in all 50 states, Australia, Austria, Malaysia, England, Scotland, Sweden, Korea, India, N. Ireland, Canada, Hong Kong, New Zealand, and West Indies. NSAI is governed by a volunteer board of directors, a majority of whom are songwriters, elected by the membership. A general membership meeting is conducted every year in March at the Spring Symposium.

Membership

NSAI features three types of membership: individual, business, and corporate.

Individual Membership. There are four categories for individual membership: professional, active, associate, and student.

1. *Professional membership* is open to the songwriter whose primary source of income is songwriting or who is generally recognized by the professional songwriting community as a professional songwriter.

2. *Active membership* is open to the songwriter who has at least one composition which has been contractually assigned to a publisher who is affiliated with a recognized performance organization (i.e., ASCAP, BMI, or SESAC).

3. *Associate membership* is open to the songwriter who is as yet unpublished, but who wishes to maintain contact with and be informed about what professional songwriters are doing

through NSAI. Associate membership is also open to those who are not songwriters but who are dedicated and devoted to songwriters and their work.

4. *Student membership* is open to full-time college students (12 hours or more) or students of accredited senior high schools. Membership fee in this category is half of the usual fee and no voting is included.

Business Membership. There are two membership categories available for business membership: patron and sponsor.

1. *Patron membership* is open to any company whose business is directly related to entertainment.

2. *Sponsor membership* is open to any business not directly related to entertainment (i.e., banks, retail stores, restaurants, etc.).

Corporate Membership. Corporate membership is open to any corporation that supports NSAI through a donation of $5,000 or more per year.

Educational Activities

NSAI sponsors a variety of educational activities.

Workshops. NSAI has fostered the formation of area workshops in cities around the country in an effort to help those songwriters who cannot travel to the major music publishing and recording centers. NSAI conducts annual "mini-seminars" at many of these area workshops, utilizing some of its professional members from Nashville.

Members who live in and around the Nashville area are invited to attend a weekly workshop. These free workshops include song critiques and rap sessions along with advice on collaboration, demos, and other subjects of interest. Guest speakers include well-known writers, publishers, and record executives.

Critique Service. Members who do not have access to an area workshop may submit a cassette tape to NSAI (one song per tape) with a lyric sheet and a self-addressed, stamped envelope. Volunteers will record a verbal critique on the tape and return it to the member. NSAI asks that members only submit one song at a time.

Symposium. The Annual Songwriting Symposium is held each March in Nashville. This three-day event features sessions to improve the writing craft, panel discussions with top industry leaders, critiques of songs by publishers, the Super Songwriters Showcase, and the Annual Achievement Awards Ceremony and Dinner.

Summer Seminar. The Annual Summer Seminar, held each July in Nashville, focuses on the craft of songwriting. This one-day event includes a songwriter showcase.

Bookstore. NSAI makes available for sale to its members a selection of reference books, textbooks, and cassette tapes aimed at improving songwriting skills and developing knowledge of the music business. These items are available at the NSAI office or by mail order.

Newsletter. NSAI's quarterly newsletter, *The Leadsheet*, keeps the membership informed of accomplishments within the association and includes articles of interest to songwriters.

Legislative Activities

NSAI has long been a champion for the songwriter on many legislative issues. Through the efforts of its membership, the association has been effective in Washington by lobbying for the revision of the copyright law and opposing such threats as source licensing. A full-time legislative committee meets to monitor and evaluate proposed or pending legislation that might affect songwriters and their families. The committee issues educational bulletins to its membership and maintains a quarterly article in the newsletter.

Recognition for Songwriters

NSAI honors songwriters at the Annual Achievement Awards Ceremony and Dinner every year during the Symposium in March. The entire membership votes on songs written by Nashville-based writers or writers whose works are generally associated with Nashville. Songs may achieve an award in the following formats: country, gospel, pop-rock, black, and adult contemporary. The Song of the Year, Songwriter/Artist of the Year, and Songwriter of the Year are also named.

Contact Information

For further information regarding NSAI, contact: NSAI, 15 Music Square West, Nashville, TN 37203, (615) 256-3354.

National Academy of Recording Arts & Sciences® (NARAS®)

The Recording Academy ®

The National Academy of Recording Arts & Sciences, Inc., is a non-profit organization of over 8,000 individual members. It represents the complete spectrum of creative people involved in the recording industry—singers, producers, musicians, arrangers, composers, songwriters, engineers, conductors, art directors, photographers, illustrators, music video producers and directors, album note writers, and more. There is one common bond: each is involved creatively in the production of all kinds of recording—from rock to classical, rhythm and blues to country, jazz to blues, Latin to polka, spoken words to children's recording, music video to Broadway.

A National Agenda. In 1957, a group of recording artists and executives in Los Angeles saw the need for an organization that would represent the creative people of the recording industry.

Sales figures and chart positions were, at this time, the only way to gauge the merit of the recording and the artist. The initial core group of the National Academy of Recording Arts & Sciences, Inc., was concerned that many artists and technicians, working in the many fields of recording, were seeing the valuable and creative efforts in the recording industry go largely unrecognized and unrewarded.

Thus, the Recording Academy came into being . . . and the Grammy® Awards process began.

Even in the 1990s, the Recording Academy has shown increasing commitment concerning issues that affect the professional life of the creative and technical community and its individuals. They range widely from the preservation and archiving of recordings to MUSICARES®, which focuses the attention of the music community on health and welfare issues affecting music people.

The Recording Academy is dedicated to protecting the creative environment, the continuing education of professionals and the recognition of excellence in recording.

The Recording Academy has also been in the front line on concerns such as censorship of recordings, labeling legislation, the protection of intellectual copyrights, home taping, record piracy, front and back announcing, and many other subjects that are monitored and addressed on an ongoing basis. The academy has represented the recording community all across the United States speaking out on these issues to the general public and politicians.

The Recording Academy is also expanding on the international front with the future intention of establishing recording academies in various countries around the world.

NARAS Chapters. NARAS has seven chapters across the United States. These chapters serve as one of the main service delivery systems from the Recording Academy to the music community and its members. Each chapter conducts educational and professional programs (seminars, membership, panel discussions, lectures, etc.) that deal with the arts and sciences of recording and how they affect the professional lives of the Recording Academy membership.

Through representatives on national committees and through national trustees from each, the chapters contribute to and participate in numerous national NARAS activities.

NARAS chapter cities are located in Atlanta, Chicago, Los Angeles, Nashville, New York, Memphis, and San Francisco.

The Officers. Administration of the Recording Academy is conducted by the national president/CEO in the national office in Los Angeles, California. The national office contains several departments: Awards, Education, Publications, Membership and Chapter Services, Finance, Special Projects, and Foundation Activities. These departments are directed by industry and Recording Academy experts.

The Recording Academy's National Board of Trustees oversees NARAS national activities. The trustees are elected by the Board of Governors of each NARAS chapter and serve a maximum of two successive two-year terms. National trustees are directly involved with the determination of the Grammy Awards categories, eligibility criteria, voting and nominating procedures, the Awards telecasts, Lifetime Achievement and Trustees Awards, the Grammy Legend Awards, NARAS membership qualifications, educational and scholarship programs, and the Hall of Fame Awards criteria and voting process.

National officers consist of a chairman of the board, first vice-chairman, additional vice-presidents, and a secretary-treasurer. They are elected by the national trustees.

The Grammy® Awards

The recording industry's most prestigious award—a golden statuette that is a composite of early gramophones—is presented annually by the Recording Academy. A Grammy is awarded for artistic or technical achievement, not sales figures or chart positions, and the winners are determined by the votes of their peers—the voting members of the Recording Academy.

The chief aims of the Grammy Awards, today, as they have been since the first Grammy Awards in 1958, are to recognize excellence and create a greater public awareness of the cultural diversity and contributions of the recording industry.

On "The Grammy Awards Show," an annual live, three-hour prime-time network TV event, the winners for the year are revealed for the first time. The telecast features performances by many of the nominees, plus appearances by other top recording artists. Winners are presented with their Grammy Awards on the show. (Some awards are made during pre-telecast ceremonies the same evening.)

The annual Grammy Awards presentations bring together thousands of creative and technical professionals in the recording industry from all over the world. The public reaction to the show is so strong that it is telecast to an international audience of over 130 countries.

Grammy Process. The Grammy Awards is a three-stage process: entering, nominating, and final voting.

All NARAS members and record companies are invited to enter recordings released during the awards eligibility year that they feel merit consideration for Grammy Awards. After these are screened for correct eligibility and then approved by the national trustees, they comprise the year's eligibility lists. These lists can contain as many as 8,000 entries annually.

Nominating occurs after NARAS' voting (active) members receive the first-round ballots and eligibility lists for all categories except those nominated by special nominating committees. In those special categories, final nominations are determined by national nominating committees of active members. The five nominations in each category receiving the highest number of votes are announced at press conferences in January. Final voting, which decides the actual Grammy winners, is also by the active members. Ballots in all rounds are tabulated by an independent firm and the results are not known until the Grammy Awards presentation ceremonies when the firm delivers the names of the winners in sealed envelopes.

All active members may vote in the general categories (Record of the Year, Album of the Year, Song of the Year, Best New Artist) but are limited, on both ballots, to a specific number of fields (rock, pop, country, rhythm and blues, jazz, classical etc.).

Education Programs

The Recording Academy has developed ongoing educational programs as well as research opportunities in the creative and technical aspects of the recording industry. The Recording Academy awards grants for research or educational projects focusing on recorded music or other sound applications. These grants, as well as significant scholarship and educational endowments, are awarded by the NARAS National Educational Committee annually.

The NARAS Foundation®, which was established by the national trustees, implements other educational goals—such as the development of the NARAS Museum—and through NARAS chapters across the United States, engages in related cultural, professional, and educational activities. The museum will eventually be home for a NARAS archival program and also the NARAS Hall of Fame. The NARAS National Archival Committee exists to examine archival procedure within U.S.

recording companies and to work toward standardization of audio preservation and cataloging of master recordings.

The Recording Academy also offers a number of regular publications, including the quarterly, *Grammy Magazine*, and the scholarly publication, *The NARAS Journal*.

Grammy in the Schools®. Grammy in the Schools is a national education program designed for high school level music students and faculty to help better define and explore all the various career opportunities available in the field of music and recording. This "career day" program is not only designed to focus on those involved in the making of music but also in other aspects of the music business, behind the scenes as well as in front of the microphone.

Organized by both national and chapter personnel, Grammy in the Schools involves workshops, panel discussions, and performances by artists, engineers, producers, and others prominent in the music industry.

NARAS Student Music Awards. These awards were established to recognize, support, and encourage exceptional creative abilities and original compositions in the recording arts and sciences at the college level.

Contact Information

For further information on NARAS, contact: NARAS, 3402 Pico Blvd., Santa Monica, CA 90405, (310) 392-3777.

Glossary

Abstruse: Hard to understand; deep; recondite. *(Webster's Dictionary)*

Accidental: Music: 1a. A sign, as a sharp, flat or natural, placed before a note to show a change of pitch from that indicated by the key signature. 1b. The tone indicated by such a sign. *(Webster's Dictionary)*

Acronym: An abbreviation which is pronounced as a word and is made up of the first letters of the title or phrase being abbreviated [(e.g., ASCAP—American Society of Composers, Authors and Publishers); snafu (situation normal, all fouled up)] *(McCrimmon)*

Adage: An old saying that has been popularly accepted as a truth (Where there's smoke, there's fire"). *(Webster's Dictionary)*

Advertise: 1. To tell about or praise (a product, service, etc.) publicly, as through newspapers, handbills, radio, etc., so as to make people want to buy it. 2. To make known; give notice. 3. To call the public's attention to things, as by printed notices; sponsor advertisements. 4. To ask (for) publicly by printed notice, etc. *(Webster's Dictionary)*

Aesthetic: 1. Of or in relation to aesthetics. 2. Of beauty. 3. Sensitive to art and beauty; showing good taste; artistic. *(Webster's Dictionary)*

Affiliation: The act of affiliating or being affiliated; connection, as with an organization, club, etc. *(Webster's Dictionary)*

Allegory: Description of one thing under the image of another. 1. A story in which people, things, and happenings have hidden or symbolic meaning: allegories are used for teaching or explaining ideas, moral principles, etc. 2. The presenting of ideas by means of such stories; symbolical narration or description. 3. Any symbol or emblem. *(Webster's Dictionary)*

Alliteration: Repetition of an initial sound, usually of a consonant, and/or the first letter of a word. *(Webster's Dictionary)*

Allusion: 1. The act of alluding. 2. An indirect reference; casual mention. *(Webster's Dictionary)*

Ambivalence: Simultaneous conflicting feelings toward a person or thing, as love and hate. *(Webster's Dictionary)*

Analogy: 1. Similarity in some respects between things otherwise unalike; partial resemblance. 2. An explaining of something by comparing it point by point with something similar. *(Webster's Dictionary)*

Analysis: 1. A separating or breaking up of any whole into its parts, especially with an examination of these parts to find out their nature, proportion, function, interrelationship, etc. 2. A statement of the results of this process. 3. Linguis: the use of word order and uninflected function words rather than inflection to express syntactic relationships.

Anapest: A metrical foot in Greek or Latin verse consisting of two short syllables followed by a long one, or in English, of two unaccented syllables followed by an accented one. Example: "And the *shine*/of their *spears*/was like *stars.*" *(Webster's Dictionary)* "She weren't *much*, to look *at*, she weren't *much* to *drive*" ("Old Yellow Car," written by Thom Schuyler).

Antithesis: A contrast or opposition of thoughts, usually in two phrases, clauses, or sentences (You are going; I am staying). *(Webster's Dictionary)*

Antonym: A word that is opposite in meaning to another word ["sad" is an antonym of "happy"]. *(Webster's Dictionary)*

Aphorism: A terse saying embodying a general, more or less profound truth or principle ("He is a fool that cannot conceal his wisdom").

Art: 1. Human ability to make things; creativity of man of nature. 2. Skill; craftsmanship. 3. Creative work or its principles; making or doing of things that display form, beauty, and unusual perception: art includes painting, sculpture, architecture, music, literature, drama, the dance, etc. *(Webster's Dictionary)*

Artist: Craftsman, artisan. 1. A person who works in or is skilled in any of the fine arts, especially in painting, drawing, sculpture, etc. 2. A person who does anything very well, with imagination and a feeling for form, effect, etc. *(Webster's Dictionary)*

Assonance: A partial rhyme in which the stressed vowel sounds are alike, but the consonant sounds are unalike, as in **late** and **make**. *(Webster's Dictionary)* The similarity of vowel sounds in words which do not rhyme [we—weep, fine—white]. *(McCrimmon)*

Bar: A vertical line across a staff, dividing it into measures. *(Webster's Dictionary)*

Beat: To mark (time or rhythm) by tapping, etc., usually on the off-beat. *(Webster's Dictionary)*

Blues: 1a. Black folk music characterized by minor harmonies, typically slow tempo, and melancholy words. 1b. The form of jazz that evolved from this. 1c. A song or composition in this style. *(Webster's Dictionary)*

Bridge: A connecting passage between two sections of a composition. *(Webster's Dictionary)*

Business: Commercial practice or policy; business is business sentiment, friendship, etc., cannot be allowed to interfere with profit making. *(Webster's Dictionary)*

Cadence: The fall of the voice in speaking, dynamics, inflection, or modulation in tone; any rhythmic flow of sound. Example: *What* am I doing; What *am I* doing; What am I *doing*. *(Webster's Dictionary)*

Childish: 1. Of, like, or characteristic of a child. 2. Not fit for an adult; immature, silly. *(Webster's Dictionary)*

Chord: 1. A combination of three or more tones sounded together in harmony. 2. To harmonize. 3. To play chords on (a piano, guitar, etc.). *(Webster's Dictionary)*

Chromatic: Music: 1a. Using or progressing by semi-tones [a chromatic scale]. 1b. Producing all the tones of such a scale [a chromatic instrument]. 1c. Using tones not in the key of a work [chromatic harmony]. 2. Music—A tone modified by an accidental. *(Webster's Dictionary)*

Circumlocution: Literally, "round-about speech." An attempt to avoid a direct statement by a circuitous reference, as in "She is expecting a little stranger" for "She is pregnant." *(McCrimmon)*

Cliche: A "trite expression," an overused or threadbare expression, or an observation which lacks originality. *(McCrimmon)*

Coda: A passage formally ending a composition or section. *(Webster's Dictionary)*

Colloquialism: Erroneously, a localism, or regionalism. *(Webster's Dictionary)* To include popular words and idiomatic construction; they also include words with popular meaning (the use of alibi to mean excuse, for example). And, constructions which are not strictly idioms, especially the abbreviated or clipped forms of more formal words, such as ad for advertisement. *(McCrimmon)*

Commercial: Made, done, or operating primarily for profit; designed to have wide popular appeal.

Commercialize: To run as a business; apply commercial methods to.

Compare/Contrast: Contrast always implies differences; Compare may imply either differences or similarities. *(McCrimmon)*

Compose: To create (a musical or literary work).

Composition: 1a. The act of composing, or putting together a whole by combining parts; specifically. 1b. The putting together of words; art of writing. 1c. The creation of musical works. *(Webster's Dictionary)*

Composer: 1. To create (a musical or literary work). 2. To create musical or literary works—a person who composes, especially one who composes music. *(Webster's Dictionary)*

Consonance: 1. Harmony or agreement of elements or parts; accord; 2. A pleasing combination of simultaneous musical sounds; harmony of tones. 3. Prosody—a partial rhyme in which consonants in stressed syllables are repeated, but vowels are not. (Example: **mocker, maker.** *(Webster's Dictionary)*

Content: 1a. All that is contained in something; everything inside (the contents of). 1b. All that is contained or dealt with in a writing or speech. 2a. All that is dealt with in a course or area of study, work of art, discussion, etc.; 2b. Essential meaning; substance (the content of a poem as distinguished from its form). *(Webster's Dictionary)*

Couplet: Two successive lines of poetry, especially two of the same length of rhyme.

Critique: (critical) 1. A critical analysis or evaluation of a subject, situation, literary work, etc. 2. The act or art of criticizing; criticism—to analyze and evaluate (a subject, literary work, etc.) criticize. *(Webster's Dictionary)*

Craft: 1. A special skill, art, or dexterity. 2. An occupation requiring special skill. *(Webster's Dictionary)*

Dactylic: A metrical foot of three syllables, the first accented and the other unaccented. Example: *"Take her up/*tenderly." *(Webster's Dictionary)* *"Ex/cuse me,* but I think you've got my chair." ("The Chair," written by Cochran and Dillon, recorded by George Strait.)

Deceive: 1. To make (a person) believe what is not true; delude; mislead. 2. To be false to; betray—deceive implies deliberate misrepresentation of facts by words, actions, etc., generally to further one's ends [deceived into buying fraudulent stocks]; to mislead is to cause to follow the wrong course or to err in conduct or action, although not always by deliberate deception [misled by the sign into going to the wrong floor]; beguile implies the use of wiles and enticing prospects in deceiving or misleading [beguiled by promises of a fortune]; to delude is to fool someone so completely that he accepts what is false as true; betray implies a breaking of faith while appearing to be loyal. *(Webster's Dictionary)*

Deceit: 1. The act of representing as true what is known to be false; a deceiving or lying. 2. A dishonest action or trick; fraud or lie. 3. The quality of being deceitful. 4. Tending to deceive; apt to lie or cheat. 5. Intended to deceive; deceptive; false, dishonest. *(Webster's Dictionary)*

Degree: 1a. A line or space on the staff. 1b. An interval between two such lines or spaces.

Demo: 1. [Colloq.] A phonograph or tape recording made to demonstrate the talent of a performer, quality of a song, etc. 2. Clipped form of demonstration. *(Webster's Dictionary)*

Design: The art of making designs or patterns.

Dialect: A pattern of speech habits shared by members of the same geographic area or social level. *(Webster's Dictionary)*

Diatonic Scale: Designating, of, or using any standard major or minor scale of eight tones without the chromatic intervals. *(Webster's Dictionary)*

Diagraph: Two letters pronounced as a single sound, as in bleed, beat, thin, stick, psychology, graph. *(McCrimmon)*

Diphthong: A combination of two vowel sounds run together to sound like a single vowel. Examples are ah-ee sounds, combining to form the vowel of hide, ride, wide and the aw-ee sound combining boy, joy, toy. *(McCrimmon)*

Emotion: 1a. Strong feeling; excitement. 1b. The state or capability of having the feelings aroused to the point of awareness. 2. Any specific feeling; any of various complex reactions with both mental and physical manifestations, as love, hate, fear, anger, etc. *(Webster's Dictionary)*

Empathy: 1. Feeling. 2. The projection of one's own personality into the personality of another in order to understand him better; ability to share in another's emotions or feelings. 3. The projection of one's own personality into an object, with the attribution to the object of one's own emotions, responses, etc. *(Webster's Dictionary)*

Engineer: A specialist in planning and directing operations in some technical field. *(Webster's Dictionary)*

Entertain(er): 1. To keep the interest of and give pleasure to; divert; amuse. 2. To give hospitality to; have as a guest. 3. To allow oneself to think about; have in mind, consider [to entertain an idea]. 4. To keep up, to maintain. 5. A person who entertains; especially a popular singer, dancer, comedian, etc. *(Webster's Dictionary)*

Epigram: A terse, witty, pointed statement that gains its effect by ingenious antithesis ("The only way to get rid of a temptation is to yield to it"). *(Webster's Dictionary)*

Esoteric: 1a. Intended for or understood by only a chosen few, as an inner group of disciples or initiates: said of ideas, doctrines, literature, etc. 1b. Beyond the understanding or knowledge of most people; recondite; abstruse. 2. Confidential; private; withheld [an esoteric plan]. *(Webster's Dictionary)*

Feeling: 1. Full of or expressing emotion or sensitivity; sympathetic. 2. That one of the senses by which sensations of contact, pressure, temperature, and pain are transmitted through the skin; sense of touch. 3. The power or faculty of experiencing physical sensation. 4. An awareness; consciousness; sensation [a feeling of pain]. 5. An emotion. 6. Sensitivities, sensibilities [to hurt one's feelings]. 7. A kindly, generous attitude; sympathy; pity. 8. A natural ability or sensitive appreciation [a feeling or music]. 9. The emotional quality in a work of art. *(Webster's Dictionary)*

Figures of speech: Metaphors, similes, personifications, allusions, and similar devices are grouped under the general name (figures of speech). *(McCrimmon)*

Filler: Matter added to some other to increase bulk. *(Webster's Dictionary)*

Fluff: Any light or trivial matter or talk. *(Webster's Dictionary)*

Foot: A group of syllables serving as a unit of meter in verse; especially, such a unit having a specified placement of the stressed syllable or syllables. *(Webster's Dictionary)*

Form: The shape, outline, or configuration of anything; structure as apart from color, material, etc.

Gender: A grammatical division of words into masculine, feminine, and neuter categories. *(McCrimmon)*

Gig: [Slang] 1. A gathering of musicians for a session. 2. A job performing music. 3. Any job, performance, or routing stint. [Slang] To have an engagement performing music. *(Webster's Dictionary)*

Hackneyed: *See* Cliche. (McCrimmon)

Harmony: 1a. The simultaneous sounding of two or more tones, especially when satisfying to the ear. 1b. Structure in terms of the arrangement, modulation, etc., of chords: distinguished from melody and rhythm. 1c. The study of this structure is called symmetry. *(Webster's Dictionary)*

Hold: When a company puts a hold on your material that means they are interested in possibly recording your work. There are three types of hold: soft hold, hard hold, and cut hold.

Homonyms: Words which are pronounced alike [air, heir; blew, blue; plain, plane; sail, sale]. *(McCrimmon)*

Hook: In lyric writing the word or words (usually the title) that the rest of the lyric revolves around, and returns to (in the chorus) and sometimes in the verses.

Iambic: A metrical foot of two syllables, the first unaccented and the other accented. Example: "To *strive*/to *seek*/to *find* and *not* to yield." *(Webster's Dictionary)* Example: "There ain't no *use*, to *sit* and wonder why *girl*" ("Don't Think Twice," written Bob Dylan).

Idiom: 1. The language or dialect of a people, region, class, etc. 2. A characteristic style, as in art or music. *(Webster's Dictionary)*

Illusion: 1. A false idea or conception; belief or opinion not in accord with the facts. (Not to be confused with allusion.) *(Webster's Dictionary)*

Immature: Not finished or perfected; incomplete. *(Webster's Dictionary)*

Impalpable: 1. That cannot be felt by touching. 2. Too slight or subtle to be grasped easily by the mind. *(Webster's Dictionary)*

Incorporeal: 1. Not consisting of matter; without material body or substance. 2. Of spirits or angels. *(Webster's Dictionary)*

Inflection: 1. A turning, bending, or curving. 2. A turn, bend, or curve. 3. Any change in tone or pitch of the voice; modulation [to signal a question by a rising inflection]. 4a. Grammar: the change of form by which some words indicate certain grammatical relationships, as number, case, gender, tense, etc. 4b. An inflected form. 4c. An inflectional element, as those bound forms used in English to form the plural and possessive case of nouns (ship, ship's) and the past tense and third person singular, present indicative, of verbs [he shipped, he ships]. *(Webster's Dictionary)*

Influence: The power of persons or things (whether or not exerted consciously or overtly) to affect others [he owed his position to influence]; authority implies the power to command acceptance, belief obedience, etc., based on strength of character, expertness of knowledge, etc. [a statement made on good authority]; prestige implies the power to command esteem or admiration, based on brilliance of achievement or outstanding superiority; weight implies influence that is more or less preponderant in its effect [he threw his weight to the opposition]. *(Webster's Dictionary)*

Intangible: 1. That cannot be touched, incorporeal; impalpable. 2. That represents value but has either no intrinsic value or no material being [stocks and bonds are intangible property, good will is an intangible asset]. 3. That cannot be easily defined, formulated, or grasped; vague. *(Webster's Dictionary)*

Interval: The difference in pitch between two tones. *(Webster's Dictionary)*

Intrinsic: 1. Belong to the real nature of a thing; not dependent on external circumstances; essential; inherent. *(Webster's Dictionary)*

Intro: An opening section of a musical composition. *(Webster's Dictionary)*

Introspection: To look within. To look into (one's own mind, feelings, etc.). A looking into one's own mind, feelings, etc.; observation and analysis of oneself. *(Webster's Dictionary)*

Irony: A mode of statement in which the writer implies almost the opposite of what he explicitly states. The writing proceeds on two levels at the same time. Ostensibly, the writer is developing the literal meaning of his message, but he counts on the reader to see the implications of each statement in the total context and so to respond at the implied level. The most famous example in English is Jonathan Swift's, *A Modest Proposal*, which under the guise of suggesting a workable plan for improving the economy of Ireland make an incisive criticism of England's exploitation of the Irish. Irony is difficult to handle. *(McCrimmon)*

ITADS: Iambic, Trochaic, Anapestic, Dactylic, and Spondiac. [See definitions of iambic, trochaic, anapestic, dactylic, and spondiac.] *(McCrimmon)*

Juxtapose: To move one phrase, clause, or paragraph to another place which makes that phrase, clause, or paragraph more cohesive, or causes the entire content to have a flow more easily conducive to understanding.

Love: 1. To be fond of, desire. 2. A deep and tender feeling of affection for or attachment or devotion to a person or persons. 3. An expression of one's love or affection [give Mary my love]. 4. A feeling of brotherhood and good will toward other people. 5a. A strong liking for or interest in something [a love of music]. 5b. The object of such liking. 6a. A strong, usually passionate, affection of one person for another, based in part on sexual attraction. 6b. The person who is the object of such an affection; sweetheart, lover. 7a. God's benevolent concern for mankind. 7b. Man's devout attachment to God. 8. To feel love for. 9. To show love for by embracing, kissing, etc. 10. To delight in; take pleasure in [to love books]. To gain benefit for [a plant that loves shade]—to feel the emotion of love; be in love—fall in love (with) to begin to feel love (for)—in love, feeling love; enamored—make love. Love implies intense fondness or deep devotion and may apply to various relationships or objects [sexual love, brotherly love, love of one's work, etc.]; attachment implies connection by ties of affection, attraction, devotion, etc. and may be felt for inanimate things as well as for people [an attachment to an old hat]; infatuation implies a foolish or unreasoning passion or affection, often a transient (passing) (not permanent) one [an elderly man's infatuation for a young girl]. *(Webster's Dictionary)*

Lyric: Music: 1. Characterized by a relatively high compass and a light, flexible quality. 2. The words of a song, as distinguished from the music. *(Webster's Dictionary)*

Lyricist: A writer of lyrics, especially lyrics for popular songs. *(Webster's Dictionary)*

Major: Music: 1a. Designating an imperfect interval greater than the corresponding minor by a semitone. 1b. Based or characterized by major intervals, scales, etc. [in major key]. 1c. Based on the scale pattern of the major mode: *see* major scale. *(Webster's Dictionary)*

Major Scale: One of two standard diatonic musical scales, with half steps instead of whole steps after the third and seventh tones. *(Webster's Dictionary)*

Manager: 1a. One who manages a business, institution, etc. 1b. One who manages affairs or expenditures, as of an entertainer. *(Webster's Dictionary)*

Material: Important, essential, or pertinent (to the matter under discussion). *(Webster's Dictionary)* Music, lyrics, and songs on a cassette, usually including typed lyric sheets. *(Jennifer Pierce)*

Mature: 1. Fully developed, as a person, a mind, etc. *(Webster's Dictionary)*

Maxim: A general principle drawn from practical experience and serving as a rule of conduct ("Keep thy shop and thy shop will keep thee").

Measure: 1a. The notes or rests, or both, contained between two vertical lines on the staff, subdividing a part of a composition into equal groups of beats; (bar measure). 1b. Musical time or rhythm. *(Webster's Dictionary)*

Melody: 1a. A sequence of single tones, usually in the same key or mode, to produce a rhythmic whole; often (song). 1b. The element of form having to do with the arrangement of single tones in sequence: distinguished from harmony. 1c. The leading part, or voice in a harmonic composition; the first vocal in the or on the air. *(Webster's Dictionary)*

Metaphor: A figure of speech containing an implied comparison, in which a word or phrase ordinarily and primarily used of one thing is applied to another. (Example: "the curtain of night," "all the world's a stage"). Mix metaphors—to use two or more inconsistent metaphors in a single expression. (Example: "The storm of protest was nipped in the bud.") *(Webster's Dictionary)*

Meter: Rhythm in verse, measured, patterned arrangement of syllables, primarily according to stress and length: or the specific rhythm as determined by the prevailing foot and the number of feet in the line (iambic meter); or rhythm in music, especially the division into measures or bars, having a uniform number of beats; pattern of strong and weak beats in a measure. *(Webster's Dictionary)*

Minor: Music: 1a. Designating an imperfect interval smaller than the corresponding major interval by a semitone. 1b. Characterized by minor intervals, scales, etc. [the minor key]. 1c. Designating a triad having a minor third. 1d. Based on the scale pattern of the minor mode. *See* Minor scale. *(Webster's Dictionary)*

Minor Scale: 1a. One of two standard diatonic scales, with half steps instead of whole steps. 1b. After the second and seventh tones in ascending and after the sixth and third tones in descending (melodic minor scale) 1c. After the second, fifth, and seventh tones in ascending and after the eight, sixth, and third tones in descending (harmonic minor scale). *(Webster's Dictionary)*

Mode: 1. A manner or way of acting, doing, or being; method or form. Music: 2a. The selection and arrangement of tones and semitones in a scale, especially any of such arrangements in medieval church music. 2b. A rhythmical system of the 13th century. 2c. Either of the two forms of scale arrangement in later music (Major mode and Minor mode). *(Webster's Dictionary)*

Modulation: 1. A shifting from one key to another. 2. To regulate, adjust, or adapt to the proper degree. 3. To vary the pitch, intensity, etc. of (the voice), often specifically to a lower degree and also, specifically to a higher degree. *(Webster's Dictionary)*

Money (monetarism): A theory which holds that economic stability and growth result from maintaining a steady rate of growth in the supply of money.

Mood: 1. A particular state of mind or feeling; humor, or temper. 2. A predominant or pervading feeling, spirit, or tone. 3. Fits a morose, sullen, or uncertain temper. 4. *Mood* is the broadest of these terms referring to a temporary state of mind and emphasizes the constraining or pervading quality of the feeling [she's in a merry mood]; *humor* emphasizes the variability or capriciousness of the mood [he wept and laughed as his humor moved him]; *temper,* in this comparison, applies to a mood characterized by a single, strong emotion, especially that of anger [my, he's in a nasty temper!]; *vein* stresses the transient nature of the mood [if I may speak in a serious vein for a moment]. *(Webster's Dictionary)*

Motto: A maxim accepted as a guiding principle or as an ideal of behavior ("Honesty is the best policy").

Music: 1. The art and science of combining vocal or instrumental sounds or tones in varying melody, harmony, rhythm, timbre, especially so as to form structurally complete and emotionally expressive compositions. 2. The sounds or tones so arranged, or the arrangement of these. 3. Any rhythmic sequence of pleasing sounds, as of birds, water, etc. 4a. A particular form, style, etc. of musical composition or a particular class of musical works or pieces [folk music]. 4b. The body of musical works of a particular style, place.

Musicology: The systematized study of the science, history, forms, and methods of music. *(Webster's Dictionary)*

Octave: 1a. The eighth full tone above a given tone, having twice as many vibrations per second, or below a given tone, having half as many vibrations per second. 1b. The interval of eight diatonic degrees between a tone and either of its octaves. 1c. The series of tones contained within this interval, or the keys of an instrument producing such a series. 1d. A tone and either of its octaves sounded together. 1e. An organ stop producing tones an octave above those ordinarily produced by the keys struck. 2. Consisting of eight, or an octave. 3. Music producing tones an octave higher [an octave key]. *(Webster's Dictionary)*

Order: A state or condition in which everything is in its right place and functioning properly.

Organization: A body of persons organized for some specific purpose, as a club, union, or society. *(Webster's Dictionary)*

Pattern: An arrangement of form; disposition of parts or elements; design. *(Webster's Dictionary)*

Pentameter: 1. A line of verse containing five metrical feet or measures; especially, English iambic pentameter. Example: "He jests/ at scars/ who nev/ er felt/ a wound." 2. Verse consisting of pentameters; heroic verse having five metrical feet or measures. *(Webster's Dictionary)*

Personification: A figure of speech in which animals, inanimate objects, and qualities are given human characteristics. *(McCrimmon)* 1. A person or thing thought of as representing some quality, thing, or idea; embodiment. Example: Cupid is the personification of love. 2. A figure of speech in which a thing, quality, or idea is represented as a person. *(Webster's Dictionary)*

Personify: 1. To think or speak of (a thing) as having life or personality; represent as a person (to personify a ship by referring to it as "she"). 2. To symbolize (an abstract idea) by a human figure, as in art. 3. To be a symbol or perfect example of (some quality, thing, or idea), typify; embody. *(Webster's Dictionary)*

Petrarchan Sonnet: A sonnet composed of a group of eight lines (octave) with two rhymes *(abba, abba)*, and a group of six lines (sextet) with two or three rhymes variously arranged (typically: *cdc dcd* or *cde cde*). The thought or theme is stated and developed in the octave, and expanded, contradicted, etc., in the sextet. Italian sonnet. *(Webster's Dictionary)*

Phrasing: 1. The act or manner of formulating phrases; phraseology. 2. The manner in which one phrases musical passages. *(Webster's Dictionary)*

Pitch: Music, acoustics: 1a. That quality of a tone or sound determined by the frequency of vibration of the sound waves reaching the ear; the greater the frequency, the higher the pitch. 1b. A standard of pitch for tuning instruments. *(Webster's Dictionary)* 2. Songs played for executives in the industry for possible recordings.

Plagiarism: The offense of representing as one's own writing the work of another. The use of unacknowledged quotations. *(McCrimmon)*

Poem: An arrangement of words written or spoken. Traditionally a rhythmical composition, sometimes rhymed, expressing experiences, ideas, or emotions in a style more concentrated, imaginative, and powerful than that of ordinary speech or prose. Some poems are in meter, some are in free verse. *(Webster's Dictionary)*

Produce: To bring into being; create, give rise to. *(Webster's Dictionary)*

Professional: 1. Of, engaged in, or worthy of the high standards of, a profession. 2. Designating or of a school, especially a graduate school, offering instruction in a profession. 3. Earning one's living from an activity, such as a sport, not normally thought of as an occupation. 4. Engaged in the professional players [professional hockey]. 5. Engaged in a specified occupation for pay or as a means of livelihood [a professional writer]. 6. Being such in a manner of one practicing a profession [a professional hatemonger]. 7. A person practicing a profession. 8a. A person who engages in some art, sport, etc. for money, especially, for his livelihood, rather than as a hobby. 8b. A golfer, tennis player, etc., affiliated with a particular club as a contestant, teacher, and the like: usually clipped to pro. 9. A person who does something with great skill. *(Webster's Dictionary)*

Promote: To further the popularity, sales, etc., of by publicizing and advertising [to promote a product]. *(Webster's Dictionary)*

Prose: The ordinary form of written or spoken language, without rhyme or meter; speech or writing that is not poetry. *(Webster's Dictionary)*

Prosody: 1. The science or art of versification, including the study of metrical structure, rhyme, stanza forms, etc. 2. A particular system of versification and metrical structure [Dryden's prosody] also: tone, accent, song sung to music.

Proverb: A piece of practical wisdom expressed in familiar, concrete terms ("A penny saved is a penny earned").

Publicist: A person whose business is to publicize persons, organizations, etc. *(Webster's Dictionary)*

Publisher: A person or firm that publishes, especially one whose business is the publishing of books, newspapers, magazines, printed music, etc. *(Webster's Dictionary)*

Quatrain: A stanza or poem of four lines, usually rhyming *abab*, *abba*, or *abcb*. *(Webster's Dictionary)*

Recondite: 1. Beyond the grasp of the ordinary mind or understanding; profound; abstruse. 2. Dealing with abstruse or difficult subjects. 3. Obscure or concealed. *(Webster's Dictionary)*

Redundant: 1. More than enough; overabundant; excess, superfluous. 2. Using more words than are needed; wordy. 3. Unnecessary to the meaning: said of words. *(Webster's Dictionary)*

Release: Music: 1a. The act or method of ending a tone. 1b. The third group of four measures in a common form of 16-bar chorus, as in a popular tune, which supplies a bridge between repetitions of the melody. *(Webster's Dictionary)*

Rhetorical Question: A question asked only for effect, as to emphasize a point, no answer being expected. *(Webster's Dictionary)*

Rhyme: 1. Correspondence of end sounds, especially at the ends of lines. 2. A regular recurrence of corresponding sounds, especially at the end of lines. 3. Correspondence of end sounds in lines (assonance and consonance). 4. A word that corresponds with another in end sound. *(Webster's Dictionary)*

Rhythm: Basically regular recurrence of grouped strong and weak beats, or heavily and lightly accented tones, in alternation; arrangement of successive tones, usually in measures, according to their relative accentuation and duration: (waltz rhythm) [time, tempo, meter]. *(Webster's Dictionary)*

Sad: 1. Having, expressing, or showing low spirits or sorrow; unhappy; mournful; sorrowful. 2. Causing or characterized by dejection, melancholy, or sorrow. 3. Dark or dull in color; drab. 4. [Colloq.] Very bad; deplorable. 5. [Dial.] Heavy or soggy [a sad cake], sad is the simple, general term, ranging in implication from a mild, momentary unhappiness to a feeling of intense grief; sorrowful implies a sadness caused by some specific loss, disappointment, etc. [her death left him sorrowful]; melancholy suggests a more or less chronic mournfulness or gloominess, or, often merely a wistful pensiveness [melancholy thoughts about the future]; dejected implies discouragement or a sinking of spirits, as because of frustration; depressed suggests a mood of brooding despondency, as because of fatigue or a sense of futility [the novel left him feeling depressed]; doleful implies a mournful, often lugubrious, sadness [the doleful look on a lost child's face]. *(Webster's Dictionary)*

Saying: The simple, direct term for any expression of wisdom or truth. *(Webster's Dictionary)*

Scale: Music: A series of tones arranged in a sequence of rising or falling pitches in accordance with any of various systems of intervals; especially, all of such series contained in one octave. *(Webster's Dictionary)* *See also* Chromatic, Diatonic, Major Scale, Minor Scale.

Semantics: The science of the meanings of words as contrasted with phonetics (pronunciation), morphology (form), and syntax (function). *(McCrimmon)*

Sensitive: 1. Of the senses or sensation; especially connected with the reception or transmission of sense impressions; sensory. 2. Receiving and responding to stimuli from outside objects or agencies; having sensation. 3. Responding or feeling readily and acutely; very keenly susceptible to stimuli [sensitive ear]. 4. Easily hurt; tender; raw. 5. Having or showing keen sensibilities; highly perceptive or responsive intellectually, aesthetically, etc. 6. Easily offended, disturbed, shocked, irritated, etc., as by the actions of others; touchy. *(Webster's Dictionary)*

Shakespearean Sonnet: A sonnet composed of three quatrains, typically with the rhyme scheme *abab cdcd efef*, and a final couplet with the rhyme *gg*. *(Webster's Dictionary)*

Simile: A figure of speech in which one thing is likened to another, dissimilar thing by the use of like or as, etc. Example: "A heart as big as a whale," "her tears flowed like wine."

Distinguished from metaphor: "We're all aging with time, like yesterday's wine." ("Yesterday's Wine," written by Willie Nelson). *(Webster's Dictionary)*

Slang: 1. The specialized vocabulary and idioms of those in the same work, way of life, etc. Now usually called shoptalk, argot, jargon. (Argot, the specialized vocabulary and idioms of those in the same work, way of life, etc., as the secret jargon of criminals: *see* slang. 2. Highly informal language that is outside of conventional or standard usage and consists of both coined words and phrases and of new or extended meanings attached to established terms. Slang develops from the attempt to find fresh and vigorous, colorful, pungent, or humorous expression, and generally either passes into disuse or comes to have a more formal status. *(Webster's Dictionary)*

Song: 1. The act or art of singing [to break into song]. 2. A piece of music sung or as if for singing. 3a. Poetry; verse. 3b. A relatively short metrical composition for, or suitable for, singing, as a ballad or simple lyric. 4. A musical sound like singing [the song of the lark]. *(Webster's Dictionary)*

Sonnet: A poem normally of 14 lines in any of several fixed verse and rhyme schemes, typically in rhymed iambic pentameter. Sonnets characteristically express a single theme or idea. *(Webster's Dictionary) See also* Petrarchan Sonnet, Shakespearean Sonnet.

Spondiac: A metrical foot consisting of two heavily accented syllables (Solemn Melody). *(Webster's Dictionary)* Example: "*Am/azing grace how* sweet *the sound.*" (Traditional hymn)

Stanza: A group of lines of verse forming one of the divisions of a poem or song. A stanza is usually made up of four or more lines and typically has a regular pattern in the number of lines and the arrangement of meter and rhyme. *(Webster's Dictionary)*

Step: 1a. A degree of the staff or scale. 1b. The interval between two consecutive degrees.

Structure: The arrangement or interrelation of all the parts of a whole; manner of organization or construction.

Studio: A room or rooms where radio or television programs are produced or where recordings are made. *(Webster's Dictionary)*

Syllable: 1. A word or part of a word pronounced with a single, uninterrupted sounding of the voice; unit of pronunciation, consisting of a single sound of great sonority (usually a vowel) and generally one or more sounds of lesser sonority (usually consonants). 2. Any of the parts into which a written word is divided in approximate representation of its spoken syllables to show where the word can be broken at the end of a line. 3. The least bit of expression; slightest detail, as of something said. *(Webster's Dictionary)*

Symmetry: 1. Similarity of form or arrangement on either side of a dividing line or plane; correspondence of opposite parts in size, shape, and position; condition of being symmetrical. The whole or the corresponding parts are said to have symmetry. 2. Balance or beauty of form or proportion resulting from such correspondence. Balance suggests the offsetting or contrasting of parts so as to produce an aesthetic equilibrium in the whole. *(Webster's Dictionary)*

Synonym: 1. A word having the same or nearly the same meaning in one or more senses as another in the same language; opposed to an antonym. 2. Same as metonym. *(Webster's Dictionary)*

Syntax: 1a. The arrangement of words as elements in a sentence to show their relationship to one another. 1b. The organization and relationship of word groups, phrases, clauses, and sentences; sentence structure. *(Webster's Dictionary)*

Synthesis: Putting together parts or elements so as to form a whole. *(Webster's Dictionary)*

Synthesize: To form by bringing together separate parts. *(Webster's Dictionary)*

Synthesizer: A person or thing that synthesizes; specifically, an electronic device containing filters, oscillators, and voltage-control amplifiers, used to produce sounds unobtainable from ordinary musical instruments. *(Webster's Dictionary)*

Tag: To end, tag line. *(Webster's Dictionary)*

Tempo: 1. The rate of speed at which a musical composition is, or is supposed to be, played. It is indicated by such notations as allegro, andante, etc., or by reference to metronome timing. 2. Rate of activity; pace [the tempo of modern living]. *(Webster's Dictionary)*

Timbre: The characteristic quality of sound that distinguishes one voice or musical instrument from another or one vowel sound from another. It is determined by the harmonics of the sound and is distinguished from the intensity and pitch. *(Webster's Dictionary)*

Theory: A systematic statement of principles [the theory of equations in mathematics]. *(Webster's Dictionary)*

Tone: Music: 1a. A sound that is distinct and identifiable by its regularity of vibration, or constant pitch (as distinguished from a noise), and that may be put into harmonic relation with other such sounds. 1b. The simple or fundamental tone of a musical sound as distinguished from its overtones. 1c. Any one of the full intervals of a diatonic scale; whole step. 1d. Any of several recitation melodies used in singing the psalms in plainsong. *(Webster's Dictionary)*

Tonic: Music: Designating or based on the first tone (keynote) of a diatonic scale [a tonic chord]. *(Webster's Dictionary)*

Tonic Accent: Emphasis given to a syllable by changing, especially by raising the pitch rather than by stress. *(Webster's Dictionary)*

Trades: Of, by, or for those in a particular business or industry [trade papers or journals]. *(Webster's Dictionary)*

Transmit: 1. To send or cause to go from one person or place to another; especially across intervening space of distance; transfer; dispatch, convey. 2. To pass along; impart. *(Webster's Dictionary)*

Transpose: To transform, convert—to play music in a key different from the one in which it is written. *(Webster's Dictionary)*

Trochaic: A metrical foot of two syllables, the first accented and the other unaccented. (Example: "Peter/Peter/Pumpkin/Eater." *(Webster's Dictionary)* "Busted Flat in Baton Rouge, Waitin' For A Train" ("Me and Bobby McGee," written by Kris Kristofferson).

Truth: 1a. The quality or state of being true; specifically: loyalty; trustworthiness. 1b. Sincerity; genuineness; honesty. 1c. The quality of being in accordance with experience, facts, or reality; conformity with fact. 1d. Reality; actual existence. 1e. Agreement with a standard, rule etc.; correctness; accuracy. 2. That which is true; statement, etc., that accords with fact or reality. 3. An established or verified fact, principle, etc. 4. A particular belief or teaching regarded by the speaker as the true one (often with the)—in truth, truly; in fact—truth suggests conformity with the facts or with reality, either as an idealized abstraction ["What is truth?" said jesting Pilate] or in actual application to statements, ideas, acts, etc. [there is no truth in that rumor]; veracity, as applied to persons or to their utterances, connotes habitual adherence to the truth [I cannot doubt his veracity]; verify, as applied to things, connotes correspondence with fact or with reality [the verity of his thesis]; verisimilitude, as applied to literary or artistic representations, connotes correspondence with actual, especially universal, truths [the verisimilitude of the characterizations in a novel. *(Webster's Dictionary)*

Turnaround: The act of turning about, as to face the other way, (turnabout). *(Webster's Dictionary)*

Twist: 1. An unexpected direction given to or taken by a situation. 2. A special or different meaning, method, or slant [a new twist to an old story]. *(Webster's Dictionary)*

Universal: 1. Of the universe; present or occurring everywhere or in all things. 2. Of, for, affecting, or including all or the whole of something specified; not limited or restricted. 3. Being, or regarded as, a complete whole; entire; whole. 4. Broad in knowledge, interests, ability, etc. 5. That can be used for a great many or all kinds, forms, sizes, etc., highly adaptable. 6. Used, intended to be used, or understood by all. *(Webster's Dictionary)*

Vacillate: 1. To sway to and fro; waver; totter; stagger. 2. To fluctuate or oscillate. 3. To waver in mind; show indecision—wavering or tending to waver in motion, opinion, etc. *(Webster's Dictionary)*

Vernacular: 1. The native speech, language, or dialect of a country or place. 2. The common, everyday language of ordinary people in a particular locality. *(Webster's Dictionary)* The shoptalk or idiom of a profession or trade. *(Webster's Dictionary)*

Vibration: One's emotional reaction to a person or thing as being in or out of harmony with one. *(Webster's Dictionary)*

Vicarious: 1. Shared in or experienced by imagined participation in another's experience [a vicarious thrill]. *(Webster's Dictionary)*

Video: 1. Of or used in television. 2. Designating or of the picture portion of a telecast, as distinguished from the audio (or sound) portion. *(Webster's Dictionary)*

Weak: 1. Lacking in moral strength or will power; yielding easily to temptation, the influence of others, etc. 2. Lacking in mental power, or in the ability to think, judge, decide, for yourself, etc. 3. Indicating or suggesting moral or physical weakness [weak features]—weak, the broadest in application of these words, basically implies a lack or inferiority of physical, mental or moral strength [weak muscle, mind, character, foundation, excuse, etc.]. *(Webster's Dictionary)*

Weakminded: 1. Not firm of mind; indecisive; unable to refuse or deny. 2. Mentally deficient. 3. Showing weakness of resolve or thought [a weakminded decision]. *(Webster's Dictionary)*

Weakness: 1. The state or quality of being weak. 2. A weak point; fault or defect, as in one's character. 3a. A liking; especially an unreasonable fondness (for something). 3b. Something of which one is unreasonably fond [candy is his one weakness]. *(Webster's Dictionary)*

Wrap: [Colloq.] 1a. To bring to an end; make final; conclude; settle. 1b. To give a concluding, summarizing statement, report, etc. *(Webster's Dictionary)* "That's a wrap." *(Jennifer Pierce)*

Writer: 1. To be the author or composer of (literary or musical material). 2. A person who writes. 3. A person whose work or occupation is writing; specifically an author, journalist, or the like. *(Webster's Dictionary)*

To obtain free copyright Form PA (lyric and music) and/or Form TX (lyric only) you may write or call the Copyright Office at:

Copyright Office
Library of Congress
Washington, DC 20559
(202) 707-3000

Bibliography

References

Definition of Music Rights, Chapter Five, SESAC, 1991.

Gene Lees, *The Modern Rhyming Dictionary: How To Write Lyrics*, Cherry Lane Books, Greenwich, CT, 1981.

James M. McCrimmon, *Writing with a Purpose*, Houghton Mifflin Company, Boston, 1967.

Roget's International Thesaurus, Revised by Robert L. Chapman, Thomas Y. Crowell Company, New York, 1977.

Kate L. Turabian, *A Manual for Writers of Term Papers, Theses, and Dissertations*, The University of Chicago Press, 1982.

Webster's New World Dictionary of the American Language, (Second College Edition), David B. Guralnik, Editor in Chief, Simon and Schuster, 1982.

Writing Aids

Richard A. Spears, *Essential American Idioms*, National Textbook Company, A Division of NTC Publishing Group, 1990.

Richard A. Spears, *Contemporary American Slang*, National Textbook Company, A Division of NTC Publishing Group, 1991.

The Lyrics of Great Songwriters
Copyright Acknowledgments

The following have issued copyright licensing permission for lyrical use in *Breakin' into Nashville*.

Business

Sidney Shemel and M. William Krasilovsky, *This Business of Music*, Revised and Enlarged Edition, 1985.

Trades

American Songwriter Magazine
121 17th Avenue South
Nashville, TN 37203
(615) 244-6065

Billboard Magazine
1515 Broadway
New York, NY 10036
(212) 764-7300

Billboard Magazine
49 Music Square West
Nashville, TN 37203
(615) 321-4290

Cashbox Publications
6464 Sunset Boulevard
Suite 605
Hollywood, CA 09928
(213) 464-8241

Close-Up Magazine
(A CMA Publication)
One Music Circle, South
Nashville, TN 37203
(615) 244-2840

Music Row Magazine
P.O. Box 158542
Nashville, TN 37215
(615) 321-3617

Music City News Magazine
50 Music Square West
Nashville, TN 37203
(615) 329-2200

*Peforming Songwriters
Magazine*
P.O. Box 158159
Nashville, TN 37215
1-800-883-7664

Musician Magazine
(A BPI Communications, Inc. Publication)
1515 Broadway
New York, NY 10036

Cashbox Publications
1300 Division Street
Nashville, TN 37203
(615) 329-2898

Inside Country Fever
LFP, Inc.
9171 Wilshire Boulevard, Suite 300
Beverly Hills, CA 90210
(800) 276-3004

Indices

Performing Rights Organizations

ASCAP
Two Music Square West
Nashville, TN 37203
(615) 742-5000

ASCAP
One Lincoln Plaza
New York, NY 10023
(212) 595-3050

BMI
10 Music Square East
Nashville, TN 37203
(615) 259-7502

BMI
320 West 57th Street
New York, NY 10019
(212) 586-2000

SESAC
156 West 56th Street
New York, NY 10019
(212) 586-3450

SESAC
55 Music Square East
Nashville, TN 37203
(615) 320-0055

Songwriters' Organizations

ACM
Academy of Country Music
6255 Sunset Boulevard
Suite 923
Hollywood, CA 90028
(213) 462-2351

CMA
Country Music Association
One Music Circle South
Nashville, TN 37203
(615) 244-2840

Los Angeles Songwriters Showcase
P.O. Box 93759
Hollywood, CA 90093
(213) 467-7823

Nashville Entertainment Association
1007 17th Avenue South
P.O. Box 121948
Nashville, TN 37212
(615) 327-4308

NARAS
National Academy of Recording Arts and Sciences, Inc.
3402 Pico Boulevard
Santa Monica, CA 90405
(310) 392-3777

National Academy of Songwriters
6381 Hollywood Boulevard
Suite 780
Hollywood, CA 90028
(213) 463-7178

NARAS/Nashville
1017 - 16th Avenue, South
Nashville, TN 37212
(615) 327-8030

NSAI
Nashville Songwriters Association International
15 Music Square West
Nashville, TN 37203
(615) 256-3354

Songwriters Guild of America
1222 16th Avenue South
Suite 25
Nashville, TN 37212
(615) 329-1782

Songs Chapter 2 (First Lines Only)

1. "My Heroes Have Always Been Cowboys"
   Writer: Vaughn

2. "Lovin' Her Was Easier than Anything I'll Ever Do Again"
   Writer: Kris Kristofferson

3. "Old Dogs and Children and Watermelon"
   Writer: Tom T. Hall

4. "The Pilgrim"
   Writer: Kris Kristofferson

5. "Mammas Don't Let Your Babies Grow Up To Be Cowboys"
   Writers: Ed Bruce and Patsy Bruce

6. "You Don't Mess Around with Jim"
   Writer: Jim Croce

7. "Me and Bobby McGee"
   Writer: Kris Kristofferson

8. "Yesterday's Wine"
   Writer: Willie Nelson

9. "That'll Be the Day"
   Writers: Holly, Allison and Petty

10. "Rapid Roy"
    Writer: Jim Croce

11. "Margaritaville"
    Writer: Jimmy Buffett

12. "That Old Wheel"
    Writer: Jennifer Pierce

Songs Chapter 3—Section 1 (Analyzed)

1. "I Saw the Light"
   Writer: Hank Williams, Sr.

2. "Amarillo by Mornin"
   Writers: Stafford and Fraser

3. "Operator"
   Writer: Jim Croce

4. "Margaritaville"
   Writer: Jimmy Buffett

5. "No Easy Horses"
   Writers: Knobloch, Schuyler, and Schlitz

6. "Amazing Grace"
   (Public Domain)

7. "Mammas Don't Let Your Babies Grow Up To Be Cowboys"
   Writers: Ed Bruce and Patsy Bruce

Songs Chapter 3—Section 2 (Analyzed)

1. "Amarillo By Mornin"
   Writers: Stafford and Fraser

2. "Mammas Don't Let Your Babies Grow Up To Be Cowboys"
   Writers: Ed Bruce and Patsy Bruce

3. "I Saw The Light"
   Writer: Hank Williams, Sr.

4. "That Old Wheel"
   Writer: Jennifer Pierce

Songs Chapter 3—Section 2 (Charted)

1. "Amarillo By Mornin'"
   Writers: Stafford and Fraser

2. "That Old Wheel"
   Writer: Jennifer Pierce

3. "Mammas Don't Let Your Babies Grow Up To Be Cowboys"
   Writers: Ed Bruce and Patsy Bruce

Songs Chapter 4 (Analyzed)

1. "That Old Wheel"
   Writer: Jennifer Pierce

Songs Chapter 6 (Analyzed)

1. "Texas When I Die"
   Writers: Bruce, Bruce, and Borchers

2. "Delta Dawn"
   Writers: Harvey and Collins

Suggested Readings

Curtis Lee Conroy, *How To Get a Record Deal (Hard Facts—Straight Talk)*, Entertainment Services (9 Music Square West, Suite 118, Nashville, TN 37203).

Scott Faragher, *Music City Babylon*, A Birch Lane Press Book, Carol Publishing Group, 1992.

Mark and Cathy Liggett, *The Complete Handbook of Songwriting*, NAL/Dutton, New York, NY, 1993.

Ben A. Mosley, Sr., *Nashville*—Film-Video-Music Creative Arts Sourcebook, Fall 1992.

The Musicians Business and Legal Guide, Edited and compiled by Mark Halloran, Esq., (Jerome Headlands Press Book, Prentice Hall), 1979, 1980, 1986, 1991.

Henry Schipper, *Broken Record: The Inside Story of the Grammy Awards*, A Birch Lane Press Book, Carol Publishing Group, 1992.

Dick Weissman, *The Music Business: Career Opportunities and Self-Defense*, Crown Publishing, Inc., 1979 and 1990.

American Songwriter Magazine, 121 17th Avenue South, Nashville, TN 37203

Word Index

296, 297, 301, 308, 309,
311
syntax 89, 90, 150, 307, 309
tenses 90, 103, 150
theory 46-49, 77, 79, 157,
201, 302, 310
time 2, 3, 7, 8, 10-14, 20,
24, 25, 27, 28, 36-38, 40,
41, 45, 47, 57, 58, 60-62,
67-69, 72, 75-77, 80-82,
84, 85, 90, 92, 93, 96, 105,
106, 107-109, 112, 118,
119, 131, 135, 148, 161,
166, 168, 171, 172, 175,
181, 185-188, 195, 196,
200, 214, 216, 217, 219,
220, 222, 228, 229, 231,
235-237, 244, 249,
251-254, 261, 266, 270,
276, 278, 280, 281, 283,
285, 291, 298, 300, 308
time frame 36, 38, 105, 107
title 5, 11, 24, 36, 37, 40, 45,
61, 105, 106, 112, 113,
220, 266, 289, 297
transmit 144, 149, 151, 311
transposed 75, 100, 110
triad 46, 79, 301
truth 11, 59, 62, 70, 71, 99,
100, 121, 166, 210, 216,
243, 289, 290, 307, 311
universal 19, 20, 22, 60, 63,
100-102, 109, 112, 120,
129, 148, 150, 151, 210,
211, 213, 214, 217, 219,
311, 312
universal emotions 211,
217
vacillate 210, 212, 312

vibration 32, 144, 304, 310,
312
vicarious 100, 130, 312
weak 108, 109, 210, 216,
301, 306, 312, 313
weakminded 210, 216, 313
weakness 210, 216, 313
writer 1, 2, 6, 12, 22, 25, 26,
34, 45, 62, 66, 69, 85, 96,
109, 112, 114, 130, 145,
146, 148, 152, 161,
163-165, 167, 168, 177,
186-191, 193, 194, 200,
201, 211, 212, 214, 217,
230, 231, 239, 242, 249,
253, 257, 258, 263, 266,
298, 300, 313, 320, 321,
322, 323